AF484512

J. Joseph Pastrana

MIRRORBALL

Reflections of Dance & Fashion

THANE & PROSE
NEW YORK • LONDON
2024

For M.S.
In another dance
to a different tune . . .

Contents

She stalked into the pool hall with not so much the gait of a dancer, rather like that of a jungle cat. Her countenance, icy, insouciant, and unflinching, issued fair warning to everyone around that they were all but easy prey. At variance with the black-clad regulars bleeding into the darkness, her dress was yellow, its gathered bodice held up by spaghetti straps, and the skirt shimmering surreptitiously in her wake. She sparked into view like a proceed-with-caution traffic signal as vibrantly improbable as the length of her legs. Indeed, so improbable was everything about this "Girl in the Yellow Dress" that she was the perfect centerpiece for the acclaimed dance-play triptych "Contact".

The character was conceived by Susan Stroman. And yet, she had not been dreamt into existence. Stro, as the five-time Tony award-winning director and choreographer is called by her peers, had actually witnessed a similar scene play out in real life.

A Delaware native, Stro had studied dance since she was five years old and eventually trained under James Jamieson (1920-1993) at the Academy of the Dance in Wilmington. After working in different capacities at community theaters in Delaware and Philadelphia, she relocated to New York in 1976. The following year, she landed the role of accused Hungarian murderess Hunyak, who plaintively (and hilariously) protests "not guilty" in "Cell Block Tango", for the national tour of the John Kander and Fred Ebb (1928-2004) musical "Chicago" after its initial run at the 46th Street Theatre (now the Richard Rodgers Theatre).

In time however, Stro realized she much preferred storytelling over performing. She swerved toward dance captain to choreographer, from assistant director to director, accruing prestigious projects along the way. When Hal Prince (1928-2019) directed the New York City Opera's 1989 "Don Giovanni", he asked Stro to create the dance sequences. In 1992, she earned her first Antoinette Perry (Tony) Award for Excellence in Broadway Theatre for Best Choreography, along with the Drama Desk Award for Outstanding Choreography, for her work on "Crazy for You" directed by Mike Ockrent (1946-1999), who she would marry in 1996.

"Then, one evening in New York," Stro says, "I stumbled on this club at the corner of Hubert and Hudson streets where I saw this woman in a yellow dress step up to the dance floor as a song began." Stro watched as the woman was approached by men offering to be her partner. She either gave an affirmative nod or a perfunctory shake of her head. After each dance, and it was always just one dance, she distanced herself with nary a backward glance. Completely enthralled, Stro recalls thinking, "Who wears yellow in New York, at night?! She's going to change someone's life," unaware then that this hunch would later apply to herself as well.

This woman had caught Stro's attention. And held it. Because she was dancing. In that dress. It was a moment that had been made indelible within the embrace of fashion and dance. As individual disciplines, each has accumulated centuries of complex rules and enviable skill sets, venerated traditions and unforgettable legacies. And they are dedicated to their own agendas. But moving in unison? Oh how they can pulsate as a singular idiom of desire. It is a seduction, aimed at each other and at the onlookers. To those who are watching, fashion and dance cast back glimmerings of their own need to see and be seen, of their ardent hopes and reveries, frustrations and heartbreak, of humanity's loftiest triumphs and abysmal failings. Going forth and back, side to side, then spinning into a kaleidoscope of images all the more breathtaking for their immediacy and impermanence. Separately and as one, fashion and dance have produced epochal performative and personal expressions that have been captivating everyone since human beings first placed one foot in front of the other. And it is certain to go on until the very final curtain.

———————————

Two weeks after her night out, Stro was summoned to the office of André Bishop, artistic director of the Lincoln Center. She presumed he planned on contracting her for a particular project. She was met instead by a proposition. Having been awed by her choreography for the Scott Ellis-directed Kander and Ebb musical "Steel Pier", Bishop said Stro should be using her talent for her own work. And if she happened to have any ideas for a show, the Lincoln Center would help develop it. So unheard of in the theater, the overture was both tacit confidence in her capabilities and the near equivalent of a blank check. After a momentary pause, she replied, of course she had ideas. One in particular sprang to mind. The unusual woman in the yellow dress that had recessed into Stro's memory resurfaced with the same purposeful stride as she had first walked in. Stro left the meeting on a cloud. She rang up librettist John Weidman (whose credits include Stephen Sondheim's "Pacific Overtures" in 1976 and "Assassins" in 1990), and together they fanned that bright yellow flicker of an idea into a narrative bonfire about human connection.

"We wanted to make something for all these New Yorkers who live on top of each other yet unable to really make contact," says Stro on the basis of the first story. Bishop and executive producer Bernard Gersten (1923-2020) liked the concept and gave the go-ahead for a workshop, installing Stro and eighteen dancers in a studio within the bowels of the Lincoln Center. Some weeks later they dropped in and left elated by what they had seen. But at only an hour max, Bishop and Gersten asked if the piece could be lengthened. Absolutely, Stro assured them. A second workshop was quickly authorized. Unencumbered by provisos, Stro and Weidman set out to complete their trilogy.

Cardinal to fleshing out the initial story was Stro's reticence about explaining "the Girl in the Yellow Dress". Rather, Stro and Weidman fixed the perspective from the world weary eyes of an ad exec who would serve as the audience surrogate. It is his slack jawed fascination of her inscrutable mystery that would provoke questions in everyone's minds. Who is she? What does she want? Is being aloof a defense mechanism? If testament had to be given on Stro's ingenuity for visual story-telling, this is it. In lieu of pat answers that were never really forthcoming, the girl in the yellow dress defies being merely an object of desire. She comes to vivid life, exerting her agency by dancing in this most conspicuous garment. And to come up with that dress? Stro thought of only one person for the job.

———————————————

William Ivey Long is to the theater born. Until around three years old he practically lived in a dressing room of the Raleigh Little Theater (Est. 1936) where his parents, William (Bill) Long (1911–1998) was technical director, and Mary Dorothy Wood Long (1919–1998) an actress. They both eventually became educators and were active with the Carolina Playmakers (Est. 1918) of University of North Carolina (UNC) at Chapel Hill (Est. 1789).

Today, William the younger is a highly distinguished costume designer who has won six of his eighteen Tony award nominations and was inducted by Stro herself into the Theatre Hall of Fame (Est. 1970) in 2006. All told his work could outfit every show on and Off-Broadway for decades. He's also created costumes for the West End, regional and touring companies, modern dance, ballet, concerts, television and film projects, even one-of-a-kind evening gowns for celebrity red carpet photo opps. So prodigious is he that designing for the stage seems to have been preordained. Except he didn't always see it that way. And therein lies an important cornerstone of what makes his work truly extraordinary.

"Fashion was already there," William discloses. "I remember when I was a child, taking needle and thread and making an Elizabethan collar for my dog out of the border of a discarded pillowcase." Despite this, it was a history degree he earned at the College of William and Mary (Est. 1693), then on to graduate studies in Renaissance art history and architecture at UNC on a Samuel H. Kress Foundation fellowship.

But theater dogged his heels. He wound up rooming in a house owned by playwright and novelist Betty Smith (1896–1972) who regaled him with her exploits. Then, for friends staging a show, he agreed to pitch in with props and sets, which he'd done for other regional productions. These, and surely other little things, brought into question where he was headed. There had been an expectation that he would be, like his father and mother, on the teaching side of an endeavor. He still harbors a feeling that he had disappointed his parents. And if there is one thing William is loath to do, it's disappoint. It was not a decision made in haste. William admits, "I wasn't really sure what path to take. All I knew was that I was reluctant to enter the 'family business'. My heart just wasn't in it." Nevertheless, he had qualms about leaving "the academic nest". It was comfortable, safe, a world he had known all his life. But he did ultimately submit to his calling and applied to the Yale University School of Drama (Est. 1924).

What did not disappoint was the detour to Yale. It was where William discovered many things that molded the rest of his life, where lasting friendships with now respected playwrights Christopher Durang and Wendy Wasserstein (1950-2006), and writer Paul Rudnick began. Then, one of his professors, the brilliant set designer Ming Cho Lee (1930-2020), became mentor, taskmaster, and confidant. Lee showed him how costumes and sets can do more than just actualize a time and place, that his creativity can also transport an audience, define characters, enrich the entire theatergoing experience. "He taught me how to 'read' a play as a designer, and how to find its moral focus," says William, tearing up at the thought of Lee's recent passing. "He made me appreciate the importance of involvement and responsibility toward the community, and was the one who urged me to apply to be in the union. To this day, everything I do is judged by 'what will Ming think?'"

No less important, it was while he was at Yale when William fell in love with fashion. "I had only taken a single course on costumes because I thought of becoming a set designer. But, I was spending a lot of time in the drama school library because my friend Wendy was working nights there," he says. "And one day, I came across a stack of the trade publication Women's Wear Daily. I hadn't been aware of it before and I was instantly hooked." He devoured every issue he could get his hands on, learning about the inner workings of the garment industry. And among its outsized yet mostly anonymous personalities, he read a story on the biggest name in fashion no one had ever heard of — Charles James (1906-1978).

William says, "I was obsessed!" And he had every reason to be. James was a visionary, a self-taught designer of erudite talent who conceived elliptical marvels of astounding mathematical precision. For instance, his Figure Eight dress (from 1933) features a skirt with a complexity that can only be truly appreciated when disassembled: its right front side wraps across the left leg, then between the legs, over to the right, and across to the left back to complete a figure-eight spiral. Made in 1953 for the third and last Mrs. William Randolph Hearst Jr., his Four Leaf Clover gown has multiple petticoats supporting a mosaic skirt of duchesse satin and Velours de Lyon with pleats that open and float the four sides up when the wearer dances. The incomparable Cristóbal Balenciaga (1895-1972) himself declared James "the greatest American couturier…who raised (dressmaking) . . . to a pure art form."

But like other artists of his rare caliber, James was tormented by his own uncompromising views and perfectionism. Some of his pieces betray tracks of several restitchings. Others he worked on for years. Because as artists are wont to do, he would either lose interest or get stymied, work on a different piece, then sometime later go back to the previous one with a fresh idea. Eventually his clients became accustomed to never knowing when or even if their dresses were ever going to be delivered. He's also been known to charge for the same order twice, or borrow a dress back from a client on some pretense, then resell it to someone else.

He was irascible, litigious, and convinced that he was constantly misunderstood, unappreciated, and that people were either conspiring against him or stealing his designs. Not that his suspicions were any less plausible. But having no qualms over escalating his grievances, James alienated friends and foes alike, stranding him amidst burnt bridges with few sources of income, much less the means to build a feasible business. By the time William read about James, the designer's halcyon days were over. He was subsisting on the largesse of a handful devotees and residing at Hotel Chelsea (Est. 1905).

James always was partial to living in hotels and the Chelsea was congruent to his temperament. Its spirit of having been once an artists co-op had carried over into its fabled period as refuge for names that weren't as boldface as they used to be. At one time or another, Jimi Hendrix (1942–1970), Jackson Pollock (1912–1956), Simone de Beauvoir (1908–1986), Dylan Thomas (1914–1953), Jack Kerouac (1922–1969), and Quentin Crisp (1908–1999) had resided at the W. 23rd Street red brick building with ornate wrought iron balconies. But the property was languishing in neglect, getting by on the notoriety of its inhabitants, and becoming a seedy magnet for drugs, prostitutes, even ghosts. It certainly wasn't causing Conrad Hilton any sleepless nights. All that made Stanley Bard (1935–2017), innkeeper to the down-and-out stars, lenient about overdue rents. And James was behind by half a year, at least. Despite his adversity, James wasn't the embittered recluse he was being made out to be, just not quite approachable.

William found that out after, in his words, "I threw myself into the deep end with all the pomposity of a three-degree graduate" and moved to New York. He took a $400 a month apartment at the Chelsea in hopes of getting an apprenticeship with his idol. "I wanted to learn from Charles," he recounts, "and for six months I tried to meet

him. I waited in the lobby, hung out in the hallways." All to no avail.
"I left entreating messages at his front door," he says, "but never heard
back. You see, he saw adulation as his due, so it had to be at
his convenience."

In the meantime, at the prodding of Lee and his pals from Yale,
William kept going to interviews for jobs he never got. He did,
however, scrounge side gigs here and there like designing party deco-
rations for an event company and making historical doll models. And
it was working on the latter that he managed to get through to James.
He recalls, "I was having problems with a piece. I couldn't make this
vintage opera capelet hang properly. So I wrote to Charles asking for
advice and slipped the letter under his door. I was walking back to my
apartment when I heard the phone ringing. From the other end he
said, 'I'd love to see what you're doing'." And so began William's novi-
tiate in the church of Charles James.

He remembers many of the famous supplicants. "Antonio Lopez
(1943-1987) made hundreds of illustrations of Charles' dresses.
Elsa Peretti (1940-2021) dropped by all the time. There was
Dominique de Ménil (née Schlumberger, 1908-1997), Paloma
Picasso, and many other fancy ladies in dark glasses." But, William
says, "He just didn't like many people and simply tolerated some.
There used to be other interns, but by then only Homer Layne and
I were left. And Homer was his assistant so he was permitted to help
make the dresses. I wasn't," William clarifies. "But I still learned so
much. A few times I did get to wear white gloves to thread mark a
dress for Homer to adjust. And I was able to sit in at some fittings.

"My tasks were mostly menial. I picked up the pins dispersed on the
floor. I cooked for him, painted the walls, walked (the dog) Sputnik,

ran errands." William also tried to tidy up the all-in-one home, studio, workshop and storage space spread across apartments 618, 620, and 624. He avers that for all of James' complaints about bugs in the apartments, he was complacent about their state of perpetual squalor. "Except for the bathroom, he dissuaded me from cleaning. He knew where everything was and didn't want anything disturbed."

Another of his unpaid factotum chores was typing James' querulous correspondences, which bore the same zeal he expended on anything he did. "He whined endlessly about Wanamaker's, raged that Halston stole his patterns. Of course, I just took it for granted he was telling the truth. I found out later Halston had already paid him for those patterns." And while it would be unfair to suppose he delighted in his many feuds, he did instigate (and actively prolonged) several of them. One involved Eleanor Lambert (1903-2003), his former publicist who is recognized for having campaigned to validate New York as an international fashion capital. On James, Lambert said, "Everyone in the fashion world knows Charlie was a genius. Unfortunately, even a genius must be part of a business collaboration. He always resisted that. He did wonderful, individual, beautifully draped clothes…the first designer I ever saw mix satin, velvet and taffeta. But that kind of dressmaking is past. It's too costly." James vehemently disagreed.

William remembers James in a heated exchange over the phone rehashing his squabble with Lambert. "He was yelling at the top of his lungs, his British accent becoming more pronounced and forceful with every word." William sighs, "It was always the same: people betrayed him, for everything he'd done for the world this was how he was being treated…" But William got used to the curmudgeon and stayed until James died in 1978 due to bronchial pneumonia. "I still miss him. He left a big void. He was self-destructive, didn't eat well, never saw a doctor. But, there was something admirable about his absolutism. There was no give and take. And he approached his art as a matter of life or death."

William's art would undergo its own rebirth after departing the Chelsea. Costumes and fashion became more important to his career, which flourished in the most New York of ways. Someone knew someone who knew someone else who knew someone from Yale who trusted William's work. He also benefited from the informal mentorship he received from respected costume designer Willa Kim (1917-2016).

His first Broadway show was the 1978 revival of Nikolai Gogol's (1809-1852) "The Inspector General" at Circle in the Square Theatre (Est. 1972). A few years later, director and fellow Yaley Walton Jones brought him into "The 1940's Radio Hour", first developed in 1974 for the Yale Summer Cabaret. As resident designer back then, William had also been part of the original, when, he says, "My budget for sets and costumes was $50." So he joined the new production, eager to see what they could bring to Broadway.

The song-and-dance 1979 revision that opened at the St. James Theatre (Est. 1927) was a nostalgic romp set during the live broadcast of "The Mutual Manhattan Variety Cavalcade" from the Hotel Astor's Algonquin Room. Chock full of WWII dancing and jazz standards, the jukebox musical revolves around a beleaguered producer and his cast, all dressed by William in handsome period suits with roomy jackets and trousers, bow ties and pocket squares. The garments were made at Barbara Matera Ltd, the once premier costume shop founded in 1968 by Barbara Matera (1929-2001) and husband Arthur (1930-2004). It attained a reputation for dependability from Matera's aptitude for translating design into superbly constructed costumes. As William worked on more projects and spent time with the shop's drapers, he bonded with Matera over his designs for dance, which was among her passions. And many of those he had the shop make ended up securing William's place in Broadway history.

For years composer and music theorist Maury Yeston had been working on a musical adaptation of *"Otto e mezzo"*, the 1963 semi-auto-biographical motion picture by Federico Fellini (1920-1993). It was known to the rest of the world by its numeric title "8½", a reference to the total of Fellini's filmography. Yeston added his version to the tally and rounded up his title to "Nine", which shares the picture's framework: the mid-life nervous breakdown of Fellini's avatar Guido Contini. But during auditions, Yeston and director Tommy Tune found that apart from Raul Julia (1940-1994) as Contini, the actors were less compelling than the actresses. This gave Yeston, Tune, and playwright Arthur Kopit (1937-2021) the impetus to bring the women to the foreground and cohere their importance in the life of the main character.

William learned about the show from Thommie Walsh (1950-2007) who also worked on "The 1940's Radio Hour". Walsh, choreographing "Nine", asked William to join the production as assistant costume designer to Lawrence Miller (1944-2009). William regretfully declined because he had never served in that capacity and wasn't entirely sure what the job entailed. Months passed when someone rang up inquiring if William could "measure all the girls today, and also do a shoe tracing?" He absently replied with his own questions, "Excuse me? What show is this?" The person on the other line said he was the stage manager calling for Nine the musical, "We're rehearsing at the New Amsterdam."

Confused, William asked why they were calling him since he had not accepted the assistant costume designer position. But, the caller countered, William wasn't on his list as assistant rather as the costume designer. Apparently, Miller was originally overseeing sets and costumes but had chosen to focus on the former and recommended they hire William for the latter. Except that everyone forgot to actually let him know.

Production meetings often took place at a pub on W. 45th Street where William expounded on his ideas, sketching them on cocktail napkins until three in the morning. Steeped in Italian *alta moda* and Venetian gothic, his designs were emblematic of Contini's overwrought hallucinations. William says, "I really love helping create a character's psychological interior." He grouped costumes in the green, red, and white of the Italian flag, rolled out a parade of dazzling 18th century gowns, and paid homage to the black-and-white Fellini picture by dressing the cast in all-black ensembles during the scenes in the white 'tiled' spa set. But the most singled out piece is the black-embroidered sheer bodysuit worn by Anita Morris (1943-1994) as Contini's mistress Carla. William created a visual and tactile medium from which the union of actress, character, and Walsh's choreography achieved an enticing performance capped by a handstand and a soprano high C.

"Nine" played at the 46th Street Theatre from 1982 to 1984, snagging twelve Tony nominations. On live broadcast, actor Hal Linden said the winner for best costume design in a musical was Theoni V. Aldredge (1922-2011). But in the next second, still looking down at the open envelope in his hands, he corrected himself and announced William's name. In that instant, William was ushered into the big leagues and the infinite world of theater and dance.

———————————

Dancing can be traced to ancient communal rites of passages, initiation, death and reincarnations, fertility and unions, or the changing of seasons. Participants to these ceremonies wore special raiments, and moved in circles and formations. An abundance of proof to this has been found engraved on cave walls in Trois-Frères, Ariège in France; the Bhimbetka Rock Shelters in India; the Tassili n'Ajjer in the Algerian Sahara; in the mountains of East Kalimantan in Indonesia. Figures in motion have also been committed to vases, urns, murals, woodcuts, vellum, as well as in numerous oral and cultural traditions. Rock carvings and potteries from predynastic Egypt depict dancing that scholars have linked to funeral rites because the looser white sheaths, collars, or hair adornments of the dancers are unlike everyday Egyptian dress.

An open chain dance of men and women holding hands and festively winding around town is the Provençal custom of farandole. But Greecian frescoes attest to a progenitor—the geranos or "dance of the crane" from the myth of Theseus. After having vanquished the Minotaur in the more well known part of the tale, Theseus returns to Crete with the fourteen other young men who were saved from being sacrificed to the monster. Enroute, they decide to pay tribute to Apollo by dropping anchor on the island of Delos where the men perform a dance that reenacts their journey into and out of the Minotaur's labyrinth. It's been described as imitating a crane, which is claimed to need eight lumbering steps before it can take flight. The Greeks took eight steps, leapt on the ninth, and repeated, while snaking around the god's temple altar.

———————————

The belief that ritualized dancing can open portals to realms of divinity are espoused in the shamanistic practices of the indigenous peoples of North America and Australia. In the 1300s, the Mevlevi, followers of renowned Persian poet Jalal al-Din Muhammad Rumi (1207-1273), originated the devotional swirling still observed today in Sufism by dervishes or *semazen.* In Islamic faith, Sufism is regarded as the purification of the inner self and thus requires proper garments—though not strictly comparable to liturgical vestments—during the worship ritual of Sema. Arising to the dance, the *semazen* divests himself of a black cloak, representing worldly life, to be symbolically reborn in a wide, white pleated frock (*entari,* or the sleeveless version called *tannur*) often secured with a 10-centimeter sash *(kemer)* wound around the waist three times, a short jacket (*destegül*), the conical camel's hair hat called a *sikke,* and soft leather shoes that reach up to the ankle.

With arms outstretched, the semazen's right palm is pointed upward, the left pointed down, channeling grace from the heavens above, bestowing it to the earth below, and upon those bearing witness. Planted on the floor, his left foot is the axis from which he spins with the right foot counter-clockwise to musical movements that progress through stages of The Four Selams. The first represents rebirth to truth; then the rapture of witnessing the splendor of creation; followed by total submission to love; and finally acceptance of destiny. The aim is renunciation of personal desires in theosophical prayer to reach the source of all perfection (dharma).

Other national dances, however, have been adulterated by colonization or secularization. The Korean Salpuri-Chum was once ceremonial, a way of banishing evil spirits. The hula, principally found in Hawai`i, Moloka`i, O`ahu, and Kaua`i is meant to honor ancient deities. It's often misrepresented to tourists as gyrations in short grass skirts, which is actually Polynesian. Real hula is said to be slow, emotive, performed by women in dignified attire, to an accompaniment of bamboo sticks and gourd drums. The form more widely known today is a mix of ancient elements with modern morality fables, backed by guitars and the ukulele. Similarly, the Philippine folk dance *tinikling* which involves beating and sliding bamboo poles on the ground while the dancer steps over and in between them, is mostly Spanish with instrumental rondalla.

In secular settings, dance was deemed a beneficial social skill by the ancient Romans, and in time, became integral to the hodgepodge shticks of the traveling entertainers of Medieval Europe. Meanwhile, it was in Northern Italy that professional dance instructors are supposed to have first taught classes to affluent families. But once dance etiquette took root, a tug-of-war between the upper and lower classes kicked off. Dance was enjoyed by commoners for its rambunctious ribaldry. But for the high-born, that sort of public display was unspeakably vulgar. They were, but of course, no less inclined from privately indulging as spectators, registering their amusement with discreet snickers and one arched brow. For hundreds of years, performers were ranked among the lower classes, and dance abided by its bipolar tangents: salacious entertainment or solemn avocations. To the elite, it was meant for private occasions, preferably at court or in noble houses, and executed with grace and decorum. Knowing how to dance was an asset but any outward sign of excitement was best left to professionals.

Fashion too imposed curtailments. Elaborate and cumbersome clothes were attributes of the leisure class. After all, one couldn't possibly get into such apparel without the help of servants, much less be expected to actually toil in them. Men wore stiff coats over brocaded tunics and knee breeches. Compensating for the towering wigs of their partners, they were shod in tight, high-heeled footwear. For women, baleen corsets, piles of silks, cottons, and tulles, wide petticoats, panniered skirts, and trains of velvet were not exactly conducive to jaunty movements. Plus, moral rectitude was somehow laughably thought to be preserved by those coverings.

By the 15th century, court dances in England, France, Germany, and Italy grouped men and women on opposite sides before launching into precise 'advance, retreat, and encircle' variations. The sequence and number of steps for each *basse danse* were inextricably timed to the exact units of measure of its own music, making it imperative to possess good ear-to-foot coordination. *Basse danse* would later be replaced by the minuet, which used to be a French folk dance. But by the time it became a staple at regal ballrooms, it had been stripped of spontaneity and became all measured steps punctuated by lots of solemn bows.

These stately dances with their processional cadences continued on through the *ancien régime* reign of Louis XIV (1638-1715) when all matters of style, art, and entertainment were arbitrated at Château de Versailles. Before then however, amidst generations of dynastic discord, tenuous world domination had belonged to the Spanish branch of the royal house of Habsburg. Under Charles V (1500-1558) their purview included the Holy Roman Empire, Castile and Aragon, Naples, Sicily, Sardinia, Germany, parts of Burgundy, and Austria. Habsburg power was perpetuated with aggressive colonization overseas and blatant displays of wealth at home. One effective way of flaunting their bottomless coffers was donning vast wardrobes of black dresses because it was common knowledge that a salient ingredient of the expensive dye needed for making them—logwood—had to be harvested from the lucrative Spanish colonies in Central and South America. Thus, every self-respecting blue blood in the continent knew well enough to only purchase clothes from Spain.

But France's Louis XIV was able to wrest supremacy from the Spaniards through a series of decrees instituting tightly-regulated trade guilds that made it unlawful to import anything that could be domestically made. *Le Roi-Soleil* then asserted absolute sovereignty from a lavishly renovated Versailles where he corralled the nobility, not just in service to his ego, but to foment rivalries and keep everyone and everything under his royal thumb and paranoid gaze. With survival as the main priority, no one stood on firm enough ground to plot against the king.

But dismissing their chicanery as the hedonistic *divertissements* of an idle aristocracy in opulent *ennui* would be a superficial reading. Were the nobles self-indulgent? They were. Could they be petty? In many cases, sure. But at Louis XIV's Versailles, hours of vacuous chatter to cultivate alliances with the right people was not frittering away an afternoon. There was nothing trivial about obsessing over the perfect frock since every *fête* was directed with great pomp. And not if any and all of it meant the difference between the betterment of one's social, political, and economic stature or being banished in disgrace and destitution. There was sycophantic fawning. Then, there was strategic scheming. Every word, step, or look was rife with innuendo, intrigue, and had all the consequences of combat. This was, quite plainly, bloodsport.

Thus, sequestering courtiers turned Versailles into an 830-hectare, 2,300-room breeding ground of hissing vipers. To those for whom it was a daily preoccupation to curry favor with the king, a signifier of having succeeded was earning a *justaucorps à brevet.* Greatly prized for nothing more than bragging rights, it was a long, light blue, collarless, and red-lined jacket with gold or silver embroidery exclusive to the king and a handful chosen nobles. The majority who didn't have one resorted to imitating Louis XIV's other sartorial cues such as his red heeled shoes, a trend that became all the rage in Europe.

But it was a groundbreaking move facilitated by the Minister of State Jean-Baptiste Colbert (1619-1683) that bestowed fashion authority to France, enduring centuries thereafter. By royal command, textiles were produced biannually: silks for summer, and satins and velvets for winter, alerting everyone to dress accordingly. Regardless of the weather, fashion dictated the start of summer on Pentecost (the seventh Sunday after Easter), and winter without fail on November 1. To have worn anything otherwise a single day off would not have been *comme il faut*.

This incessant updating of wardrobes, propagating excitement over newness, was a welcome boon to the French economy and national pride. And perhaps even more pointedly, it ran contrary to the Spanish way of valuing constancy and the delineation of the classes by way of dressing. Soon, Paris as *le dernier cri* and France's political and economic leadership were acknowledged by other nations—at least, until 1789 at the swift and deadly fall of the guillotine.

In the aftermath, egalitarianism prevailed over Parisian cultural life and attracted wider audiences to the bourgeoisie's cobbled stomping grounds of the *18e arrondissement.* The neighborhood had once been dotted by windmills. And still there today are the Moulin Radet and Moulin de la Galette, along with the sweeping view of Paris. But a third, the most internationally recognized attraction, is the windmill that was converted into a cabaret (by Catalonian entrepreneur Joseph Oller, 1839–1922 and business partner Charles Zidler 1831–1897) to coincide with the 1889 Paris Expo: the Moulin Rouge. Among the many lewd entertainments of Montmartre's pantomimes, jugglers, and spine-tingling feats of acrobatics, the red structure with neon-lit sails stands as the birthplace of an obstinately working class dance, devoid of pretensions and as thrilling today as when it debuted: the cancan.

Since skirts of the period were a bundle of layers, women needed both hands to gather and lift them up so the dance's high kicks could be managed. And as their legs rose and dropped, the dancers wove their skirts and intermittently flashed gartered black stockings and frilly colored knickers of embroidered silk and lace. One tricky maneuver involved using one hand to catch and hold the ankle at the kick. The dancer then spins on her supporting foot, jumps, and finishes with a full drop and split. The liberating jubilation of the cancan was in tandem with the bawdy complexion of the rhinestoned dresses and ruffled petticoats of silk taffeta and organza in crimsons and blue stripes, pink trims, and embellished with velvet ribbons.

For those more inclined to dance than watch, hundreds of places from taverns and public halls to private clubs and salons opened in England. Two of the most frequented were the gardens of Ranelagh and Vauxhall, both of which had quaint Rococo rotundas. The one at Ranelagh, designed by a minor architect called William Jones, had a central fireplace surrounded by columns and an orchestra stand from which Wolfgang Amadeus Mozart (1756-1791) at age nine performed. The rotunda at Vauxhall was designed by enameller George Michael Moser (1706-1783) who ornamented elegant timepieces, candlesticks, bracelets, and snuff boxes. While both were destinations for lazy promenades and listening to orchestras, they became packed venues for dancing. At the cost of a guinea, over three hundred of London's nobility and gentry showed up at Vauxhall for a masquerade ball with outdoor dancing, and Frederick, the Prince of Wales (1707-1751) as a special guest.

A little over a thousand kilometers east, in Vienna, the composers, dance orchestra conductors, and friendly adversaries—Johann Baptist Strauss I (1804-1849) and Joseph Franz Karl Lanner (1801-1843)—were enchanting locals with the waltz. Strauss brought even more attention to it during tours with his band to Britain, Belgium, and the Netherlands. The son, Johann Baptist Strauss II (1825-1899) would surpass his father's accomplishments and be renowned for his 1866 masterpiece *"An der schönen blauen Donau"*, Op. 314 (commonly called the 'Blue Danube'), which debuted a year later at the concert of the *Wiener Männergesang-Verein* (Vienna Men's Choral Association). The eminence of the music at these "participatory" concerts also challenged the belief that one should only be seated and listening to fine compositions.

The usual *sturm und drang* roiled over the unappealing antecedents of the waltz itself, of course. It had been a boisterous dance for peasants in which couples rapidly rotated around the room while holding firmly to each other so as not to be flung aside by the centrifugal force. Vociferous objections over both velocity as well as the close contact of the dancers were made. Why, it was simply outrageous that any virtuous couple would show such intimacy in public! Clerics bellowed from their pulpits that this new dance was indecent and could only lead to sin. And enough people must have been convinced since the waltz was banned in certain regions of Switzerland and Germany.

It probably didn't help when the waltz became a plot point in the scandalous 1856 novel "Madame Bovary" by the French novelist Gustave Flaubert (1821-1880). In chapter 8, the titular character is at a ball when she is approached for a dance by a man only identified as a viscount. Ignorant of the waltz, she demurs. But he insists on teaching her. It is three in the morning. It's the last dance. And while the husband distractedly plays at a card table, stealing glances at her, she is in the throes of an indiscreet and intoxicating waltz with a total stranger.

All the protestations only underlined the futility of even trying to curb the demand for dancing. Perhaps wanting to capitalize on its notoriety or recognizing the cursive handwriting on the dance floor, or both, instructors took it upon themselves to redeem the waltz. The dichotomy of right and wrong ways of dancing eased it into tolerable legitimacy. The accepted first English language treatise on it is 1816's "A Description of the Correct Method of Waltzing" by Thomas Wilson (1774-1854) of the King Theater Opera House in London. Anxious for guidance on how to infiltrate the right social circles, many snapped up such dance manuals. And those how-to books made dancemasters the self-appointed authorities on the subject, while simultaneously promoting their studios and services.

Fragments of assorted documentation imply that the waltz washed up on U.S. shores sometime around 1815. And while there was still reticence over the decency of public dancing, the skill itself was valued by the upper classes. By 1823, dance was an official course at The United States Military Academy, better known by its metonym, West Point (Est. 1802). Floridians say they have been waltzing in Tallahassee since the 1820s. But it was in 1834 when American high society made its acquaintance at a party given by Mrs. Harrison Gray Otis (née Sally Foster, 1770-1838) at 45 Beacon Street. And right on schedule, the parlors of Boston's upstanding citizens echoed with dismayed gasps, the clutching of pearls, and whispers of what had happened at the Otis house the night before. But, the edges of their disapproval were blunted by the two prominent personalities who had led the waltz: dancemaster Lorenzo Papanti (1799-1872) and Mrs. Otis, who was the undisputed queen of Boston society and had married (senator Otis, 1765-1848) into the illustrious Beacon Hill brahmins.

The word "brahmin"—the highest (and priestly) of the four Hindu castes in India—had been co-opted by author and physician Oliver Wendell Holmes, Sr. (1809-1894) to describe well-shod

Bostonians in his 1861 novel "Elsie Venner". Henceforth, Boston Brahmin referred to the city's old families, characterized by their subscription to the same tenets as the puritans from whom they were directly descended. From that unyielding, puritanical streak came the assertion one should only deign to appear in print thrice, at the announcements of one's birth, marriage, and death. Never mind how incapable they actually were of staying out of the papers in between those milestones. The Boston brahmin class betters, by a hair, their rivals from the main line families of Philadelphia and the knickerbockers of New York because many of them were already rich before they immigrated to the new world in the 17th century. There is an old joke that their servants had been sent ahead on the Mayflower to prepare their 'summer cottages'.

The waltz could not have received a seal of approval more definitive than from a family of that pedigree. Then, there was Signor Papanti, who had arrived from Italy a mere seven years prior, and opened a dance school, at the time only the second in all of New England. Against the odds, he gained entrée into the city's upper echelons by having befriended Mrs. Otis, about whom author Cleveland Amory (1917-1998) wrote, "It amused her to do things other Boston ladies didn't do, and to do them first" in his 1947 book "The Proper Bostonians". Mrs. Otis took her role of society figurehead very seriously and her willingness to champion something as fresh and exciting as the waltz verified Papanti's reputation.

Soon after, Papanti presided over Boston's most spoiled children in his stiff suit, powdered wig, and patent leather pumps, standing ramrod straight with bow in hand for keeping time with the music. He also brandished it as a switch to correct every sign of misbehavior, or mistake in steps or posture. By 1837, he was doing all that from his splendid new Tremont Row ballroom, with its massive chandelier, dressing rooms, a main floor bracketed by benches, a minstrel's gallery for musicians, and opposite that a wall of tall mirrors. It became the venue of the can't-miss Boston Assembly balls, and from where generations of future city leaders learned the Boston Waltz, a more languid, Americanized version of the Viennese with extra to-and-fros. It has since been modified further into what is currently the International Style Waltz. Before the close of the 1800s, the waltz was a regular part of the dances held twice a month at the White House of President Stephen Grover Cleveland (1837-1908).

In New York City, composer and band leader Allen T. Dodworth (1822-1956) opened the Dodworth Dancing Academy north of the Grace Church rectory, within 806-808 Broadway, a double-wide Italianate brownstone designed by architect James Renwick, Jr. (1818-1895) that eventually came to be known as Dodworth's Hall. The school was hailed by the New York Times in its September 16, 1852 issue as "the most splendid private dancing academy in this country." In a way, Dodworth was to New York what Papanti was to Boston. Except Dodworth's charges were mostly the offsprings of the infamous "Robber Barons".

At the dawn of the 20th century, industrialization fueled extraordinary innovation and growth in the United States. The newly laid railroad tracks made the transport of people and goods faster and more efficient. But like a steel web it had also ensnared businesses and workers in the clutches of a few men. To some, they were "Captains of Industry", to others "Robber Barons". The latter phrase came from a moniker for feudal lords who hijacked travelers in Medieval Europe, and was used by the New York Times as a derisive descriptor of Cornelius "The Commodore" Vanderbilt

(1794-1877) for how he rapaciously conducted his enterprises. Later, this unflattering sobriquet encompassed the rest of his business cohorts. Because, while there was a surge of opportunities for unskilled laborers, the haves were making unconscionable fortunes off the backs of the have-nots and the disparity between them was beyond bridging. The teeming masses huddled in the neighborhood slums of Hell's Kitchen and lower Manhattan were wallowing in extreme poverty.

A turbulent sea of industrial, economic, and cultural change was inundating the city. But high and dry on an island of privilege were a handful of men from a freshly burnished merchant class, leading historians to call this era, twenty years after it ended, "The Gilded Age". Though often romanticized as a time of splendor, it was in fact one of harsh inequities, 'gilded' by the unchecked ostentation of greedy capitalists and social climbers. The name was intended as a pejorative. And the virtues, or lack thereof, of the robber barons have been and will be debated for years to come.

What is incontrovertible was the contentious ascension of the Hills, Goulds, Fisks, Vanderbilts, Rockefellers, Carnegies, Morgans and their ilk. To the old families, the Stuyvesants, Schermerhorns, Newbolds and Livingstons, the upstarts were a narcissistic, pernicious lot, for whom there wasn't a problem that couldn't be solved by throwing enough money at it. From the opposite end, the arrivistes felt they were being made to squirm under the heel of well-bred tyrants who, blind to their own impending extinction, were only upholding the status quo out of self-preservation. Veiling their hostilities in figurative chess matches of social one-upmanship couldn't hide the truth of both those points of view.

Curiously enough, the main objective of the new people was to become exactly like the old. Even as they built their homes on Fifth Avenue into ever taller, bigger, gaudier show palaces, they sought the means by which they could scrub away the parts of themselves that looked or sounded as though they had just disembarked at Ellis Island, albeit with carpetbags of cash. And so they got their clothes from Henry Poole & Co on Savile Row, gowns from *maison* Félix or the House of Worth in Paris, crystal from Baccarat, and flowers from Mr. Charles Thorley of The House of Flowers. They adorned their walls with pictures by Paul-Jacques-Aimé Baudry (1828-1886) and François Boucher (1703-1770). They attended the opera at The Academy of Music on E14th Street, bitterly seated orchestra because they couldn't buy their way into a box seat. They learned how to ride, tried to speak French, and sent their children to Dodworth.

Wise to the ways of the wealthy, Dodworth made his school more desirable by not accepting just anyone who showed up at his door, requiring at least three letters of introduction from all would-be applicants. His bona fides became more impressive after the 1888 publication of his dance manual with the much too verbose title "Dancing and Its Relations to Education and Social Life, With a New Method of Instruction Including a Complete Guide to the Cotillion" from Harper & Brothers (now just Harpers as part of HarperCollins). The inclusion of cotillion as part of the title is indicative of its importance. Although the version to which New Yorkers had become accustomed is slightly different from the former incarnation—*contredanse française*—of the previous century. The cotillion that was being emulated in the city's ballrooms was Germanic, which incorporated flirtatious games of choosing and mixing partners. Its first publicized appearance was at 49-51 W. 23rd Street during the 1854 winter season costume ball thrown by the William Colford Schermerhorns (1821-1903). They were joined by a hundred or so of their closest friends including the Redmonds, the Van Nests, and the Iselins.

Dodworth's book helped further the cotillion until it became an anticipated full-on performance by trained dancers at the conclusion of a soiree. Then, the events themselves came to be called "cotillions" and taking over the floor were quadrilles, which were so complicated it took on average twelve hours to rehearse. And, that was taking for granted that one had already spent years under Dodworth's tutelage.

By all accounts, Dodworth was an excellent, well-liked instructor. He designed a creative set of guidelines and imparted good manners and refinement. Eventually, Dodworth's Hall couldn't contain everyone who wanted to study there. So, he followed most of his clientele who had already wriggled their way uptown. From a new space on Fifth Avenue and 26th Street, Dodsworth continued to teach New Yorkers how to dance with decorum at all the city's debutante balls and grandest social functions. Dodworth's Hall, incidentally, would thereafter house many tenants from the garment industry such as shirtmakers Lubell Bros. Mfg. Co. and Criterion Shirt Band Co. as well as Eastern Textiles Co. A costume shop at the street level of the building is there today.

The Gilded Age's supercilious principles tainted its fashions. The dignified neutrals that have always been at home in the grimy environs of an unforgiving city were replaced by conspicuous jackets and skirts awash in bright colors and patterns. Hats too became more decorative, cradling flowers and feathers. More radical still, horizontal seaming was abandoned. Dresses, bodices, and corsets with vertical seams—starting from the shoulders or at the armholes—elongated the line of the body. This also made it appealing to heighten the neckline with a standing collar. Then, the ensemble was festooned with plastrons, beads, bows, silk cords, and laces. Looking "pulled together" in convoluted clothes was more apt to be admired since comfort was more closely associated with being indolent.

Likewise, men were wearing leaner and more intricately layered pieces under frock and morning coats with top hats. The average man had to make do with bowler hats over a sack, double, or single-breasted suit minus waist seams. The dinner jacket, popularized by Albert Edward (1841-1910) or "Bertie" (not yet Edward VII, King of the United Kingdom of Great Britain), made its transatlantic crossing and was rechristened the "tuxedo" after the Tuxedo Club (Est. 1886) in Tuxedo Park, some forty miles north of Manhattan. A shortened modification of the tailcoat, per Bertie's request to his Savile Row tailor Henry Poole & Co, the dinner jacket was allegedly, with scant and doubtful substantiation, worn at that country club by coffee broker James Brown Potter (1853-1922). Regardless, it ended up becoming the tuxedo and the de-facto American formal wear.

The finest menswear came from England, and Paris was still the capital of women's wear. But one Englishman—Charles Frederick Worth (1825-1895)—was able to beguile the French when he opened an atelier there in 1858. After he had won over Empress Eugénie de Montijo (1826-1920), titled Parisiennes, followed closely by ambitious Americans, beat a path to the House of Worth. Its salon on rue de la Paix bustled with aristocrats and socialites who were there for fittings or deciding next season's wardrobes. The conventions of labels with the designer's signature sewn onto garments, and having clients view the collection on live models originated there. Supposedly at the behest of the empress, Worth earnestly pursued ways to make his designs practical. First, he altered the crinoline's unwieldy breadth by gravitating its bulk to the back. Then he disposed of it altogether for straight silhouettes. He also raised hems to the ankles, keeping skirts from raking against the ground. These were risky changes but clients stayed loyal to Worth because he never stinted on the richness of the kind of gowns women loved to wear.

The American rag trade, meanwhile, traversed new avenues for selling its wares. Because shopping had been, questionably yet chiefly, designated as a pursuit for women, department stores were among the few public places where they could go unchaperoned without imperiling their reputations. It's almost unfathomable that there was a time when women were made to believe they were helpless past the thresholds of their homes. They may rule their roosts, but servants were the ones expected to venture out to buy supplies and run errands. Not only were women not allowed in public spaces without being escorted by a man, even idling along the sidewalk to peer into a store window was frowned upon since this would leave them vulnerable to an assault. The imaginary potentials for an attack and having their reputations besmirched beyond bearing kept women indoors. Few truly realize that it was in the contrivance of the department store where women were first 'permitted' freedom from their households. And, down the road, enabled them to exert power via what they chose or refused to purchase.

The department store hails back to Harding, Howell & Co (Est. 1796) in London. But the accretion of what makes up the modern department store took place in a roughly twenty-eight New York city block perimeter called the "Ladies' Mile" shopping district. It was here in the mid-1840s when an Irish immigrant called Alexander Turney Stewart (1803-1876) paid $70,000 for a section of Broadway upon which he had architects Joseph Trench (1815-1879) and John Butler Snook (1815-1901) build for him the A. T. Stewart & Co store, which came to be known as the "Marble Palace". This was followed twenty years later by the "Iron Palace", a six-story Italianate edifice surrounded by arched windows, tall sheets of plate glass, and Corinthian columns. It was crowned by a picturesque dome skylight shining down over some nineteen departments that sold dresses, carpets, fabrics, toys, and other home goods.

Since the fight for women's suffrage was already underway, the whiff of condescension wafting from the very name "Ladies' Mile" was conspicuous even then. After all, these emporiums were conceived specifically for women as larger, more 'genteel' dry goods stores, as though the departments within them were all that should matter to 'proper' ladies. And questioning entrenched gender roles wasn't done. But lulling women into submissive domesticity must have been inadvertent since the trailblazing purveyors of luxury were more fixated on the bottom line. They did everything they could to please their customers and make shopping as convenient as possible. Shelves were stocked with finds from all over the world, bought wholesale for reasonable pricing. Outside innovations helped as well. The installation of street gas lamps in Manhattan, from 1825–1840, brought illumination to the stores on Broadway in the evening. The Interborough Rapid Transit (IRT) Sixth Avenue El (elevated) train began operations in 1878, making it easier for women, at least those who didn't own their own carriages, to come to the stores and carry their shopping home with them.

Inside, to encourage women to squander their clothing allowances as well as their days in each other's companies, stores opened restaurants. These were even strategically ensconced at the topmost floor so that women would have to wend their way through every department, dawdling over the hats, dallying among the dresses, fussing over the gloves, before they could sit for a spell at the restaurant. And there, whilst sipping Ceylon tea and nibbling cucumber sandwiches, they would be entertained by a live band and professional dancers. Soon, the customers joined in the merriment. Thus, the afternoon tea dance became quite the fashionable public gathering.

The inclusion of dancing during afternoon tea is supposed to have happened naturally, not long after having tea between 4 to 7pm was ritualized in British country homes. Such jovialities were referred to as a *thé dansant,* supposedly because afternoon tea came to England from Paris. In the famous letters of Marie de Rabutin-Chantal, the marquise de Sévigné (1626-1696) to her daughter Françoise-Marguerite de Sévigné, the comtesse de Grignan (1646-1705), she wrote of how French royalty had taken to drinking copious amounts of tea as some sort of miracle cure-all and how a particular lady was responsible for adding milk to it.

Whoever came up with *thé dansant* and how that was simplified as 'tea dance' are unknown. What is on record is the mention of it in an essay on "Slang" that appeared in an 1853 edition of Charles Dickens' weekly 24-page periodical called "Household Words", which came out every Saturday in London for a mere tuppence a copy. Attributed, but not verifiably so, to journalist George Augustus Sala (1828–1895), the piece was a scathing indictment of the misuse and corruption of words. The author offers *thé dansant* as an example and contemptuously points out its translation: "A dancing tea. Does tea dance? Can it dance?" But like other slang words of yore, the name stuck. Well, the English translation did anyway. The tea dances in private residences and at department store restaurants continued through the next century because they were a more manageable, and frankly less expensive, alternative to balls. But for those who could afford to, a ball was exactly what they couldn't afford not to throw.

As a matter of fact, a combination of fashion and dance in the form of a costume ball was how the William Kissam Vanderbilts finally gained social entry. In early 1883, the cement had yet to dry at their just erected mansion, sprawled on an entire block on Fifth Avenue, when word circulated about plans for its housewarming. Champing at the bit to give all New York an eyeful of their price-be-damned taste, the couple had decided to throw a ball to end all balls. Twelve hundred invitations, hand-delivered by liveried servants, went out well in advance. And so in the weeks prior, the Vanderbilt abode, and indeed the entire city, was abuzz with anticipation and activity. Quadrilles were practiced. Whimsical costumes were handcrafted. Select members of the press "previewed" the house's interiors so they could report, with breathless superlatives, on the height of the ceilings, the antiquity of the furniture, and the provenance of the paintings and tapestries on the walls.

On March 26, 1883, the house designed by architect Richard Morris Hunt (1827-1895) on 660 Fifth Avenue opened its doors at 10:30pm. A procession of costumed revelers passed through the vestibule and made their way into a gothic, two-story high banquet hall. Everyone all but gawked in wonderment and envy at the majesty of their surroundings. Surely the value of their names and fortunes paled in comparison to all this. The baronial room framed an august stained glass window painted by Eugène Stanislas Oudinot (1827-1889). An orchestra played from a musician's gallery opposite a gigantic double fireplace with an overmantel and marble caryatids by Austrian-born sculptor Karl Theodore Francis Bitter (1867-1915). Every room seemed filled to overflowing with orchids, bougainvilleas, and the unrestrained awe of the guests.

Quadrilles, five in all, began an hour later, after which, the floor was opened for everyone else to dance. Dinner catered by Delmonico's (Est. 1827) was served promptly at 2am, followed by more dancing and drinking, which lasted well into the dawn. As the remainder of her guests took their leave, Alva Vanderbilt (née Smith, 1853-1933) of Mobile, Alabama retired to her suite with relief that all had gone well, and the satisfaction of having, at long last, reached the top of the ladder she had so tenaciously climbed. Though the voracious acquisition of property absorbed most of the rest of her life, she is also remembered for helping found the Metropolitan Opera (Est. 1883). And after divorcing Vanderbilt and remarrying into the Belmont banking family, she became very active in the fight for women's rights.

Meanwhile, high society's gatekeeper, Caroline Webster "Lina" Schermerhorn (1830-1908) or Mrs. Astor, as she was called, still regarded the new people as an affront to propriety. But, she was perfectly aware the sharply drawn battle line against them had eroded. She reluctantly and wordlessly conceded that efforts to thwart their incursion had failed. The only course left was to negotiate the transition on her terms, with a little help from unctuous accomplice Samuel Ward McAllister (1827-1895). They formed the Society of the Patriarchs (Est. 1872) to gradually bring into the fold select new people, whose acceptance was made official the moment they passed through the 44th street entrance of Delmonico's on Fifth Ave for the society's seasonal ball. Dancing to two orchestras preceded epicurean feasting on the lower floors, amidst bouquets of tulips and roses and endless bottles of Moët & Chandon.

Then, for 12 weeks in winter, it seemed like no sooner had one stumbled home from a party when an invitation to the next appeared at the door. Aside from said Patriarch balls, there was the one for the start of the opera season, another for the New York Horse Show, followed by a whirlwind of debutante balls through the holidays, then Mrs. Astor's annual ball every third Monday in January. And in a way, those society balls—evenings enchanted by waltzing in a gorgeous ball gown—were emulations of the Cinderella story. Fashion and dance as one in a pair of glass slippers that made wishes come true. But another form of dance dwells in fairy tales where ugly ducklings dream of growing up to be graceful swans. Because as every dancer ought to know—everything was beautiful at the ballet.

CHAPTER TWO
Endless Flight

Natalia Osipova raced across the floor to gather momentum. Her front leg shot straight up. She pushed down with her back leg, and used the thrust to spring off the floor. While her torso appeared steady, she had shifted her weight forward so her body sailed along the arc of the leap. At the very apex, she reached full split, arms stretched out and parallel to the spread of her legs. She coursed through the air like a javelin, forever it seemed, suspended in time and space. In reality it was mere seconds. She was floating, gliding, and landing back on the floor with the front foot first. The impact rippled along her toes to the ball of her foot, ending at her heel as her back foot followed the descent.

In ballet, this is called a *grand jeté,* for which Osipova, principal dancer since 2013 with the Royal Ballet (Est. 1931), is much admired. Her technical prowess and acuity for externalizing emotional depths through dance have garnered her praise from critics and balletomanes alike. The mesmerizing whirlwind of pirouettes she unleashed in the role of Kitri towards the end of Act I of Alexei Fadeyechev's 2007 staging of "Don Quixote" at the National Theatre (Munich, Est. 1818) was met with thunderous ovation.

In 2015, as a guest artist of the American Ballet Theatre (ABT, Est. 1939) in the title role of "Giselle" she was expectedly an explosion of supernatural physicality, sacrificing some traditional steps for surprising 'method acting' choices to accentuate narrative. Unexpectedly, at the closing of her Act II solo, as she landed the last in a series of breathtaking jetés, a miscalculation sent her hurtling to the floor. A collective gasp filled the theater. But after a momentary silence, she pulled herself up and moved with a detectable limp to her appropriate mark down stage. Then without further ado, and still completely in character, she carried on *en pointe* to the end, eliciting deafening cheers from the audience and applause from the other dancers. The seemingly effortless virtuosity of Osipova's soaring jetés have become exemplary of ballet's gravity-defying wonders enveloped in costumes like spun gossamer.

The life and career of a dancer are governed by many things—not the least are agility, stamina, an aptitude for grace, and infallible metric and spatial awareness. Random luck of the genetic draw accounts for some of these. The others can be learned or improved by training. But it's being in possession of a dancer's mettle that enables someone to push on, especially after interminable hours of grueling practice, chronic aches, or when rejections come, as they sometimes must. Depending on the perspective, it is admirable or sad that a higher threshold for pain is taken for granted as part of the job description.

It's widely acknowledged that any serious pursuit of a career in ballet must begin at around seven or eight years of age when the body and brain are still malleable enough to condition. It is advisable though to wait until age ten when bones are thought to be strong enough to don pointe shoes. Still, this does beggar the question of autonomy. In the past, young girls were entirely at the mercy of men, and life was a fixed trajectory. In this world, it was a glissade from father to *regisseur* to husband. If she was lucky. And she may well make it into the corps, but the potential for injuries, stress fractures, long-term issues with joints are more whens than ifs. Dancers and fashion models share similar burdens—held up to unreasonable, sometimes arbitrary, physical standards, which require excruciating dietary and exercise regimens, only to face very few opportunities to excel before being aged out entirely.

The cultural cachet of ballet was hard earned, freighted by both the prestige of its ethereal qualities and its somewhat blemished beginnings. In the entertainment sphere, prostitution has always lurked behind the scenes. And because they are in the spotlight for their desirability, performers—female and male—are either exploited for their vulnerability or enter into unsavory arrangements by their own volition. But it was always the women who suffered censure.

When bereft of religious purpose, dancing in public, especially as a performance, has an unavoidably confrontational carnality. But while men were somehow mostly excused for failing to resist their baser instincts, women were not. Motivations and viewpoints also differed. For women, dance as a profession was a means with which to eke a living, a matter of survival if the 'protection' of a father or husband was unavailable. To men, a female dancer was temptation incarnate, dangerous, to be adored, feared, and condemned.

Published in 1463, the book *"De pratica seu arte tripudii"* (On the Practice or Art of Dancing) by Guglielmo da Pesaro (1420-1484) dates how far back dance was becoming structured. Another book *"De la arte di ballare et danzare"* (On the Art of Dancing and Choreography, 1445) by Domenico da Piacenza (1390-1477) helps pinpoint the origins of the word "ballet". Although *"danzare"* is more appropriate, for some reason da Piacenza preferred the informal *"ballare"* leading to his work being referred to as *balletto*.

The earliest known ballet performance was in Tortona, the Italian town where Isabella of Aragon (1470-1524) and Gian Galeazzo Sforza (1469-1494), the sixth Duke of Milan, stopped over on the way to their official wedding ceremony in Milan. There in 1489, the betrothed couple was honored with a banquet by dance master Bergonzio di Botta who had each course served with specific dances including a ballet. A hundred years later, Catherine de' Medici (1519-1589) commissioned the performance of *"Ballet comique de la reine"* for her son Henri III (né Alexandre Édouard, 1551-1589), king of France to celebrate the *alliance* he had arranged for Anne de Batarnay (1560-1587) and Marguerite de Lorraine (daughter of Nicholas, the Duke of Mercœur, 1524-1577).

Naturally, present day ballet is hundreds of years removed from when it was less created performance and more like staged social dancing (and often included the minuet). Among the many breakthroughs that elevated its status was allowing women to finally appear onstage by command of the British king Charles II (1630-1685). In time, ballet was also enfolded into opera and became a regular spectacle at royal courts. And as more public performances were mounted, music and dramatic orations, scenery and costuming, technical training and complex choreography were elaborated.

More headway was made under the aegis of Louis XIV. By royal edict in 1661, the Académie Royale de Danse was founded in Paris, overseen by thirteen of the French monarch's personally handpicked dance masters. One of them was Pierre Beauchamp (1631-1705) who documented dance forms and movements using figures, counts, symbols, and path mapping. This came to be known as the "Beauchamp-Feuillet notation" after appearing in *"Chorégraphie, ou l'art de décrire la danse"* by Raoul-Auger Feuillet (1659-1710), published at the king's bidding in 1700. It codified classical ballet's five positions of the feet and paved the way for the "turnout" to become fundamental to dance technique.

Turnout is when the feet are faced outward sideways in opposite directions, inherently unnatural since the human anatomy is predisposed to forward motion. It's up to the upper leg (and to a lesser extent the ankle) to direct the foot. But it's the hip rotators and the spherical top of the muscles in the upper thigh that enables turnout. Even in the 1700s, dance masters were aware an individual's conformation determines the breadth of their turnout. An average person can do a 45 degree turnout, while most dancers are able to do 55 degrees. It's a rare person who can achieve a functional 90 degrees in which the feet are diametrically aligned in first position while keeping the knee directly above the toe. And that's why a good part of ballet training is dedicated to strength and flexibility to avoid undue stress to joints, knees, feet, and lower back.

Up until this point, most shows were held in open air ampitheatres with the stage surrounded on almost all sides by attendees who could watch everything 'in the round'. But proscenium stages facing rows and columns of seats arranged in a rectangular block became more common. This reoriented the view to a 'frame' straight ahead. The frontal perspective diminished the appearance of any performance with only onward and backward dancing. Lateral movements became necessary and the turnout made that possible. Moreover, it enabled dancers to raise their legs higher, change directions faster, and appear lighter, expanding what could be done in choreography. The external conditions and articulations of dance continued to evolve. But internally, it was, is, and ever will be the body's way of physically manifesting an array of emotive tales of the human condition.

————————————

For many years, dancers didn't really wear 'costumes' as such, rather, they performed in garments current to them. So when Marie-Anne Cupis de Camargo (1710-1770), a principal ballerina with the Paris Opera, appeared onstage with her thirty yards of tulle and tarlatan skirt chopped off at the hems, it was met with shock. This prototype "tutu" (conjectured to have come from "tulle") is widely attributed to illustrator Eugène Lami (1800-1890). The shortened dress displayed Camargo's vigorous footwork, but it was her exposed ankles that titillated spectators. Another dancer, Marie Sallé (1707–1756), countered by performing in wispy cotton muslin. Subsequently, women's fashions lost its more constricting elements. And dancers duly adapted with sleeveless and high waisted outfits, shorter skirts, and flats. Thereafter, theater people more readily remodeled costumes in service of aiding mobility and for clearer articulation of the legs.

Costumes and a great deal more of what an average person now associates with ballet may be traced back to Imperial Russia. In the 1700s Tsar Pyotr Alekseyevich (1672-1725), or Peter the Great, was steadfast in disabusing the world of the presumption that the country was but a frozen hinterland. Part of his plan was to enrich the cultural life of St. Petersburg by hosting balls grander than those in other European courts. These were called "assemblies" so there were to be no misunderstandings that attendance was mandatory. The old boyars were none too pleased with these decadent indulgences. It didn't take them long though to enjoy, even look forward to, an assembly until the social calendar was crammed with them from December to March.

Routinely, everyone was given a week or so to prepare, especially if the event was themed. But as a general rule, men came in tails or suits, women in ravishing gowns, while officials wore dress uniforms. And because dancing was salient to the proceedings, the tsar hired French dance masters to tutor the nobility. Led by the host and hostess, festivities were held in a commodious hall lit by wax candles fastened to chandeliers and candelabras. A master of ceremony called out the dances: an hour of the polonaise, followed by a waltz, then a Krakowiak, a pas-de-quatre, quadrilles, and culminating in a spirited mazurka.

The aristocracy's penchant for all things dance made possible the founding of the Imperial Ballet School (Est. 1738) at the Winter Palace under Jean-Baptiste Landé (1697-1748). It was later renamed after the Mariinsky Theatre to which it relocated as the company in residence (briefly referred to as the Kirov under the Soviet Union). An amalgamation of French, Italian, Danish, Slavic and Austrian styles flourished under its innovative dancemasters. The Mariinsky grew with the steady influx of major international talents. Foremost among them was another Frenchman, Charles-Louis Didelot (1767-1837), whose reputation was made by his landmark production of "Flore et Zéphire" at the King's Theatre in London. It was in that one-act ballet when dancers were first seen *en pointe,* if only as sleight of feet since Didelot had them held up by wires and balancing on their toes in flat, satin slippers with leather soles.

Another import was someone in that same production, the woman considered to be the greatest dancer of her time—Marie Taglioni (1804-1884, the Comtesse de Voisins by marriage). Born in Sweden to a family of dancers, Taglioni was with the Paris Opéra in 1832 when she headlined the acknowledged first romantic ballet—"La Sylphide". Created by her choreographer father Filippo (1777-1871) as a showcase for Taglioni, its mythical and tragic love story lent itself well to emotive dancing in ethereal costumes of tight fitting bodices and gauzy calf-length tulle skirts. But most important of all, this was the piece for which Taglioni is supposed to have brought attention to pointework.

Still, technique was circumscribed by whatever makeshift or rudimentary pointe shoes were available. Everyday footwear, made of felt, leather, silk, or velvet wasn't sturdy enough. Men's low heels were fine but women had higher, thin ones. And the pointed toes weren't practical for balance. Italian ballet slippers in the 19th century adopted a flattened toe cap 'box' stuffed with burlap and reinforced with crushed paper and flour paste. Serviceable but hardly ideal since functional requirements, different feet shapes and flexibilities, had to be considered.

Prima ballerina Anna Pavlova (1881-1931) entrusted her formidable arches to shoemaker Romeo Niccolini in Milan. Another master craftsman was Salvatore Capezio who opened his New York shop close to the Metropolitan Opera House in 1887. The years have seen improvements such as baking the shoes in an oven to preserve the contour and harden toe boxes. Dancers then stuffed them with cotton, tissues or jelly molds. Because the entire body bears down on the ankle and toes, the box has to provide ample support, but not so much the dancer can't feel the floor, or worse thud on the floorboards and contradict the notion of weightlessness.

Given the punishment they had to endure, pointe shoes were good if they lasted through a single show. And surely those were a well-made pair worn by Pierina Legnani (1863-1930) for the 1893 "Cinderella" (choreographed by Enrico Cecchetti, 1850-1928, and Lev Ivanov, 1834-1901 to music by the Baron Boris Fitinhoff-Schell, 1829-1901). Legnani was the Mariinsky's prima ballerina assoluta, a most exalted position since "ballerina" is an official title in Russia. And hierarchy in this world climbs up from the corps de ballet to first artist, soloist, to principal (etoile in Paris) and finally prima.

As Cinderella, Legnani brought down the house with 32 consecutive *fouettés en tournant,* which hinged on rotating en pointe using one leg for support and the other to propel each turn. Spinning like a top, her uncanny balance and control astonished those in attendance. One dance critic described the feat as "sparkling as the facets of a diamond", while another averred how she did it "without traveling one inch" from her mark, a chalked outline of a rouble on the floor. Her extraordinary prowess placed pointework in the limelight. And there it has stayed.

Of those who've basked in that light, none remain as brightly lit today as Marius Ivanovich Petipa (1818-1910) whose stagings through thirty years as the Mariinsky's *premier maître de ballet* continue to inspire, be revived or reinterpreted. There isn't anyone in the civilized world without even a passing acquaintance of "The Sleeping Beauty" (premiered in 1890) and "Nutcracker" (1892 in a double bill with the opera "Iolanta", music for all three commissioned from Piotr Ilitch Tchaïkovski, 1840-1893).

Then, there's *"Le lac des cygnes"* (Swan Lake)—the best-loved and most performed of them all, with music by Tchaïkovski and choreography by Petipa for the Mariinsky in 1895. But any balletomane knows this wasn't the original. Tchaïkovski had actually composed the music for a new ballet company based in Moscow. It was that, with a different choreography by Julius Reisinger (1828-1893), the first "Swan Lake" which opened at the Bolshoi Petrovsky Theatre in 1877. It took a couple more decades for the Bolshoi to become any kind of serious rival to the Mariinsky. It wasn't until 1900 when choreographer Alexander Gorsky (1871-1924) took the helm that the vivid colors and visceral daring of the Bolshoi's productions distinguished themselves from the patrician finesse of Mariinsky's shows. In the wake of both companies, many aspects of ballet cannon became ingrained: fairy-tale romances in exotic settings, star-crossed lovers and otherworldly characters in diaphanous costumes.

An even shorter tutu became acceptable when Virginia Zucchi (1847-1930) was invited to debut with a revival of *"La Fille du pharaon"* (choreography by Petipa) at the Mariinsky in 1885. After her request for a shorter skirt was refused, Zucchi slashed her costume anyway. Eventually, more dancers preferred wearing the flared, circular skirt—now typically made with fourteen layers of tulle—to show off their legs and uphold the illusion of floating.

Illusions, however, are inadequate balm for harsh reality. The peasantry's dissent from 1905 on culminated in the violent abolition of the monarchy twelve years later. In the interim, ballet faltered. Its close links to and reliance on the aristocracy became handicaps. Art patron Sergei Diaghilev (1872-1929), who had a law degree but preferred to dabble in theater, was promoting cultural tours around Europe when suddenly government financing for his 'elitist' pursuits was severely curtailed. After wrangling for outside investment, he managed to present *"Saison Russe—opera et ballet"* from May to June 1909 at the Théâtre du Châtelet (Est 1862) in the *1er arrondissement* of Paris. Though the show's

Slavic tone was a trifle heavy-handed, sufficient success laid the groundwork for Diaghilev's founding of Ballets Russes in the French capital.

Already, the city was primed for it. Parisians delighted in romantic ballet and frequented the Palais Garnier (Est. 1875, named after its architect Charles Garnier, 1825-1898) home to the Paris Opera Ballet. An avid supporter was the artist Edgar Degas (1834-1917) whose paintings of ballet and horse racing were popular. His oil-on-wood "The Dancing Class" (now at The Metropolitan Museum of Art, Est. 1870 in New York) was the first of over fifteen hundred oils, pencil sketches, sculptures, monotypes and pastels that he did on ballet alone. The vitality that still emanates from them comes from Degas' rejection of the idyll for an often voyeuristic realism. Instead of glamorizing the life of dancers, he sought beauty in their quotidian moments: stretching at the barre, loitering in the wings, practicing, soothing fatigued muscles, exchanging backstage palaver. It helped that though headliners were being idolized, the corps consisted of impoverished and agreeable girls.

It was common for theaters to have affluent male benefactors called *abonnés* who preyed on the dancers with impunity. And even if most of the girls, and even their families, were complicit in trading sex for money or other forms of favors, the imbalance of power is there. Degas himself was an *abonné,* but no evidence exists that he ever indulged in sexual congress with any of the dancers. He was often observed backstage crouched on the stairs, furiously sketching them swarming about. And even when a dancer was hired to pose at his Montmartre studio—untidy with paintings piled against the walls, a bathtub, a piano—he was nothing less than paternal. Once, questioned about why he painted dancers, Degas explained his impulse thusly, " "(It) lies in rendering movement . . . and painting pretty clothes."

Meanwhile, after the Bolsheviks had confiscated their possessions, legions of Russian blue bloods descended on Paris without so much as two *sous* to rub together. In their hurry to evade the horrendous fate of their Tsar, few had the wherewithal to snatch whatever baubles were on the dresser before heading West. But inured to a cosseted existence, these émigrés who settled in the *16e arrondissement* were not amenable to a Gallic, much less humble, way of life. Instead, they clung to each other and anything that reminded them of the motherland. And Diaghilev's Ballets Russes became a cherished distraction from their ignominious downfall.

Despite his ill-disguised disdain for ballet (and the dancers) Diaghilev, more than anyone, became its most diligent ambassador to the world. A natural impresario, he brought promising Russian talents-in-exile together with other artists to create shows by committee. It's what's called *Gesamtkunstwerk*—that is, synthesizing disparate artistic elements (in this case set and costume designs, choreography and storytelling, music and themes) into a cohesive whole. Many were the gifted contributors to Ballets Russes including choreographers Michel Fokine (1880-1942), who brought the male dancer to the forefront; and Léonide Massine (1896-1979), who utilized folk dances to drive narrative; as well as composers like Claude Debussy (1862-1918), Erik Satie (1866-1925) and Sergei Prokofiev (1891-1953), painters Henri Matisse (1869-1954), Marc Chagall (1887-1985), and André Derain (1880-1954). But second only to Diaghilev was Léon Bakst (1866-1924) whose orientalist sets and costumes were stamped all over productions like *"Cléopâtre"* (1909, originally *"Une nuit d'Égypte"*), *"Le carnaval"* (1910), *"Narcisse"* (1911), and *"L'après-midi d'un faune"* (1912).

For "Schéhérazade" (1910), Bakst dressed Vaslav Nijinsky (1889-1950) in a bejeweled bandeau and gold harem pants, and festooned him with a gold turban, pearl earrings and multi-colored rings. The look played up the flagrant sensuality of both the slave character he portrayed as well as Nijinsky himself. The dancer (and later choreographer) had already caused scandals including having been dismissed from the Mariinsky in 1912 for going onstage in revealing tights when male dancers were still expected to wear breeches. The passage to leotards and tights for better demonstrating leg articulation didn't happen overnight. Originally referred to as a maillot, the leotard was created by French acrobat Jules Léotard (1838-1870) whose one-piece form fitting outfit aided his trapeze act. But it was finding the right fabric—from cotton jersey that deformed too fast to resilient wool jersey to silk and finally to synthetics —that standardized tights.

The Ballets Russes lunged forward when the singular designer Gabrielle "Coco" Chanel (1883-1971) got involved. Not exactly a stranger to the Russians, she had a brief affair with the Grand Duke Dmitri Pavlovich (1891-1942) whom she found "tall and handsome and splendid" yet later conceded, "Behind it all? Nothing…just vodka and the void." But it was actually through her somewhat mercurial friendship with Misia Sert (1872-1950) that Chanel met Diaghilev. Misia was already on her third marriage, to the muralist José-Maria Sert (1874-1945) scion to textile manufacturers from Barcelona, when she became the toast of Parisian society and got to know Diaghilev.

On a sojourn in Venice, Chanel and Misia ran into the ballet manager who, as he perennially was, desperate for backing. The next Ballets Russes project was a revival of its own *"Le Sacre du printemps"*, first mounted in 1913 with choreography by Nijinsky and music by Igor Stravinsky (1882-1971). The original showing made headlines for the bedlam incited by the sexually-charged dancing and atonal score. Booing from some and cheers from others sent fists flying across the aisle. Performers valiantly continued, to a commotion so loud no one could hear the music. The dancers were only able to keep the tempo because Nijinsky was hollering out the count from the wings.

Thanks to a generous capital infusion from Chanel, the show Le Figaro had once summed up as "puerile barbarity" was revived in 1920 to a less factious reception. Despite an entirely new choreography by Masine, it still managed to astonish. And it would take many many more years for people to catch up with Stravinsky's unpredictable rhythms and time signatures and this composition's forgoing melody for beats. *"Le Sacre du printemps"* is now believed to be ballet's transition from classical to contemporary.

Coasting on anodyne, well-trodden repertoire could've kept ticket sales brisk. Probably. But Ballets Russes had cosmopolitan French and international intellectuals occupying many of those theater seats. And the company's artistes were devoted to furthering their disciplines, experimenting with abstractions and looking ahead to what could be done in this medium. So when Diaghilev came calling on Chanel once more, it was for something more overtly up to date. And the first sign of this was he wanted her to do the costumes.

The show was 1924's *"Le train bleu"*, choreography by Bronislava Nijinska (1891-1972), libretto by Jean Cocteau (1889-1963), music score by Darius Milhaud (1892-1974), sets by the sculptor Henri Laurens (1885-1954). The painted scenic drop curtain was a replica of *"Deux femmes courant sur la plage"* by Pablo Picasso (1881-1973), who also created cubist sets for the company. The titular locomotive is the Calais-Mediterranée Express, colloquially named after its remodeled blue cars with gold trims and the midnight blue velvet interiors of its ten sleeping compartments. The overnight shuttle, departing the Northern French coast at 1pm and arriving in the Riviera the following morning, was convenient for the leisure set. The train functions comparably in the ballet—as simply a vehicle to flaunt a beach holiday.

The show itself is loosely connected picture postcard vignettes—a flock of beautiful people in sunglasses, posing for photos and engaging in romantic dalliances and sporty activities such as gymnastics and tennis. Since these upper class archetypes were the sort who mingled in her salon, bringing Chanel in to do the costumes was genius. Her first boutique had been in the seaside resort of Deauville, by the by, so all this was very much terra cognita for the designer. She came up with sleeveless bathing outfits in striped ocean blue and baby pink knits, handsome V-neck sweaters and tweed plus-fours, white tennis ensembles, and emerald robes with diagonal stripes. All very *au courant.* But, they also served a lesson in making stage costumes. One of the male leads had trouble articulating in his layered look. The corps strained to grasp the knit fabric for partnered lifts. Some say Chanel reworked some of the garments. Presumably, it was a lesson learned. Because when she was asked in 1929 to create new costumes for a restaging of *"Apollon musagète"* (choreographed by George Balanchine, 1904-1983, to music by Stravinsky) she came up with flowing, pleated short silk togas cinched with Charvet men's silk cravats— obviously better suited to dancing.

Later that same year, Diaghilev died in Venice. And although he had been staying at the Grand Hotel des Bains (Est. 1900, slated for redevelopment as a condominium since 2019), he was, unsurprisingly, destitute. Chanel helped pay for his burial at the city's cemetery on the island of St. Michel. His death brought an abrupt end to the Ballets Russes.

Its legacy scattered to the four winds on the wings of everyone who had ever been with the company. As its last choreographer Balanchine was set adrift. He took on whatever projects he could find from Monte Carlo to Copenhagen until he was cajoled into coming to New York by Lincoln Kirstein (1907-1996). The son of the chairman of Filene's department store in Boston, Kirstein was an enthusiast who had hoped world class ballet could be produced in the U.S. In his journals, he wrote of having met a Balanchine who was "not desperate, exactly, but without any hope."

Admitting to Kirstein his dream of working in the new world, Balanchine relented. Together with Kirstein and Edward M.M. Warburg (1908-1992), he opened the School of American Ballet, an outlet for his inclination toward neoclassicism and the foundation of the New York City Ballet. In 1935, the first American ballet from Balanchine —"Serenade"—was introduced at the Adelphi (originally the Clark Theatre in 1928, and demolished in 1970). Set to "Serenade for Strings in C, Op. 48" by Tchaikovsky, it's a pioneering piece that remains a testament to Balanchine's brilliance. Before there was such a thing, it was everything an American ballet could have been: a minimalist, geometric swirl of dancers breaking apart then coming together as a whole, unadorned by any ancient folklore. There's even a neurotically New York way Balanchine kept revising it in the following years. After artists like Jean Lurçat (1892-1966) and Candido Portinari (1903-1962) tried, the costumes, for instance, only arrived twenty years later in their conclusive version courtesy of Barbara Karinska (1886-1983). It is her leotard fastened at an angle to a gauzy powder blue tutu that is still seen today.

Balanchine also made his mark on Broadway, choreographing four shows for Richard Rodgers (1902-1979) and Lorenz Hart (1895-1943), the first of which "On Your Toes" in 1936 is noteworthy. The "book musical" as is generally understood today—having a complete story with plot driving music (often) composed specifically for the show—did not exist in those days. Instead, Broadway put on revues, thematically but tenuously strung-together music, dances, and comedic skits. And while "Oklahoma" (by Rodgers and Oscar Hammerstein II, 1895–1960) and "Show Boat" (by Jerome Kern, 1885-1945 and Hammerstein) are considered the prototypes of the book musical, an argument can be made that "On Your Toes" got the ball rolling. It had a fleshed out story, and the two ballets Balanchine conceived—"La Princesse Zenobia" and especially the climactic 27-minute "Slaughter on Tenth Avenue"—were germane to the hijinks.

On the morning of April 30, 1983, Balanchine was pronounced dead, reportedly by cardiac arrest caused by the pneumonia he had contracted from having long suffered a neurological disorder. The deterioration of Balanchine's faculties—worse, his equilibrium—had been observed with some alarm by those around him. It wasn't until after an autopsy when it was diagnosed that he had Creutzfeldt-Jakob disease, a degenerative disorder often confused with other forms of dementia. It was later speculated he may have contracted the disease from dodgy 'rejuvenation injections' he had been getting from a spa in Switzerland.

Balanchine's life had been every bit enigmatic. He was schooled in the florid glory of Russian ballet, and yet better known for his avant-garde choreography and by his Americanized sobriquet "Mr. B". He adored his ballerinas, each of his four marriages was to one. But they had to be obsequious. And it was easy to incur his ire. He was vindictive to anyone with the temerity to have a life outside the company, get married, pregnant, or gain by so much as an ounce of weight. His stern and dogmatic ways have doubtlessly resulted in monumental works and generations of choreographers following in his footsteps. But these are still debatable for what they cost to so many dancers who had and are still trying to live up to impossible standards.

As more Americans acquired a taste for recondite ballets, the resurgence of melodramatic Russian ones became a foreseeable reaction. During the Cold War, the polarity of American and Russian styles were cast in sharper relief when art forms like dance were weaponized as ideological propaganda. Western countries positioned art as voices of individualized choices, while the Union of Soviet Socialist Republics (U.S.S.R.) promoted them as examples of solidarity, discipline, and national pride. This is why on June 17, 1961 newspapers all over the world—with the exception of the U.S.S.R.—front paged the defection of the most celebrated male ballet dancer of that generation, with one too on-the-nose headline: "Dance to Freedom".

The drama unfolded the previous day at Le Bourget airport in Paris where members of the Kirov (as the Mariinsky was called under Soviet Russia) were boarding a flight to London, the next leg of their cultural tour. There are variations of how events transpired, each more histrionic than the other, but the facts are the same. As the corps was being handed plane tickets, Rudolf Nureyev (1938-1983) was held back for rerouting to the U.S.S.R. instead. The socialite (later press officer for YSL Rive Gauche) Clara Saint, who had befriended Nureyev during the Paris stop, was present and had alerted the French police on the premises of the situation. At her whispered urging, Nureyev bolted for a secure room where he formally asked for asylum.

Most attest this a spur-of-the-moment resolution. But there had been cause to worry long before the airport impasse. From the outset, Nureyev's open defiance of authority was known to the Soviet Union's security agency, the *Komitet gosudarstvennoy bezopasnosti* (KGB). In Paris he repeatedly ignored his handlers' admonitions against fraternizing with the locals. He struck up an acquaintance with Saint and her circle. He'd gone to gay bars and clubs. And while that's often soft-pedaled in most accounts, it can't be ignored that his first taste of freedom in Paris greatly factored into his decision to defect. Being gay is a punishable offense in the U.S.S.R., while same-sex relationships over the age of 21 were legal in France.

There are also divergent particulars about who knew what and when. In one, Nureyev was being summoned back for a gala performance at the Kremlin. Another claim was he was told his mother was gravely ill and he should come home. Some say he had already been informed the night before that he wasn't joining the rest of the troupe in London. Others say he only found out about it at the airport. Whichever was accurate, as far as the KGB was concerned Nureyev was clearly a flight risk. On his part, the dancer was acutely aware returning to the U.S.S.R. meant imprisonment and never again setting foot on Western soil. The incident received the cinematic treatment in 2018's "The White Crow" directed by Ralph Fiennes with Oleg Ivenko as Nureyev.

After severing ties with his homeland, the dancer's career flourished for thirty years, performing for the ABT and perhaps more notably for the British Royal Ballet where he partnered with the great Margot Fonteyn (1919-1991). His dancing was bolstered by real acting chops and his magnetic intensity made him an international celebrity, bringing renewed focus on the male ballet dancer. In paparazzi photos he was often seen in leather jackets, jeans, and turtlenecks. On stage, he seemed to prefer costumes by Nicholas Georgiadis (1923-2001) who brought emphasis to his trim waist, broad chest, and the muscular lines of his legs. He was appointed ballet director of the Paris Opera in 1983, but died only ten years later from complications due to AIDS.

Back in the U.S.S.R., the Soviet Union sentenced Nureyev to prison in absentia, an ineffectual retaliation for lost credibility. And this would only be the first of several high profile defections. Natalia Makarova defected to London in 1970. Four years later, while on tour in Toronto, Mikhail Baryshnikov dashed out of the O'Keefe Centre (Est. 1960, today Meridian Hall) to an idling car. This kickstarted Baryshnikov's fame in the West. On May 19, 1975 both Time magazine and Newsweek placed him on their covers. He was called "Ballet's New Idol" in the former, while in the latter he is with Gelsey Kirkland as "Ballet at Its Best".

But the defection that tops all in high stakes intrigue was that of Bolshoi's *premier danseur* Alexander Gudonov (1949-1995). In 1979, on tour with the company in New York, Godunov eluded his KGB handlers and sauntered into an Immigration and Naturalization Services (INS) office to demand political asylum. As soon as the KGB got wind of this, eight U.S.S.R. diplomats boarded Godunov's wife Lyudmila Vlasova (a soloist for the Bolshoi) on an Aeroflot flight back to Moscow from John F. Kennedy (JFK) international airport. But before the plane could taxi out, a squad of police cars swarmed the tarmac and blocked the takeoff. Then acting secretary of state Warren Christopher had ordered the grounding of the flight on the assertion that Vlasova was being repatriated under duress. After the news broke, the official Soviet news agency, Tass, publicly retorted that the U.S. was holding her as a political hostage.

With Godunov in protective seclusion, deputy U.S. ambassador to the United Nations Donald McHenry made repeated formal requests to speak with Vlasova, denied by his Soviet counterpart Yevgeni Makeyev. Ten hours later, the over one hundred Americans and foreign nationals on the plane were ordered to disembark while the Soviets stayed put. Eventually two state department officials were permitted to board and ask Vlasova if she wanted to return to the U.S.S.R.. She answered in the affirmative, but she did so with a scowling Soviet entourage stationed by her side. U.S. officials proposed interrogating her in neutral surroundings, but this was refused. The standoff lasted three days until the state department, though still unconvinced, conceded that Vlasova was returning of her own accord. Godonuv, meanwhile, went on to a career in the U.S. He was with ABT for a while, then branched off into acting, most memorably as a Teutonic villain in the 1988 John McTiernan action picture "Die Hard".

The Russia of nimble kulaks, brooding royals, and fairy creatures traipsing in dark forests and frozen mountains was a construct exported to the West via ballet. It was the imaginary backdrop of many important fashion collections by designers like Paul Poiret (1879-1944) and Jeanne Lanvin (1867-1946). But none achieved glory as great as the *Opéras-Ballets russes* collection by Yves Saint Laurent (1936-2008).

By 1976, fifteen years had been enough time for the fashion set to believe they knew all there was to know about chez Yves Saint Laurent. Practically the poster boy of the tortured artist, its designer was brilliant yet volatile, his moods susceptible to his four food groups: alcohol, cocaine, tranquilizers, and the fumes of his Lucky Strikes. That year, his partner Pierre Bergé (1930-2017) had moved out of their shared apartment. To Saint Laurent, this placed their business relationship, on which he was inextricably dependent, in jeopardy. And a new collection was due. His modernist riffs on streetwear, intuitively refracted through the lens of couture, had always served him well. But of late they had taken on a been-there, worn-that tedium.

From his tribulations Saint Laurent ran, hiding out in the two story pink riad he and Bergé refurbished in Marrakech called Dar es Saada (Arabic for The House of Happiness). When designing a collection, it was his habit to initially render only black line drawings, then gradually finalize fabrics and embellishments along the way. But for the upcoming season, he sketched everything out completely, detailed, accessorized, and in full color. They were unlike anything he had ever attempted before.

Saint Laurent returned to Paris more exhausted than when he left. Fearing for the designer's very sanity, Bergé admitted Saint Laurent into the Hôpital américain de Paris (Est. 1906) in Neuilly-sur-Seine where he rested overnight and most of the day. But in the late afternoons, the designer was chauffeured back to 5 Avenue Marceau to supervise work. In the blinding beauty of the sketches before them, whatever respect the harried patternmakers, seamstresses, beaders, and tailors had for Saint Laurent was elevated to unadulterated worship. Their faith would be justified at the collection's unveiling.

The raised catwalk in the middle of the Salon Imperial at the Hotel Intercontinental Paris (Est. 1862), a first for Saint Laurent, did not seem to arouse any suspicions in the minds of the editors, buyers and house clients that there might be something different about this showing. Nor did the opera music (another first, and Verdi according to those who were present) signaling the start of the show prepared them for what they were to witness. Then, the deafening bravos and jubilant clapping came when models marched down the runway in dresses gleaming like garnets, rubies and sapphires worthy of a tsarina. Piece after piece of regal silks, gold lamés, velvets and furs were met with gaped jaws and open weeping. There were printed shawls, jeweled turbans, fox toques. Never were there peasant skirts, satin capes, or cossack coats so extravagant. The Bernadine Morris (1925-2018) review on the front page of the New York Times, gushed that it was "revolutionary". To Vogue, for its September 1976 issue, Saint Laurent cited Bakst paintings, the odalisques of Delacroix, and Degas' ballet dancers among his inspirations. Dissenters opined that the collection had no bearing on reality. And they weren't wrong. They just didn't realize, because no one did then, that this was when couture seriously became haute. Whereas it used to be just loss leaders costing the GDP per capita of France, from that moment haute couture became pure fantasy, reaching apotheosis in the works of Alexander McQueen (1969-2010), Karl Lagerfeld (1933-2019), and John Galliano in the 1990s.

Countless productions have benefitted from the partnerships sealed between ballet and fashion. When Baryshnikov revived *"Gaîté Parisienne"* for ABT in 1988 (fifty years after Massine's original), he inveigled Christian Lacroix into dressing the company in a cyclone of polka dots and stripes, crimson and emerald shades, and gold trims. The costumes' reported cost of up to half a million dollars was no doubt off-set in part by tickets to the premiere that sold for $1,000 a seat. After the show, Baryshnikov crowed, "Lacroix's wild imagination fits this ballet perfectly."

Today's most appreciable merging of fashion and ballet has to be the New York City Ballet's Fall Fashion Gala annual fundraiser. It was inaugurated by board vice chair Sarah Jessica Parker with *"Bal de Couture"* featuring dancers in Valentino suits and dresses performing to selections from Tschaikovsky's "Eugene Onegin" at the Lincoln Center. Since then, fashion darlings such as Thom Browne, Peter Copping for Oscar de la Renta, Prabal Gurung, Carolina Herrera, Zac Posen, Gareth Pugh, Narciso Rodriguez, Olivier Theyskens, and Dries Van Noten have worked with the company's director of costumes Marc Happel to have their designs constructed in-house. Not all companies have that capability, of course. And for large-scale productions even the New York City Ballet outsources to reputable costume shops. When it restaged Tchaikovsky and Petipa's "The Sleeping Beauty" in 1991, two hundred costumes designed by Patricia Zipprodt (1925-1999) had to be made at Matera.

———————————

It just so happened that William was also there that year. On his own project, he was judiciously at work with one of Matera's adept drapers, Werner Kulovitz, finishing the gowns Joan Collins would be wearing for her Broadway debut as socialite Amanda Prynne in the Noël Coward (1899-1973) comedy "Private Lives". Collins first took on the role in London before going on a national U.S. tour enroute to New York. But because the actress will never ever be able to pry herself away from her bitch queen "Dynasty" alter ego Alexis Carrington, the costumes were as much (if not more) the subject of curiosity as the performance. Rumors had been circulating that Gianni Versace (1946-1997) was designing them for the play's American stops. In the end, William got the gig and he would only entrust the making of his designs to the people at Matera.

By serendipity, a floor above, at the studio of scenic designer Robin Wagner, a minor crisis was brewing. The costume designer for a show Wagner was working on had been indefinitely detained in Bali. Wagner rang downstairs, got a hold of Arthur Matera, and asked if he happened to know a designer who could create great showgirl costumes? Why, the guy who did "Nine" was right there.

In 1991, both the Matera atelier and Robin Wagner Productions were still housed within the Lawrence A. Wien Center for Dance and Theater at 890 Broadway. Other tenants had included Theoni V. Aldredge, a wigmaker, and a shoemaker for theater. The edifice is to dance what 550 Seventh Avenue had been to fashion, and 1619 Broadway to pop music. Few know though that the eight story-building, today the base of operations for ABT, Gibney Dance, and Ballet Tech, was once tenanted by dress and shirtmakers and belt manufacturers. In 1978, the property pivoted from fashion to dance when it was acquired for $750,000 by choreographer Michael Bennett (1943-1987).

Up on the sixth floor, William walked in and introduced himself to Wagner, director Mike Ockrent and the choreographer with whom William would strike a lasting friendship and professional camaraderie: Susan Stroman. "Usually, I've already studied the play before I meet with the director," says William. "But I knew nothing about their show when I first met Mike, Stro, and Robin." They spent the next few hours getting acquainted and talking about the new musical. Not long after that meeting, William had to jet off to Nice for Collins' final fittings at the same time Ockrent was going to be in Provence. Once William made certain Collins was caparisoned in the manner to which she was accustomed, he gladly rushed over to Ockrent and commenced work on "Crazy for You".

Very loosely based on the George (1898-1937) and Ira Gershwin (1896-1983) musical "Girl Crazy" from 1930, the new show is set in the same period and features more songs from the brothers' substantial catalog. Of course, designers investigate the era-specific fashions relevant to their shows. But any designer worth his mood boards knows how to use them as just the starting point for their own elucidations on character and story. A tale properly told is greater than the sum of artistic flourishes devised to foreshadow, advance plot, or shade character. And everything must cohere in a way that, no matter how implausible the story, is consistent with its own internal logic. Moreover, if these stories are to live on, they have to be imbued with nuance, meaning, and truth by those doing the telling. Fantastic creators like Stro and William steep themselves in the history of bygone worlds so they can build castles in the sky even as they bring the audience along to the very brink of reality.

CHAPTER THREE
Sketches of Spain

Patient 3929 was wheeled along the silent corridors of Long Grove
Asylum (Est. 1907) to an examination room for a post-mortem. The
results have never been disclosed. His death certificate dated March 18,
1941 indicates he'd been afflicted by dementia praecox. But even after
twenty-two years of being cloistered in this facility with some two
thousand other patients, Félix Fernández García remained shrouded in
mystery. More truth may be gleaned from a Picasso drawn sketch of
the dancer in rehearsal, and the traces of his technique in the works of
Massine. The man's history comes chiefly from his brief tenure at Ballets
Russes, the specifics of which are unverifiable at best.

It was in 1917 at Café Teatro-Salón Novedades in Sevilla when a then
21 year-old García met Diaghilev and Massine who'd been entranced
by one of his adroit performances of flamenco. They invited him to join
Ballets Russes in London where he spent the following year teaching
Massine the fundamentals of flamenco and working with the troupe
on *"El Sombrero de tres picos"*. García is said to have labored under the
impression he was headlining the show. But because of his predilection

for spontaneity he couldn't adhere to a set routine, even for one Tarantella solo. García is purported to have come undone after finding out someone else, a non-Spaniard at that, was dancing the lead. Others claimed he had already been spiraling before that. He was seized for public disturbance at the church of St. Martin-in-the-Fields in Trafalgar Square. But that he was taken to the Union Fulham Road workhouse by order of not the police but a certain Dr. Sandiland supports the subsequent transfer to Long Grove Asylum. The lack of any official details about his 'arrest', however, has led some to doubt García was ever truly mentally disturbed. None of this detracted from Massine's praise of García as one of the finest flamenco dancers of all time.

Flamenco is one of the most recognized of the Spanish dances, of which there are many. Due to centuries of Spain's colonial dominance, most dances were fettled by the back and forth between their genesis, the cultural sensibilities of the communities that adopted them, and the caprices of the motherland. The Sarabande originated in Central American colonies, sailed to the continent in the late 1500s, and was expeditiously acclaimed and impetuously condemned. But once the French stepped in, it slowed down to an acceptably dignified pace. Seguidilla (that appears in the first act of Petipa's "Don Quixote") later spawned the Bolero, which transfigured into the Beguine in the West Indies. The Fandango from Portugal morphed into Málaga's Malagueña.

Any effort of learning how flamenco came to be must follow the trail of the wandering Romani caravans that settled in Catalonia and Aragon in the 15th century. Rightfully or wrongly, the locals ascribed tarot cards, tambourines, motley garments, and passionate music to these outlanders they named Gitanos. For reasons unclear, the Spaniards conflated the Gitanos with the soldiers of Spanish-occupied Flanders, hence use of their word for Flemish—flamenco—in reference to the music and dance, which grew richer from the continued mingling of the locals, the Gitanos (Romani), and the *moriscos.*

Regional differences and types (such as Bulerías, Alegrías, Seguiriyas) of flamenco arose but still shared characteristics such as clacking castanets, drumming of heels on the floor, and accompanying songs of faith or love or sorrow. These songs are usually categorized by emotional heft, chord structures, and subtle inflections. The profound *"cante jondo"* is reckoned to be the oldest, laden with agony or mourning; the intermediate *"cante flamenco"* has stylistic deviations; and the jejune *"cante chico"* deals with lighter, humorous matters, or perhaps love's first blush. The song's protagonist narrates through the sinewy movements of the arms, hands, fingers and torso, peppered by fiery and tempestuous footwork and heel stamping. Technical prowess is important. But valued even more is one whose intensity takes him to a trancelike state of *"duende"*, or being possessed by something called *"los sonidos negros"*.

Nowadays, the guitar is taken for granted as intrinsic to flamenco. But early on, everything was actually instrumented a *palo seco,* ie. by clapping, rapping knuckles on a wooden surface, or pounding a stick on the floor. The uninhibited, blurred strumming of a guitar was added later, mostly due to master luthier Antonio de Torres Jurado (1817-1892). Emitting rounded tones of vibrant clarity, his guitars were a vast improvement on the string instruments of the time and were copied the world over. Nearly every modern guitar is a derivation of his design.

Another important change was flamenco's move from family camp-fires into the public arena of the *café cantantes* of the 1800s. These local hangouts with musical entertainment proliferated in Córdoba, Granada, and Sevilla and exposed more people to the dance. By 1910, these were displaced by the *tablao flamenco,* venues with raised stages and arranged seating which better showcased the art form and its artists. But it took events of graver import and unintended consequences to give flamenco the international praise it deserved.

From 1936 to 1939, the *Guerra Civil Española,* opined by some as the 'dress rehearsal' to WWII, pitted Spaniards against one another. Power was relinquished to Francisco Franco (1892-1975) whose oppressive government condemned artistic freedoms. But this actually enhanced flamenco's international profile with performers seeking refuge in other parts of the world. And more ironic still, the same Francoist dictatorship that had denounced flamenco as immoral reversed course in the 1950s and used it to campaign for tourist *pesetas.* Twenty years and millions of visitors later, the resilience of dynamic *bailaors* and *bailaoras* had prevailed. Flamenco was finally an indelible facet of Spain's cultural identity.

Outside of Spain, flamenco found a home away from home in the crossroads of tradition and tomorrow that is New York. Here stars were made of Encarnación López (1898-1945), who founded *Compañía de Bailes Españoles,* and Carmen Amaya (1913-1963), who rebelled against convention by dancing in trousers. In the city's tangle of ethnicities, an Italian-born and Brooklyn-reared Costanzo Greco (1918-2000) could grow up to be a handsome flamenco star called José Greco; and an Irish lass christened Joan Fitzmaurice could so completely make herself over into a Spanish dancer called Maria Alba (1910-1992) that very few were ever aware she could actually speak English. Only here could flamenco be a spectacle at a club with kitschy Polynesian trappings or go cheek-to-cheek with belly dancing and hip hop at a rehearsal studio owned by a former cabbie.

At present, no talk of New York and flamenco would be complete without Carlota Santana, founder of one of the city's premier dance companies—Flamenco Vivo Carlota Santana. "I have always loved to dance and took classes in tap and ballet while I was growing up," she says. She wasn't schooled in flamenco until later. But she was taught by none other than Alba. Recounts Carlota, "I spent a number of years in Spain and I returned to the city in the 1980s with more than just newfound skill and experience." She brought with her an abiding need to perpetuate the traditions of flamenco.

"I was teaching Phys Ed and staging small shows for NYU (New York University) when Bobby (Roberto Lorca, 1938-1987) and I talked about starting a dance company," she says. "It wasn't easy, but he was able to get a $3,000 grant from the National Endowment for the Arts." Lorca, sadly, passed only a few years later, leaving Carlota to carry on alone with their mission. "I had to keep going. And for many years, putting on blinders and moving forward was how we survived." She clarifies, "I'm not a choreographer. My role is finding great talents and bringing them together to make something extraordinary." Not, as it happens, a trouble-free undertaking.

"New York has an endless number of great musicians, but it's hard to find local singers and guitarists who possess genuine knowledge of flamenco," she professes. For the annual four-to-six-week tours and two-week season, Carlota often has to recruit abroad to compensate for the lack of domestic talents. This probably explains why putting on shows is simply a means to the company's true goals of nurturing flamenco as a living art form, an integral part of Hispanic heritage and vital to its future. And to Carlota, education is the way.

"We have some twenty trained teaching artists who bring the history, geography, and culture of flamenco to kids. We have a *certamen* for next generation artists who can win mentorship, and a consorcio program to instruct those who want to start their own companies." She relates, "Ours is a story of different ethnic groups coming together to make flamenco accessible to everyone. Each year we bring this message to different communities through free performances around the city." Wherever that may be, she goes through a ritual before every show. "I always walk around the theater, mostly to make sure everything is in readiness because it's like inviting people into my living room. I want them to feel part of the family. We reach out to multicultural audiences in the tens of thousands nationwide and hope we break down barriers."

In 2022, those barriers were opposed by José Maldonado and Karen Lugo's choreography and performance of Flamenco Vivo's "Fronteras", with a score and live accompaniment by José Luis de la Paz, at the Joyce Theater (Est. in 1941 as a movie house, the Elgin, then into a dance theater in 1981). The 13-movement piece opened with Maldonado, Lugo, and six members of the company trapped inside a white-taped area, grappling against unseen impediments, physical, emotional, spiritual, and some possibly self-inflicted. Maldonado explained through a translator that he wanted to show that flamenco "doesn't understand or accept boundaries…it can be used to connect, unite (us) . . . to be stronger, and achieve goals together."

Individually and in banded formations, the dancers push against confinement, cleverly underscoring commonality by switching accessories —a shawl, a fan, a hat. And the company was also united by costumes designed in modernized cuts and a luminous palette by Belén de la Quintana. Carlota understands and appreciates the need for flamenco to advance and find fusion with other disciplines. But she doesn't deny that her personal taste leans toward the traditional. And that means the established *bata de cola* with its fitted bodice and trailing skirt of tiered ruffles. This may sometimes be complemented by a shrug, a *mantón de Manila,* or an *abanico,* each serving some form of expression. Hair is pulled into a tight bun bedecked with flowers or other decorative items. Men wear snug, high-waisted trousers with cummerband, and a *traje corto.* Options like suede in footwear are out there, but the smarter choice is the durability of leather, with the embedded nails in the toe and heel for the requisite call-and-response between the footwork *(zapateado)* and the singer.

The inexorable collision of flamenco and couture came at a distinct phase in the work of Balenciaga when he brought in elements of the *bata de cola* and *torero* outfits to his collections in the 1950s. In his determination to frame the body with the dress, many are witnessed accounts of the master molding a piece of fabric into a gown with just his will and a handful of pins. In its Sept 15, 1950 issue, Vogue effused, "(Balenciaga's skirts were of) taffeta as thin as burned paper . . . (inspired by) the women of Ibiza, who look like clouds walking." The Baroness de Rothschild (née Pauline Potter, 1908–1976) described how her Balenciaga silk gazar flamenco gown's gatherings undulated when she danced, "(It) billow(s) out just so much, front, back and sides…round out each in turn, imperceptibly, like a sea-swell."

Today, friend to Flamenco Vivo, and indeed to all things flamenco, Emmy-winning (for "One Life to Live") costume designer Sally Lesser custom makes romantically ruffled outfits for professional dancers and casual fans alike. On a much larger scale is *casa* Menkes, founded in 1950 by Marcos Menkes who apprenticed with Catalan costume designer Marbel. Its workshops in Madrid, Bilbao, Sevilla, Barcelona, Alicante, Zaragoza, Santander, Murcia, Valencia, and Paris, produces a range of dancewear for international dance companies.

Flamenco Vivo commemorated its decades-spanning work in 2023 with a show at the Joyce, *"El Cuadragésimo"*, created and directed by Emilio Ochando. It was a celebration, a reunion with luminaries who've collaborated with the company—Andrés Peña and Maria Bermudez—and a redux of flamenco's dazzling range.

———————————

An even more circuitous route brought another dance to its current form—the tango. At the nethermost parts of its roots are women's solo and partnered dances (with hints of flamenco and the habanera) observed in Andalusia and Cuba. But after another prototype—between two men—situate itself in Argentina—in the residential barrio of San Telmo where couples dance there still on Sundays at its main square Plaza Dorrego; in Avenida Corrientes where milongas (tango halls) stay open until 4am; and in the souls of every Argentine.

The word "tango" was documented in a 1789 government proclamation banning gatherings around the dance. Authorities were unduly wary of commotions in quarters of ill-repute where immigrant Spanish, Italian, Polish, British, Russian, and African *peones* and *jornaleros* were contributing their histories, sensibilities, rhythms to the nascent dance. While an iteration called *Baile con corté* was a favorite in the Barrio de las Ranas neighborhood, the name tango only became official once solo guitars and entire ensembles of violins, piano, flute, double bass and two bandoneons (from Germany) were orchestrated around it. Eventually, tango migrated to Paris on the polished shoes of Argentine novelist and poet Ricardo Güiraldes. At a soirée hosted by the Jean de Reszkes (1850-1925), Güiraldes is said to have led an unwitting Yvette Gueté in a tango, to which an onlooker murmured for all to hear, "Is one supposed to dance it standing up?"

When learning tango, men are usually obligated to learn his partner's steps first in order to lead by anticipation. Movement, with sensitivity to one another's energy, is mostly guided from the torso and solar plexus, pulling back then stepping forward, faint signals issued through shifts of the shoulder or the chest, a lift of an arm, or a squeeze of the hand. Tango at its finest is a conversation conducted by action, reaction, hesitation, interruption, and negotiation. The music plays at a tempo of thirty-three bars per minute and often conveys a power struggle fraught with danger and misery. Still, unlike most dances, no one was able to standardize tango. It seemed different from teacher to teacher, all of whom made things more perplexing by alternating between usage of Spanish and French titles for the steps.

Back in Buenos Aires respectable people still viewed this product of the slums with abject contempt. It was a sentiment muddled by the identity crisis Argentine essayist Jorge Luis Borge said plagued his fellow *porteños, "El argentino es un italiano que habla español, piensa en francés, y querría ser inglés"* (The Argentinian is an Italian who speaks Spanish, thinks French, and would like to be English). Consequently, after tango gained *entrée* into Parisian salons, the mansions, theaters, brothels, and nightclubs in Argentina finally welcomed it home. It was almost predestined that the greatest tango singer of all time Carlos Gardel (1890-1935) was an Argentine, born Charles Romuald Gardès in Toulouse to a washerwoman and a married man called Paul Lassere, who disappeared before his birth.

New York read about Paris' *tangomanie* in the first, September 1913, issue of publisher Condé Nast's (1873-1942) Dress and Vanity Fair magazine. (Ballerina Anna Pavlova was on the December cover, its last issue before relaunching as just Vanity Fair the following year). Noting that tango had not hit New York, yet, the uncredited article described gowns fashionable Parisiennes wore to tango. Yes, those long and lean dresses held the posture while leaving the feet to do the work, but their actual relevance to tango was tenuous since these were fashions of the moment. Dresses specifically catering to tango only came out after the dance gained traction and just as corsets were loosening. Tango dresses usually came in orange and yellow satin, with plunging décolletage, side slits, and hemline at mid-calf. Men's outfits grew from its gaucho foundation to more sophisticated satin shirts and black tapered trousers. Modifications were made as warranted. When material became scarce, skirts got shorter. When showmanship was necessary, decorative fringes that would slap with each shimmy were attached.

Demand for twinkling costumes and experienced tango dancers surged from the restaurants, theaters, and casinos of holiday destinations from Dinard to Deauville. Tea dance was now "Tango Tea". And despite another sanctimonious damning—Pope Benedict XV (1854-1952) huffed over the "pagan dance"—it was spreading so fast across Europe, dancers without so much as a drop of Spanish blood joined in. British vaudevillians George Grossmith (1847-1912) and Phyllis Dare (1890-1975) appeared in the 1913 film short "The Argentine Tango and Other Dances". In the summer of the following year, husband-and-wife Maurice Mouvet (1889-1927) and Florence Walton (1890-1981) tangoed for HRM Mary of Teck (1867-1953) at a ball given by Grand Duke Michael Michaelovitch (1861-1929) at Kenwood House where he was in residence after his exile from Russia.

Americans too opened their hearts to tango. But one made chaste by Vernon (1887-1918) and Irene Castle (1893-1969), whose immensely successful stage revues and motion pictures capitalized on a wholesome veneer. Compared to *el auténtico* McCoy, the Castles' tango was vapid, yet more palatable to proudly prudish folks. Fans copied the way the couple danced, the way they dressed. She was partial to simple dresses with hems that hovered above the ankles. He made it okay to sometimes dance without a jacket, though never without a waistcoat.

The press affixed the title "America's Best Dressed Woman" to Mrs. Castle, cavalierly though not without reason. She modeled her own looks in magazines, and once, dresses from the Mexixe line by silk manufacturer M.C. Migel & Co (Est. 1895, renamed H.R. Mallinson & Co). And in conjunction with the Nonotuck Silk Company (Est. 1832), she later produced branded Corticelli Silk ready-to-wear gowns for about $62. In the fourth chapter "Modern Dance as Fashion Reformers" of the couple's book "Modern Dancing" (published 1914 by World Syndicate Company, Est. 1902), Mrs. Castle wrote of how dance liberated fashion: "All wore tight shoes and heavy petticoats and high, stiff-boned collars. Then Paris began to dance . . ."

The couple's multiple enterprises—Castle House school on Madison Ave, Castles in the Air supper club on Broadway, and Castles by the Sea nightclub along the Long Beach Boardwalk—prospered on their conservative, unmarred reputation, which belied their personal liberal attitudes. Their manager was a lesbian. They went on tour with the all-black James Reese Europe's Society Orchestra. Later in life, Mrs. Castle founded an animal shelter in Illinois. In April 1964, she told the New York Times, "When I die, my gravestone is to say 'humanitarian' instead of 'dancer'."

Of course dancers can also make a difference just by dancing. Talia Castro-Pozo is active on several fronts of bringing New Yorkers to the floor. "I started ballet when I was four years old," she says.

At fourteen she was the youngest soloist at Escuela Nacional de Ballet Peru. After her family relocated to New York, she resumed her studies at the School of American Ballet, and expanded her skills with jazz and ballroom along with voice training. Nowadays, she serves on the board of Ballroom Basix USA which teaches dance classes to more than twenty thousand kids in 150 schools around the five boroughs. The program deliberately uses partner Latin and ballroom dancing as a way of encouraging social interaction among children while reinforcing the importance of etiquette and respect.

For those old enough to drink, Talia warms up her Latin Mondays parties with primers on salsa at Taj lounge in the Flatiron district. For more than a decade, Peruvians, Cubans, Puerto Ricans, Dominicans, Spaniards, and Asians have been intermingling over salsa, timba, bachata, merengue, cumbia, and champeta to live music at the weekly shindig. But in the summertime, couples in every imaginable configuration of races, genders, shapes, and sizes in even larger numbers come to Talia's Sunset Salsa for Hudson River Park (HRPK) at the piers.

Operated by its Trust and fundraising arm Hudson River Park Friends, HRPK oversees the maintenance and community activities of the West Side's public waterfront areas. A highlight in its cultural and public entertainment calendar, Sunset Salsa was inaugurated in 2010. "Someone from HRPK was at Taj and had such a good time they asked if I could produce a similar concept for them." recalls Talia. "At our first event, we couldn't have imagined the crowd would grow by hundreds to a thousand people," Ever exuding vivacious and contagious *buena onda,* Talia indulges in forgivable exaggeration when she proclaims, "Salsa is the most popular partner dance worldwide and New York is its capital!"

As what happened to salsa, ballet, flamenco and tango, legitimacy was accorded ballroom dancing when someone seized the reins of authority and codified the steps. In England, that someone was Victor Sylvester (1900-1978) of the Imperial Society of Teachers of Dancing (Est. 1904) who was instrumental in formulating the dance known today as the International Style. In the U.S., it was Arthur Murray (1895-1991) of the eponymous dance studios, franchised worldwide in the thousands at its zenith, and a couple hundreds still in business in 2020. Murray was already teaching dance at the ripe old age of 19. In his twenties, he had a thriving dance instruction business by mail order. He studied further at Castle House and went on to devise the six basic steps of ballroom with illustrated foot imprint how-tos. Murray graduated to owning a small dance studio on Madison Avenue, then franchised the brand and fueling it with aggressive ads and promotions with eye-rolling promises that anyone who enrolled could have a vibrant social life—from only one lesson besides.

As the franchises multiplied, Murray's legacy became more about his savvy business sense. This doesn't negate how the Arthur Murray system enabled countless people to learn the in-demand dances of the age: the Cuban rumba, which was all about buildup and release while staying on a square spot on the floor; Samba, bouncing from the knees and shifting the weight from the ball to the flat of the foot; and the zigzagging Chacha with its five count of "1, 2, 3, cha, cha".

———————————

With so many professionals strutting for fame, it was only a matter of time when they would squabble over who was best. Organized competitions were first spearheaded by entrepreneur Camille de Rhynal before others cropped up in Berlin, London, and Paris with separate professional and amateur level qualifications. Ballroom dance competitions differ in that everyone takes to the floor simultaneously to flaunt their skills. From arbitrary vantage points, judges move around the room observing the contestants' posture, timing and rhythm, body line, hold, movement, interpretation, footwork, floor craft, and how they appear as couples in their chemistry, costuming, and appearance.

Although various groups held different contests, organizers eventually fell into lockstep and formed the International DanceSport Federation, renamed World DanceSport Federation in 2011, to which one must be a member in order to compete. It's been noted that competitions held outside the U.S. tend to attract a bigger pool of superior dancers. And while there are many such events, the dream has always been to make it all the way to the big leagues. For half a century, it didn't get any bigger than the championship at the Blackpool Dance Festival.

Since the 1900s, the coastal town of Blackpool has been thronged by tourists who wander about the promenade, play in the arcade, or take rides on the Big Wheel overlooking the Central Pier. But on and off since the 1920s, those who arrive in May, spend most of over a week at two of the ballrooms in the Winter Gardens, to either watch or enter the dance competitions. More than a thousand couples from some sixty countries endure seven rounds of six to seven minutes each at amateur or professional levels in Ballroom (waltz, foxtrot, tango, and quickstep) and Latin (cha cha, samba, rumba, paso doble, and jive) categories.

This is the Olympics of dance. No one here is less than a serious athlete with personal motivations beyond coveted trophies and monetary prizes. Most have been training all year, some coached by previous winners. They will need to harness skill and concentration in order to dance while ignoring the stares of the eleven judges circling the Empress Ballroom. And heaven forfend they overperform, which counts as a demerit and may cause injury. Though the 1176-meter floor is equipped with coiled springs, a feature in the very best dancefloors to improve performance and absorb shock, mishaps are always possible. Bad enough there are several dancers who will be alleviating previous injuries with painkillers, anti inflammatories, and cortisone shots. Twisting an ankle during a routine would be a catastrophe.

Some ado is also made over costumes, which can only be mistaken for chic by someone astigmatic or residing in Las Vegas. In fairness, the garish mess of synthetics, neon colors, and hologram effects make form more prominent while facilitating movement. They are also, apparently, governed by random trends. One year it's beads and sequins, then crystals the next. And if they weren't conspicuous enough, slathering on bronzers and shellacking hair and makeup are acceptable. The only thing that isn't is being eliminated too soon in the rounds. In the thinning of the herd, excitement builds. Many wait for the paso doble, the swiveling dance that supposedly recalls the maneuvering of the French infantry or the tantalizing pivots in a bullfight. The kill or be killed metaphor is hard to ignore. But at another seaside resort, endurance was the objective of a different kind of dance competition.

Ice cream and hot dogs, penny arcades and carousels are, historically, boardwalk attractions for the hoi polloi. But, a stone's throw away from the swanky hotels and racetracks of Gravesend and Sheepshead, where the moneyed set puttered, Coney Island became the convergence point for these polar classes. In the 17th century Dutch colonies of New Netherland, spanning Delaware all the way up to Cape Cod, the original "Conyne Eylandt" referred only to the westernmost tip of today's

Coney Island. Hotels and restaurants arrived on the steel heels of the railroads and made West Brighton, Brighton Beach, and Manhattan Beach the domains of, respectively, the working, upper middle, and leisure classes.

Changing the makeup of the neighborhoods further were fair compounds—Sea Lion in 1895, Steeplechase in 1897, and ultimately Luna Park (taking over Sea Lion in May 1903)—boasting a slew of innovative rides and roller coasters, alongside circus and carnival acts, dining and dancing. Dreamland next door went even bigger, throwing in beachfront access. From all ethnic and economic backgrounds they came, queuing to put the downpayment on what became the amusement park. Not even bothering to wait for the dramatic effect of sunset when the million electric lights that had been installed would go on, Dreamland threw its gates open midday in May 1904. Good thing too because by late afternoon a cold, thick fog crawled along the oceanfront. Most of the over a hundred thousand people who were there crowded into the just built 25,000 square-foot dance hall, astride a brand new steel pier.

Inside, a dance marathon took place. Because stamina was more consequential than skill, these contests attracted more participants, especially during the Depression when the cash prize was a strong incentive. Those who entered had to abide by very strict rules. No shorts, smoking or spitting. Couples have to be appreciably moving at least forty-five minutes out of every hour, after which they are allowed ten minute rests and two minute bathroom breaks. Showering after a twelve-hour stretch was sanctioned. Apart from the numbers attached on the backs of the dancers, they were permitted to wear the logos of local companies that may be sponsoring them. The longest marathon reported was nine and a half hours in England, and twenty-seven hours at New York's Audubon Ballroom.

Beneath the glow of incandescent lamps, men and women propped themselves up on one another, trying to ignore the burning of their feet, swol-
len in scuffed working class shoes scraping on the wooden floorboards.
Now and again, a salty breeze pierced through the dense stench of per-
spiration, giving the contestants reason enough to believe they just might
make it through another hour. And in this universe unto itself, the dance
marathon musical "Steel Pier" reunited Stro and William. It had been years
since "Crazy for You". Although they had worked on Ockrent's 1994 take
on Charles Dickens' (1812-1870) "A Christmas Carol" at Madison Square
Garden (Est. 1968), this was their return to Broadway.

The everyday Depression era costumes for the marathon participants jig-
gled in contrast to the steadiness of the double-breasted suit on the nefar-
ious master of ceremonies played by a dulcet Gregory Harrison. William
took inspiration for the former from the social commentary drawings of
illustrator Reginald Marsh (1898-1954). But unlike Marsh's proclivity for
capturing destitutes as a collective, William's designs were for individual
characters. Variety's Greg Evans praised Stro's choreography and William's
costumes, noting "how the shuffling of the ghostly dancers in the first
scene mimics the sound of ocean waves" and "the women don cellophane
gowns for a publicity-stunt wedding". Unfortunately, the show ran for a
mere hundred performances. It may have been hampered by comparisons
to another Kander and Ebb musical that was revived just a year prior, coincidentally costumed by William and one Stro had been in—"Chicago".

The 1926 play written by Maurine Dallas Watkins (1896-1969) from
her stint as a beat reporter for the Chicago Tribune, was the basis of
Kander and Ebb's "Chicago: A Musical Vaudeville" starring Gwen Verdon

(1925-2000) and Chita Rivera, choreographed by Bob Fosse (1927-1987). But the public couldn't fully apprehend a cynical satire about incarcerated sociopaths when it ran in 1975. Twenty years hence, a better appreciation for gallows humor and an understanding of the cult of celebrity made a reassessment possible at the City Center's Encores! Great American Musicals in Concert with Ann Reinking (1949-2020), Bebe Neuwirth, Joel Grey, and James Naughton, directed by Walter Robbie.

"My title was 'apparel coordinator' because all we had for costumes was a thousand dollars, a pair of scissors, and nine days," quips William. So he rummaged through department store racks and the showrooms of Capezio and Danskin for whatever he could use to cobble together danceable 1920s looks by way of the 1970s. "City Center had never done a dance show before," he says. "But they wanted to honor Fosse, so Ann (Reinking) recreated the original choreography while Walter said I should use Bob's favorite colors—black and flesh."

Its critical and commercial triumph quickened the way to a full-on revival. Cinemagoers too were given 'the old razzle dazzle' in an Academy Award-winning version directed by Rob Marshall in 2002. It's had many touring companies and is currently the longest-running show on Broadway. William's task of hastily stitching outfits for a limited engagement turned into decades of revising the lead costumes for the revolving door of actresses who've slipped into and out of them. It must have, at least, ameliorated the sting of seeing "Steel Pier" close too soon. And William is no stranger to the vagaries of Broadway. He's always viewed his work on the Frank Loesser (1910-1969) musical "Guys and Dolls" directed by Jerry Zaks to be among his strongest, yet it was passed over during awards season. No matter, for Stro and William, the best was yet to come.

———————————

Majority of the population unable or unwilling to enter exhausting dance marathons looked elsewhere for hope. When the Great Depression blanketed the U.S. in the shadows of crippling poverty, the light most people counted on was the one glimmering from the cinema projection booth above their heads. Motion pictures had done what was thought to be impossible—capture the ephemeral aspect of dance. For a couple of hours and a measly quarter, people could at least lose themselves in music and dance and romance.

Strangely auspicious yet ominous "The Broadway Melody" won the Academy Award for Best Picture in 1929, the year the stock market nosedived. Directed by Harry Beaumont (1888-1966), it was the first ever "talkie" and musical from Metro Goldwyn Mayer (MGM, Est 1924). The opening aerial shot of Manhattan was scored to "Give My Regards to Broadway" (composed by George M. Cohan, 1878-1942). MGM later came to be known as much for dispensing such lustrous diversions as its roaring lion vanity card. The studio's "Born to Dance", directed in 1936 by Roy del Ruth (1893-1961), featured the balletic tap dancing of Eleanor Powell (1912-1982) and the now classic "I've Got You Under My Skin" by Cole Porter (1891-1964).

Others produced their own musicals. RKO (Radio Keith Orpheum, Est. 1929) pictures hit the jackpot by pairing Fred Astaire (1899-1987) with Ginger Rogers (1911-1995) in nine dancetravaganzas including "Top Hat" and "Shall We Dance" (1935 and 1936, directed by Mark Sandrich, 1900-1945). Bernard Newman (1903-1966) who'd been a window dresser for Bergdorf Goodman (Est. 1899) created many of Rogers' costumes. From "Follow the Fleet" (1936) was a silk gown that had been dyed blue so its embroidered glass beads would glisten under lights when shot on black and white film. It's currently at the Smithsonian's National Museum of American History. After Hollywood, Newman returned to the city's finest department store as Bergdorf Goodman's in-house head designer. Astaire and Rogers made their tenth and last picture together "The Barkleys of Broadway" in technicolor for MGM.

"Crazy for You" and "Steel Pier" are set in the dimming twilight of the Jazz Age. The term was solidified via "Tales of the Jazz Age", the 1922 F. Scott Fitzgerald (1896-1940) anthology of his previously published short stories. In France, these *"Années folles"* was when the fabled author was also among café society's so-called "lost generation" of writers and artists, exiles and expats who carelessly tossed off bon mots at La Coupole or La Closerie des Lilas. And if they weren't at the usual guinguettes, they were at Gertrude Stein's (1874-1946) salon at N° 27 Rue de Fleurus, the Paris apartment she shared with brother Leo (1872-1947), and her partner Alice B. Toklas (1877-1967). Stein surrounded herself with the likes of Fitzgerald, Ernest Hemingway (1899-1961), Virgil Thomson (1896-1989), Ezra Pound (1885-1972), and Paul Cézanne (1839-1906) to pontificate on matters of art and literature, bestow benediction on a favored few, and indulge in her own cruel and indelicate semblance of *brouillé*.

Up north, the prosperity of the Weimar Republic's "Golden Twenties" gave thousands of Germans occasion to cram into the Admiralspalast (Est. 1910) and marvel at the dancers in the latest musical revue. The wanton combinations of gold knickers and velour brocades or the skimpy lace with light crepe worn by the dancers were designed by Otto Haas-Heye (1879-1959) who worked on many of the city's shows and ballets. Still, these were but incidental spectacles in a more formidable tempest of art, architecture, motion pictures, and literature. Walter Gropius (1883-1969) founded his Bauhaus movement. *"Der Dreigroschenopera"*, a "play with music" by Bertolt Brecht (1898-1956) and Kurt Weill (1900-1950) debuted. Enormous movie palaces unspooled terror and wonder in the expressionist films "Nosferatu" by Friedrich Wilhelm Murnau (1888-1931) and "Metropolis" by Fritz Lang (1890-1976).

But it was also when Berlin was said to have been "dancing on the edge of a volcano". The phrase—a romanticized allusion to the time's unbridled liberality—is often attributed to either literary critic George Steiner (1929-2020) or historian Walter Laqueur (1921-2018), although it could also have been appropriated from a letter by Austrian composer Alban Berg (1885-1935). To moralists this meant shameless hedonism, to cynics, tourist attraction slogan. So prevalent was the depravity of drugs, alcohol, and sex in Berlin's hundreds of clubs and bars that describing these hotspots as underground really only served to make them more enticing. Even the most guileless of travelers could find some of them listed in guidebooks.

The Moka Efti, located on Friedrichstrasse is most familiar now for having been a setting in the 2017 neo-noir TV series "Babylon Berlin" (based on the novels of Volker Kutscher). Of course there are differences. The original interiors weren't impersonally industrial as depicted on the small screen. It was more like an agreeable Moorish sitting room. It did have a barber, pastry shop and billiard hall, but definitely no brothel. Nevertheless, it's fair to assume the male and female dancers were open to side transactions. Other popular clubs of the era, the Eldorado and the Topp, though meant for gay men, brought in an affable clientele of straight men, women, and cross-dressers. At least Berlin's excesses were borderline legal. Across the Atlantic, a misguided law was transforming cities into playgrounds of booze, broads, and gangsters.

CHAPTER FOUR
Mecca for Moderns

In the pre-dawn hours, a cab screeched to a halt in front of the building on W. 44th where the New Yorker magazine (Est. 1925) was temporarily ensconced (before relocating over to W. 45th where it stayed until 1991). In the 1920s, a columnist called Lois Bancroft Long (1901–1974) frequently arrived here after a night on the town and, still inebriated, staggered up to her office. Having rifled through her purse and failing to find the key to her cubicle, Long never hesitated to hoist herself over the partition in full evening dress and heels, stumble to her desk, and type out her cognac-flavored misadventures in the trenches of New York nightlife.

In 1919, the passage of the National Prohibition Act had rendered the production, sale, and transportation of alcohol illegal. But regarding it an inconsequential folly, most New Yorkers flouted this law. If anything, Prohibition only served to fuel their appetites for wild revelries at illicit speakeasies like Chumley's in the West Village. And the flapper—the Charleston dancing, hard drinking, chain smoking party girl—became the era's societal totem.

"Flapper" was what Britons called actual fledglings trying to fly by repeatedly flapping their wings. At the end of the 19th century, the word was used to describe vivacious teen girls. By the time the New York Times got a hold of it in 1912, "flapper" was synonymous with debutantes. Eventually, the word characterized young women deemed frivolous and morally deficient by some, while embraced as carefree and independent without apology by others.

A card-carrying flapper, Long (no relation to William) once described in an interview a typical night for her: "We start at '21' (officially founded in 1922, moved to several locations before it settled on W. 52nd Street, and shuttered in 2020), then Tony's (59 W. 52nd, where the Rockefeller Center is today, owned and operated by Tony Soma, 1890-1979, the grandfather of actress Anjelica Huston)…(and) usually wound up in Harlem." The Vassar (Est. 1861) grad worked at Vogue and Vanity Fair, but found her niche writing the weekly New Yorker column "When Nights are Bold" (changed later to "Tables for Two") under her nom-de-plume "Lipstick". The column had been running mere weeks, penned by the painter Charles Baskerville (1896-1994) alias "Top Hat", before Long took over and the logo was changed to a silhouetted woman in a cloche and cape escorted by a man beaming a flashlight on the words "Night Club".

Because the magazine was still finding its footing, Long's editor gave her latitude to pontificate beyond the who-what-and-where of it all. She railed against the police raids of speakeasies. She bemoaned the slim pickings of bluechip bachelors in Manhattan. And she got away with everything because she never failed to give subscribers an intelligent yet fizzy read. Hers was the voice of the flapper as modern woman. To cap it off, Long also served as an astute fashion critic in her other column "On and Off the Avenue" to which she became more dedicated after being appointed the magazine's fashion editor. In the July 31, 1974 New York Times obituary for Long, her editor William Shawn (1907-1992) hyperbolized that Long had "invented fashion criticism". She most assuredly did not. "The Philosophy of Dress" by Oscar Wilde (1854-1900) was published in the New-York Tribune in 1885. And many were the fashion essays he wrote 1887-1889 for The Woman's World magazine. Still, Long's articles are an invaluable diary of 1920s-1930s fashion and nightlife from a fiercely emancipated woman who wrote, as Shawn pointed out, "with independence, intelligence, humor, and literary style."

Fashion, of course, provided fillip to the power of the flapper, a collective identity telegraphed by what they wore. Sans corsets, dresses now hung straight down, from the shoulders to around the calves. Sleeves during the day, sleeveless for evening. If there were shoulder straps, they were thin. If there was a waistline, it was low. Some were tiered, and most with oscillating fringes. The *Arts décoratifs* (Art Deco) movement in design and architecture seeped into the flapper look with geometric or scallop patterns, the use of metallic tones especially silver and gold, shiny sequins or beads. Mass produced imitation pearls hanging in one or more strands straight down the front flattered the vertical silhouette. Short bobbed hair framed rouged faces and bright red lips. The finishing touches? High heels, a jeweled headband or fringed flapper cap, and a long cigarette holder, maybe one from jeweler Auguste Bonaz (1877-1922).

Interviewed for the July 1927 issue of Motion Picture magazine, Fitzgerald mused over the flapper. "The girls I wrote about were not a type—they were a generation," he said. "In my day, they had just made their escape from dull and blind conventionality. Subconsciously there was a hint of belligerence in their attitude, because of the opposition they met, but overcame. It's rather futile to analyze flappers. They are just girls—all sorts of girls. Their one common trait being that they are young things with a splendid talent for life."

Curiously, although the flapper look remains firmly of its time, many menswear items from the same period became quintessential. Brands staked niches—Brooks Brothers (Est. 1818) in Ivy League looks, Champion (Est. as Knickerbocker Knitting Mills, 1919) and Lacoste (Est. 1933) in sporty attire, and Gucci (Est. 1921) in continental flair. Argyle patterns in socks and sweaters were extrapolated from the clan tartan of the Campbells of Argyll, Scotland. Pinstriped or checked, tweed, flannel, or linen suits; single or double-breasted jackets; blazers; V-neck pullovers and cardigans; slim, high-waisted and pleated trousers—these defy anachronism. They were reimagined for a new generation in the 1950s, and again in the 1980s by the likes of Ralph Lauren. Oxford shoes, bow ties, pocket squares, and tank watches are also still in use. Some items however—detachable shirt collars, spats, walking sticks, silver cigarette cases and flasks, straw boaters and top hats—didn't quite cross over to the next century.

A sober, slightly hungover mood had descended on the country following the Crash of '29. The Great Depression dried out the deluge of bathtub gin more efficiently than Prohibition, which only lasted four more years before being repealed. For majority of Americans, the good times were over, curbing most flamboyant inclinations. Hemlines lowered, instigating the nonsense that is the "hemline index", which alleged some spurious correlation between the stock market and hem length. Fashion in the 1930s abjured the flippant, tart-tongued bon vivant and embraced the wide-eyed ingénue. Designers tossed out linear for hourglass silhouettes. The couturier Madeleine Vionnet (1876-1975) accomplished this by cutting diagonally on the bias so the fabric draped closer to the body. At chez Chanel, the period is known as her most romantic. Her signature flower, the camellia, appeared along with many other floral motifs on printed fabrics, appliques, lace details, even jewelry to relay innocence and purity.

Contrary to what those who traffic in social media would have everyone believe, cultural shifts are never abrupt, nor do they occur in a vacuum. They may take some inciting incident, but that is caused by something else preceding it, which triggers contrary or complimentary responses. Some things take root, others not so much. But all those impel more feedback and more still after that. They have a glacial way of toppling over one another, these dominoes of fashion, music, literature, art, even politics. And, vestiges of what came before lives on in what's next.

Jazz wasn't completely forgotten. Collectively recognized as the Great American Songbook, jazz standards from Broadway shows and films were the pop music of the 1920s to the 1940s. Music composed by giants like the Gershwins, Rodgers and Hart, Irving Berlin, Jerome Kern, Cole Porter etc have been covered by hundreds of instrumentalists and vocalists and are still on every cabaret repertoire to this day. But its rhythmic, danceable subgenre called Swing was what dominated the infancy of recorded sound.

Thomas Edison (1847-1931) (yes, *that* Edison) had invented the cylinder phonograph years prior. But it wasn't until Emile Berliner (1851-1929) designed the flat disc-playing gramophone and Eldridge Johnson (1867-1945) founded The Victor Talking Machine Company (later known as RCA Victor) that record players were mass marketed. The first flat disc records were made from weighty yet fragile shellac resin and played at 78 revolutions per minute (RPM). Decades of technological advancements in sound quality recording and tinkering with formats and players transpired before the public was able to afford and accept the standards of vinyl records in 12" playing at 33⅓ RPM or 7" at 45 RPM. From 1907 on, the wood base Victrola with the hand crank turntable, tonearm with diamond stylus for reading the disc's grooves, and the protruding metal horn was the most recognized record player.

But the average American household couldn't afford novelties. Basic models cost around $60 to $100 while top-of-the-line sold for as much as $1000 (over fifteen thousand in today's money). Instead, families bought a radio. Market surveys of the time estimated radio's reach at 23 million households or over 90 million individuals. Even hotel ballrooms and dance halls were wired for music provided by live broadcasts from local radio stations. Dance-related programming did so well that corporate America sponsored entire programs. "Saturday Night Dance Party" was brought to radio listeners by tobacco company Lucky Strike in 1928, then "Dance Hour" in 1930. "Let's Dance", a five-hour long broadcast from the East Coast, aired in three-hour blocks from 10:30pm in the three time zones. It was the show that made Benny Goodman (1909-1986) and his Orchestra a national sensation.

Swing and Big Band orchestras with ten or more musicians with horn and rhythm sections ruled over the airwaves and dance venues. Each bandleader played to his forte and for different audiences. Goodman, for instance, refused to accept "white only" gigs and boasted some of the best black musicians like Lionel Hampton (1908-2002). Classically-trained Paul Whiteman (1890-1967) couldn't improvise to save his life, and followed his own carefully written out music sheets. But this "sweet" sound made him that much more appealing.

There were other 'sweet' bands such as the one fronted by Glenn Miller (1904-1944), 'hard' bands by the Dorsey brothers (Jimmy 1904-1957 and Tommy 1905-1956), and latin sounds by Xavier Cugat (1900-1990). Latin, particularly the Afro Cubans led by Machito (1909-1984) and Mario Bauza (1911-1993), was vital in fusing percussion instruments like maracas, bongos, congas, and timbales with jazz. Certain bands concentrated on their audiences. Guy Lombardo (1902-1977) catered to high society. Glen Gray (1900-1963) and the Casa Loma Orchestra played mostly for the Ivy leaguers. All the while, everyone found any excuse to go slumming in Harlem. The elegant brownstones that line these streets used to belong to Irish, Dutch, and German immigrants who scurried out the neighborhood the second they were able. That's when African Americans from the South moved in and imprinted the neighborhood with their culture. Despite being on their own territory, they still had to make concessions to entrenched racism. Cotton Club (Est. 1920 by bootlegger and mob boss Owney Madden 1891-1965), for instance, had headliners Duke Ellington (1899-1974) or Cab Calloway (1907-1944), but the patrons were rich caucasians. Chick Webb (1905-1939) and his orchestra, on the other hand, could play music for a mix of black and white dancers that filled the Savoy Ballroom's (Est. 1926) 4,000 capacity.

———————————

While the public swang, stage performance was being redefined by daring female pioneers. Isadora Duncan (1877-1927) spent part of her European tour at the turn of the 20th century squaring off with critics who couldn't reconcile her free flowing movements with their rigid view of technique. Duncan was undeterred. The notoriety of her performances was magnified by heretofore uncommon aspects such as appearing with shaved underarms and legs, dancing barefoot, and wearing ankle length muslin chitons or yards of wavy silk shawls.

For a time, her career and the dance school she opened were funded solely by her lover, the sewing machine heir Paris Singer, with whom she had her second child. There is an unsubstantiated anecdote that Bakst once read her palm and predicted she would gain glory yet lose what she loved the most. Then one rainy night in 1913, Singer, Duncan, their son and her daughter were out to dinner when it was decided the children should return ahead to the apartment after the meal. Along the way, the car sputtered to a stop on a bridge over the Seine, forcing the driver to get off to manually crank the engine. Suddenly, the vehicle jolted forward and plunged into the river with the children trapped inside. Duncan was inconsolable. By 1925 she was penniless and holed up at the Hotel Negresco (Est. 1912) in Nice. Her final tragedy occurred two years later. She was driving an open top sports car when the long red shawl she was wearing twisted around a wheel axle, and strangled her to death.

Another truly notable dancer of this time was Joséphine Baker (1906-1975) who refused to let the systemic racism of her native country victimize her. American born but French naturalized, she actually got into theater as a costume designer for dancers touring the racially segregated Southern states. Searching for less oppressive conditions, Baker eventually made her way to Paris and became a headliner at world renowned cabaret hall the Folies Bergère (Est. 1869). Believe it or not, this headstrong black woman's energetic "Danse Sauvage" number was somehow less remarkable than her accomplishments as a spy.

She may have been scantily-clad onstage, but off it Baker was resplendent in Poiret and Erté (1892-1990). During WWII, she exploited her glamour to infiltrate embassy affairs and the get-togethers of the crème de la crème. She cozied up to German, Italian, and Japanese officials, plying them with flattery and liquor to extract counterintelligence information for the resistance. For the rest of her life she fought for important causes. She was among the main speakers at the 1963 March on Washington rally. In 2021, Baker became the first black woman to be symbolically interred at the Pantheon, France's national museum of heroes, in a ceremony officiated by the French president Emmanuel Macron.

Dance truly became modern when Martha Graham performed her 1930 watershed solo "Lamentation" to Zoltán Kodály's 1910 Piano Piece, Op. 3, No. 2 at Maxine Elliott's Theatre (Est. 1908, demolished in 1960). Graham dispensed with flow for contraction and release in communicating emotion. Throughout the performance, she was encased in an elastic tubing of her own creation to depict tension and extension with every shift of limbs and torso. Minus intricately detailed costumes, modern dance removed concealments or anything that might distract from the purity of a body in motion. What mattered were the colors, the weights and textures of the materials, how they were cut or pleated. Throughout her prolific career she chased after paradox and complexity with the barest requisites to espouse revelation out of stark, sculptural forms.

Young people and dancers alike acclimatized to this aesthetic by wearing leotards and tights for sporty activities until they were subsumed into casual wear. The cover of Life magazine's September 13, 1943 issue announced "Leotards: Acrobats' tights make news in this year's college fashions". The same year, Harper's Bazaar extolled "the 21st century and the cosmic costumes of Flash Gordon" silhouette based on "every ballet dancer's traditional rehearsal costume". The leotard also figured in the work of theater and fashion designer Mildred Orrick (1906-1944). Archived at Parsons School of Design (Est. 1896) are her sketches of pants and leggings in yoga poses to stress anatomy and motion. Her extensive studies in folk dress from Turkey, China, Native American and Inuit tribes supplemented her ideas for 1940s fashions.

After the U.S. entered WWII, a compeer of Orrick's, Claire McCardell (1905-1958) responded to supply rationing and the new reality of more women in the workforce. She pioneered American sportswear with functional ideas like coordinated separates to produce multiple looks. And due to the shortage of leather, she engaged Capezio to make ballet slippers that matched her designs. Preserved at the MET's Costume Institute is her hunter green bodysuit with a wraparound tweed dress, matching belt and tweed ballet pumps. Experts pointed at the parallels of Graham and McCardell's works, analogous in how both depicted motion even while stationary, concurrently existing within the liminal space of the collective yet individual sense of American identity.

Fashion and dance fed into the notion of an 'American' identity, wars in the making. In 1775 it was about dissociating from any dependence on a monarchial past. The one between the North and South was supposed to institute "inalienable" rights for all. The moral imperative of WWII came with a halo of heroism. Now, the aww-shucks, mother's apple pie image was sunkissed with a fit body in sportswear. It was a prophecy, the media said, that could be self-fulfilled by beauty and weight loss regimens and modern fash- ions. Reality had other ideas. Women especially were periodically reminded of their failings by cinema and magazines, which offered renegotiations in the guises of more things to buy.

In 1942, director Busby Berkley (1895-1976) introduced the world to Gene Kelly in "For Me and My Gal". In spite of Kelly's regular guy persona being in opposition to the dandy often portrayed by Fred Astaire, the two shared strong creative proprietorship over their routines and preferred them shot wide and almost in their entirety. This often had Astaire butting heads with Berkley, the master of overhead kaleidoscopes of multiple chorus girls. Just before the end of the war, the heir presumptive to Astaire's title of the greatest male dancer on celluloid became apparent when Kelly played Danny McGuire in Columbia Pictures' "Cover Girl".

Another difference between them, Astaire is best remembered dancing with Ginger Rogers while Kelly's most iconic partner is his umbrella in the 1952 Stanley Donen (1924-2019) picture "Singin' in the Rain". From his soaked Norfolk tweed suit (by costume designer Walter Plunkett, 1902-1982) in that picture to the blue-striped muscle T and high waist trousers in "Anchors Aweigh" (1945 by director George Sidney, 1916-2002, costumes by Irene, 1901-1962), Kelly danced his way into the hearts of millions looking dapper in whatever he wore.

As wartime caused incomprehensible devastation abroad, a heavy pall of fear and uncertainty engulfed the U.S.. To galvanize the motion picture industry without seeming to endorse propaganda and censorship, the federal government established two agencies within the Office of War Information (OWI). The Bureau of Motion Pictures produced educational films and reviewed scripts submitted by the studios The Bureau of Censorship was in charge of film exports. Hollywood acceded to this federal oversight, conforming to a nationalistic narrative. But what that looked like exactly caused endless bickering. The more obvious goals were addressed faster: sell war bonds, rally the troops, and boost morale. Ratchet up sentimentality. Now, do it with song and dance. Thus, audiences watched patriotic boys in the barracks, sailors on shore leave getting into hilarious situations, and zany entertainers putting on a show.

A resurgence in vaudeville on film provided comforting nostalgia. But at urban centers, tickets for live vaudeville were cheaper. So Hollywood repackaged their pictures as "revivals" of Broadway hits. The 1942 Anne Sothern (1909-2001) vehicle "Panama Hattie" was advertised as "Broadway's famed musical on the screen" (based on the 1940 Cole Porter musical) and trumpeted as having "more talent than in ten vaudeville shows." At the height of the war, an estimated 90 million Americans went to the movies every week.

On actual Broadway, shows were being restructured into cohesive book musicals, and importantly, being imbued with real substance. Chief among them were three shows from composer Richard Rodgers and librettist Oscar Hammerstein II: "Oklahoma!" (March 1943) an adaptation of the 1931 Lynn Riggs (1899-1954) play "Green Grow the Lilacs"; "Carousel" (April 1945) based on the 1909 Ferenc Molnár (1878-1952) play "Liliom"; and "South Pacific" (February 1949), an amalgamation of plots from the anthology "Tales of the South Pacific" by James A. Michener (1907-1997). All those musicals were revolutionary for songs and dances that advanced the story in lieu of pointless gags and throwaway numbers. They also resuscitated an almost forgotten practice of having dancers take over the actors in performing a ballet as an interior monologue of the main characters. Although this "dream ballet" in act one of "Oklahoma!" only serves to underline what the audience already knows, the act two routine in "Carousel" does provide a vision of the future.

Unavoidably, since shows were behooved to send people out of the theater with smiles on their faces and humming show tunes, productions could only really mature in increments. The pastoral backdrop of "Oklahoma!" is practically a cardboard rendering of a settlement outpost where the characters were reduced to a 'white hat' Curly versus a 'black hat' Jud. And the 'accidental' death of someone who was clearly the villain is brushed off as a nuisance to the happily wedded after. Though still distanced from its grim source, "Carousel" dared to have a more complicated, well, frankly abusive and problematic main character. At last, "South Pacific" went fully confrontational in dealing with racism. And having the promising life of Lt. Joseph Cable cut short was surely provocative at wartime. All three musicals were diluted into motion pictures in 1955, 1956, and 1958, respectively. Nevertheless, all received accolades, proving how their inherent profundity makes them topical for recurrent re-examinations and revivals.

Next up in the Rodgers and Hammerstein streak was 1951's "The King & I", adapted from a rather trifling Margaret Landon (1903-1933) novel "Anna and the King of Siam", itself based on a travel writer's memoirs of having been in service as governess to the Siamese royal household. A pivotal ballet in act two necessitated the hiring of a choreographer called Jerome Robbins (1918-1998), who'd also been a Broadway hoofer then soloist at ABT. In 1944, this native New Yorker conceived the sailors-in-the city musical "On the Town", from which came the Leonard Bernstein (1918-1990), Betty Comden (1917-2006) and Adolph Green (1914-2002) geography lesson "the Bronx is up and the Battery's down". It is also notable for the racially diverse dancers Robbins brought together to better capture the city's complexion.

"The King & I" producers' faith in Robbins was validated after they saw his "The Small House of Uncle Thomas" ballet, patterned after poses of the majestic mythological figures and deities hewn into the Grand Palace in Bangkok. They relented to his wish of adding to "March of the Siamese Children" and "Shall We Dance". Again, social messages are but hinted. The presence in the cast of Baayork Lee and Yuriko (1920-2022, the Graham dancer who returned to "The King & I" as director for the 1977 revival) was already a coup.

For his 1957 vendetta musical "West Side Story", Robbins substituted blood with race, the tiles and stones of Verona with the fire escapes and concrete of (now razed) San Juan Hill, the Montagues and Capulets with the Jets and Sharks. Eight weeks—double the norm—to learn the routines was the first indication dance would be on par with plot, dialogue, and music (Bernstein and Stephen Sondheim, 1930-2021) in this modernized "Romeo and Juliet". Another was declaring its central conflict from the jump with a dance-off for turf. Because of its setting, Robbins' choreography is deemed modern jazz. But Robbins, neither tap nor jazz dancer, always was a ballet dancemaster. And classical ballet is in the bones of the choreography, for which Robbins won the Tony. With Robert Wise (1914-2005), he helmed the unavoidable film version, which swept the academy awards voters off their feet, winning 11 Oscars including Best Picture.

———————————

Pop music from these Broadway shows and Hollywood movies trickled down to the public through printed music sheets, live bands, radio, and records. In another instance of disruptions by the war, the bulk of shellac resin supplies for making wax records was reallocated by the government toward the production of explosives and coating for artillery shells. Shellac was so badly needed that Americans were encouraged to donate unwanted or even chipped records to the war effort. In Pittsburgh, people who brought in five records were admitted into the "War Records Dance" at the William Penn Hotel (Est. 1916).

Vinyl proved to be more than adequate a substitute for producing records. From 1943 to 1949, thousands of 12" "V Discs" were distributed to servicemen in the Army, then the Navy and Marines. These contained music especially recorded by band leaders like Glenn Miller and jazz greats like pianist Art Tatum (1909-1956) and saxophonist Coleman Hawkins (1904-1969). After the war, affordable and better made players ensured vinyl's takeover. Then came RCA's launch of the one song-per side 45 RPM record, which served as grist for the new mill being referred to as a jukebox. In small venues—diners, malt shops, dives and hole-in-the-wall restaurants—all across the country, the jukebox was everywhere. By the 1950s, nearly a million units, stocked with a hundred singles, offered wider music selections from rhythm and blues and country to rock and roll. To music they could now personally select, teens found new ways of contorting their bodies—The Locomotion, the Mashed Potato, and the Bugaloo.

One dance, very easily accomplished from the hips, became a breakout favorite, stoked by Chubby Checker's 1960 hit "The Twist" (a cover of Hank Ballard and the Midnighters from 1958). In 1961, Paramount Pictures made a movie around the dance—"Hey, Let's Twist!"—set in the Peppermint Lounge, an alternate reality of a deliberately unremarkable gay bar on W. 54th Street that barely held 180 people. Among many Mafiosi-owned Manhattan watering holes, the real Peppermint Lounge (Est. 1958) was nicknamed "the Pep" by patrons who elbowed each other over the mahogany bar or danced discreetly in back. In Esquire (Est. 1933), author Tom Wolfe (1930-2018) essayed how everything changed "One week in October 1961 (when) a few socialites, riding hard under the crop of a couple of New York columnists" blundered in, probably because it was next door to the Knickerbocker. Both the Pep and the twist were 'discovered'. A juicy blind item later and the male regulars were jostling with the likes of Audrey Hepburn (1929-1993), Greta Garbo (1905-1990), and Lee Radziwill (1933-2019).

From there the Pep's cash registers were sustained by the motion picture, the dance, and hit records like Joey Dee and the Starliters' "Peppermint Twist" and Sam Cooke's "Twistin' the Night Away". Meanwhile, Checker wrung what he could from the fad with a follow up single "Let's Twist Again" in 1961, and starred in back-to-back pictures "Twist Around the Clock" and "Don't Knock the Twist". But another song brought hordes more to the bar. Released in advance of the Beatles first-ever visit to the U.S., "I Want to Hold Your Hand" was the Billboard Hot 100 chart topper by the time they arrived. Over seventy million viewers tuned in for their 1964 appearance on The Ed Sullivan Show. Immediately after, the band ran from the studio of squealing fans and spent the rest of the night at the Pep.

When Robbins co-directed "The Pajama Game" with George Abbott (1887-1995) he handed choreography duties to 27 year-old Bob Fosse (1927-1987) who'd been working both coasts as a stage and motion picture dancer. The year after saw Fosse's sophomore effort "Damn Yankees". The Tonys bestowed on him the first and second Best Choreography awards of his career. Those shows also set in stone Fosse's unmistakable dance vocabulary: isolated gestures, snapping fingers and jazz hands, the shoulder and pelvic rolls, turned in knees, forward movement at an incline, even white gloves, all-black outfits, bowler hats, and the use of canes and chairs. In the following years, Fosse assumed more control by directing and choreographing his projects. 1972 was a very good year for him. He picked up yet another Tony in choreography and direction for "Pippin", followed by a night at the Oscars where his motion picture version of "Cabaret" collected eight statuettes.

It is largely unacknowledged that these accolades for "Cabaret" are about Fosse's interpretation and not any kind of fidelity to the material. The public often takes it for granted that they are watching something definitive when in reality the "Cabaret" they saw onscreen bore closer resemblance to 1970s Hollywood than it did to 1930s Germany. As a matter of fact, Fosse's version was a striking departure from the 1966 stage musical directed by Harold Prince (1928-2019) and choreographed by Ron Field (1933-1989), as that was from the John Van Druten (1901-1957) 1951 stage play, as that was from the source stories in the 1939 novel "Goodbye to Berlin" by British-born writer Christopher Isherwood (1904-1986).

It is incumbent upon any artist not to just replicate a pre-existing material, rather find something relevant to the times. Isherwood was said to have been dismayed by each successive iteration for arbitrarily plucking parts of previous versions as well as from his original work. Even Kander and Ebb reworked numbers from their musical for the film. "Cabaret" went through another overhaul when Sam Mendes presented it in 1993 at the Donmar Warehouse (Est. 1977) in Covent Garden, then again in 1998 as a Broadway revival with Rob Marshall signed on as co-director and choreographer. And for costume design duties? William Ivey Long, *aber natürlich.*

In Mendes' 1998 self-proclaimed "fully realized version," Fosse's glossy and stylized routines were peeled away to reveal the bruised hearts and tortured souls in the Kit Kat Klub as they tried to drown out the sound of approaching jackboots with music, alcohol, and sex. So instead of formal tails, the Emcee enters the spotlight in a risqué trench coat and body harness. Gone too is the cheery glamour of Sally Bowles, replaced by a tremulous voice, needle track marks, and tattered fishnet stockings. Of course, with William involved, the perforations on the hosiery aren't random. Holes were deliberately placed for different performers, hemmed to prevent runs, and stitched with stray yarn to appear as though they were naturally fraying. William's granular attention to costumes and Robert Brill's night club set enfolded the audience into the production. The Emcee's "Willkommen" pulled them into their seats. And Sally's conspiratorial "Don't Tell Mama", *bitte,* kept everyone glued for the rest of the night.

As if a reminder was necessary on how small the world is, the next defining dance spectacle of this generation was made possible by a man Fosse had met when they were both serving in the Navy onboard the U.S.S. Solomons aircraft carrier stationed in the South Pacific during WWII. Joe Papp (1921–1991) was a Brooklynite who entertained the troops with vaudeville sketches and roped in Fosse to perform. After being discharged from the services, Papp studied acting and directing (under the GI Bill) at the The Actors' Laboratory Theatre (Est. 1941) in Los Angeles. As an understudy and assistant stage manager, he toured with a production of "Death of a Salesman" and ended back in New York where he got a job stage managing a couple of shows at the CBS Broadcast Center on W. 57th while directing plays on the side.

Papp then spent years roaming the five boroughs with a rag tag crew and makeshift stages, mounting his New York Shakespeare Festival (Est. 1954). That was until the itinerant company settled into an 1,800-seat open air Central Park theater financed by and named after George (1894-1991, founder of Dell Publishing) and Valerie Delacorte (1914-2011). Papp's passion project aimed at bringing the Bard to all New Yorkers, particularly the young and indigent. Having been both himself once, Papp never forgot how he'd felt transformed by theater. So no amount of pressure from the parks commissioner could convince him to charge the public one thin dime to watch George C. Scott (1927-1999), James Earl Jones, Martin Sheen, and Meryl Streep soliloquize in iambic pentameter.

With the Shakespeare Festival nestled at the Delacorte, Papp set his sights on a rusticated brownstone on Lafayette from where to incubate new work. Designed in 1853 by Alexander Saeltzer (1814-1883), it used to be the Astor Library until the books (all reference not lending) were reshelved at the Beaux Arts Public Library on Fifth Avenue. The building then housed the Hebrew Immigrant Aid Society. By 1965 it was a deteriorated, desolate husk awaiting the business end of a wrecking ball, had the Landmarks Preservation Commission not swooped in, declared it a historic site, and brokered a deal for Papp to take ownership. Architect Giorgio Cavaglieri (1911-2007) renovated it into performance spaces comprising The Public Theatre.

On October 17, 1967, the Public announced its intent in no uncertain terms with the sex, drugs, profanity, and pacifist message of "Hair: The American Tribal Love-Rock Musical". For Papp, championing the arts was a civic obligation. His support of playwrights made the Public the birthplace of works that may have otherwise never seen the light of the stage. And one singular critical and commercial sensation of a dance musical high kicked Broadway into the future.

The Great White Way's nadir was apparent in its far too many extinguished lights in 1973. And those to whom this caused the most worry were at the bottom rung—the dancers on the chorus. Two of them—Michon Peacock and Tony Stevens (1948-2011)—and choreographer Michael Bennett toyed with some amorphous idea of organizing a dancers repertory. At nigh the witching hour on January 26, 1974, those with gigs hurried out stage doors and taxied down snowed over streets to E. 23rd. Above a Dunkin Donuts, at the Nickolaus Exercise Centers, they sat in a circle and uncorked bottles of red wine. Without an agenda, Bennett led the powwow with, "I really wanna talk about us, where we came from, why we're dancers . . ." It took a few more swigs of vino before the dancers got veritas, unburdening themselves of things they probably would have preferred to forget. Recorded on a Sony reel-to-reel, the soul-baring and cathartic confessions yielded hours of tapes, which Bennett later brought to Papp.

Papp heard potential and gave Bennett and his team a working space and $100 a week to workshop it. The creative team (including Marvin Hamlisch, 1944-2012, and Edward Kleban, 1939-1987 for music, James Kirkwood Jr., 1924-1989 and Nicholas Dante, 1941-1991 for the book, and co-choreographer Bob Avian, 1937-2021) then grafted fragments of dancers' personal stories onto composites. A few, however, were tethered directly to a dancer. Connie's diminutive stature and Asian heritage was baked in from Baayork Lee, born in Chinatown to an Indian mother and Chinese father. Thus the role was almost always assigned to an Asian dancer. The tone deaf Kristine, meanwhile, came from Renee Baughman's inability to stay on key. Anyone who eventually took on this role might be a good singer but sometimes would recite the lyrics instead, or intentionally go in and out of tune, which really isn't how a tone-deaf person sounds. The story of Sheila's mother who gave up dancing for a loveless marriage then foisted her ambition on her daughter was from Kelly Bishop (who famously played other kinds of mothers in the 1987 motion picture "Dirty Dancing" and the 2000 TV drama "The Gilmore Girls"). Cassie was mostly Donna McKechnie (who was above 'chorus', and even achieved an entirely different kind of fame for being a part of the gothic soap "Dark Shadows"), though some aspects were culled from Bennett's personal history with dancer Leland Palmer.

An early pass was an unwieldy four hours of depressing stories which kept getting whittled down until it was a manageable two-hour show without intermission. In April 1975 a voice at The Public Theater barked: "Again! Step, kick, kick, leap, kick, touch . . . Again!" thrusting the audience in media res of an harrowing audition called "A Chorus Line". Until the Public ran out of money. Bennett rang Bernard B. Jacobs (1916-1996) of The Shubert Organization and offered the show to them. Jacobs protested, "I can't do that to Joe." He counter-offered "We can lend him some money, and if it works, we'll put it in one of our theaters."

By summertime, the show did move to the Shubert Theatre (Est. 1913). Broadway audiences were riveted from the moment the dancers launched into "I Hope I Get It". Not only did it have all the earnestness of a traditional 'I Want' song for inciting plot, but its visceral yearning rollercoasted from blustering heights to bottomless insecurities. Each "I hope I get it…" was a gut punch to anyone who's ever wanted, needed, a job, which, at the end of the day, is everyone. Still, its specificity to dancers is unrelenting—from Cassie's affirmations of "I am a dancer . . . " to the uplifting climax. Everyone gets to do the triumphant finale song and dance, made bittersweet however, since the dancers retreated once more to the similarly costumed, anonymous line, singing about the "second best to none" qualities of the unseen 'real' star of the show.

"A Chorus Line" was a runaway smash that 'saved' The Public, the Shubert, and perhaps all of Broadway since overall attendance increased by a million the next year. Some of the original dancers opened the San Francisco show. For fifteen years, at the time the longest-running show on Broadway, it raked in money by the hundreds of millions. It won nine out of its fifteen Tony nominations and a Pulitzer Prize (Est. 1917) for Drama in 1976.

Time magazine heralded the decade of dance with a 1971 cover story on Broadway's "Follies", directed by Bennett and Hal Prince. That same year, the ballerina Suzanne Farrell was the face of Nina Ricci's L'air du Temps perfume. In December of 1975, Vogue featured a Richard Avedon full-bleed layout on troubled prima ballerina Gelsey Kirkland, while Newsweek raved about "Broadway's New Kick" with McKechnie on the cover. It's not all national covers and cosmetics contracts, the life of a dancer. Neither is it just devastating elimination rounds. Otherwise, there wouldn't be another hundred people who just got off of the train, or off of the bus, and off of the plane. But fluctuations in the number of arrivals from elsewhere, counted against those who depart, then replaced by another batch of newcomers, add up to only a U.S. Census Bureau estimate of 17,500 who move into the city annually. Chances are that tally includes dancers.

"It was really supposed to be just a visit," Seán Martin Hingston insists. "I had a friend who offered to put me up at his place while he was out of town." But, a dancer's gonna dance. No sooner had his bags plopped down the apartment in New York when the Australian was out the door to open-call auditions. "I arrived late to one. The men's call was done and they were trying out the women. Before I could leave someone told me to just hang around because that sort of thing happened all the time and they might be able to see me after. I did, and they did, and I got the gig!" A week to the day, he was booked for "Broadway Tonight", a sort of compendium of musical numbers scheduled to tour Europe. "I think my being Australian helped," Seán conjectures. "There weren't many of us then." It couldn't have hurt that he was good and had already been in major shows down under. With the skills he'd been honing in tap and ballet classes since age fourteen, Seán had starred in school productions in Melbourne and joined the Sydney production of Andrew Lloyd Weber's "Cats".

He was raring to go on the European tour. Except there was a catch. Seán didn't really have a work visa. "Not even a bank account," he admits. "So I convinced the producers to pay me cash under the table." He adds, "The show was billed as 17 Broadway Stars from 17 Broadway Shows! … well, 16 Broadway stars and one Aussie on a tourist visa." When he returned to New York a close friend from acting class who knew of his predicament offered to marry him so he could get a green card. The couple got hitched at city hall. The best man was Seán's buddy Nathan Fillion (then an actor on the daytime sudser "One Life to Live", now lead in ABC's "The Rookie"). And in a playful tribute to Ang Lee's 1993 "The Wedding Banquet" about a marriage of convenience to obtain a green card the party had their reception at a Chinese restaurant.

Seán's amiability and work ethic endeared him to the Broadway community. In no time, he was upgraded by casting directors to invitation calls, which expedites the hiring of performers who've proven reliable in previous shows. One call gave him his biggest break yet. "I was taking over for an ensemble part from a friend (Rob Ashford who would later carve his own career as choreographer and director) in 'Crazy for You'," he recalls. "You usually have two weeks, sometimes less, to rehearse and you're expected to watch the show as much as you can—especially if there's dancing involved. So I was at the Shubert watching when I saw Stro for the first time. I'd auditioned for Mike and had been cast when she had been out of town. She was in back taking notes when I caught her eye, and without a word she walked over and gave me the warmest hug. She's a good hugger. I was so touched that this legend was welcoming me to her show."

He continues, "In the world of dancers Stro is known specifically for using props to drive narrative and reveal character." This made it all the more mortifying when he failed to catch a pickaxe during his first performance in "Crazy for You". He laughs, "The sight of it flying into the front row of the audience is burned into my memory!" Seán is unstintingly effusive in his praise of Stro, "As a human being, she is generous, warm, loving. As a professional she is unflappable, never raises her voice. But she sees and hears everything. Meeting and working with her was a true joy." In 1999, Stro brought the band back together for "Contact"

On a frigid winter's day, Stro demonstrated swing dancing to the assembled company at the Lincoln Center workshop. Then the dancers were really put through the paces of East Coast Swing, Ballroom, Lindy Hop, the Shag, and Rhythm Steps. Sro says, "I had them learn a routine, which they had to do under different states of emotion—happy, angry, drunk, flirty. I then had them switch partners to see how they interacted with one another. It helped us match them up and choose the characters who would inhabit the club."

She recalls, "The dancers were especially good at improv and made the characters richer by the minute. There were three solo men at the club—Jack Hayes, Seán, and Robert Wersinger—all magnificent, athletic dancers and skilled actors. And they have to be powerful personalities so they can serve as obstacles to our leading man." For that role, Stro wanted Juilliard-trained and multi-award winning actor Boyd Gaines. She says, "He was perfect because he did not look like a dancer and, in fact, could not dance at all, which is crucial for the role." Furthermore, Gaines was capable of crafting a believable Wiley, treading between boys club insider and someone emotionally adrift on whom viewers could imprint their own doubts and fears. As for the Girl in the Yellow Dress? Stro knew the minute Deborah Yates walked in the audition room. "I just kept thinking 'I hope she can dance'." She could. "She was beautiful, tall, had a mysterious aura about her, and she danced with terrific confidence."

With her cast in place, next up was a call to William, who picked up the phone on the first ring. "William, I need a yellow dress," Stro's voice came over the receiver. "Oh," he responded. Momentarily caught unawares, confusion creased his brows. "Why yellow?" In summary she told him she was at Lincoln Center doing a workshop and asked him to come over and see what they were doing. He continues, "I went and she told me about being commissioned by Andre to do this show. I watched them working and she related seeing that woman in the club. She never did tell me what the dress looked like, just that it was yellow and how it came into the light then pulled back." Armed with those simple instructions, off he went. But, William avers, "I'm telling you, simple is hard. A lot of work goes into simple." Little did William know just how much.

William headed for the nearest subway station to return to his studio. All gripes against the MTA aside, it's still the quickest and most convenient way of getting around town. Besides, William prefers it. "It's a way of being among other city folk. I always look around and try to figure out the people around me. And I make up stories in my head about who they are, why they are wearing these clothes. It's exhausting. You can't just take the subway without looking at every single person. There's a lot you can learn on the subway."

What he had yet to learn then was although he and Stro routinely wore dissimilar outfits, these serve as uniforms. She had a propensity for being in black, often baseball-capped, he in a striped tie and natty blue blazer or full suit. Both contend that doing so telegraphs professionalism and consistency. For Stro this also usually means spaces as sterile as a dance studio or her office where all she wants to see are clear surfaces and her writing implements. "No show posters," she says. "I don't want anything that distracts from the project I'm working on." And this kind of compulsive and scrupulous fervor with which they approach their work is another thing Stro and William share. Never far from reach are their show bibles brimming with information, ideas, and images. Of late though Stro has been foregoing her binder for compiling and tracking of routines and blocking and using instead the Stage Write computer application (created by Jeff Whiting), which conveniently does all that on a tablet.

That William's Royal typewriter, in perfect working order, sits at the ready on a table in a vast room below street level in lower Manhattan, suggests new fangled apps and minimalist rooms are where the road diverges for Stro and William. On all sides of his atelier are memorabilia and show records stored on shelves and tall flat filing cabinets, the ones architects use to keep blueprints. His hand-made maquettes line mantels. Sketches are heaped upon enormous tables and paper the walls alongside photographs and greeting cards from friends. And hidden somewhere must be a Dorian Grayesque portrait of William since many have noticed how the passing years have had little effect on his youthful, elfin visage.

Working down here preserves his privacy as much as, he admits, those of the staff's on the upper floor. There, mere feet away from the cubicle of his trusted and hyper efficient adjutant Donald Sanders, a massive mirror leans against a wall. The glass is spotless. But the gilded frame bears the years it had spent on a tavern wall from which it had been rescued by William just before the place was torn down. But the mirror isn't here to be decorative. William uses it to get a read on costumes from a distance doubled by the reflection to twenty feet. He demonstrates with a recent acquisition. "This fabric looked so good. We loved its texture and pattern. But," he says dejectedly, "see, from this distance, you can't really make out the stripes anymore."

William adds that the recent changeover to LED lighting in theaters has brought up new issues, "Standard lighting is already tricky since it underlights nylon and makes black look brown. Now, LED lights cast a blue tint onto everyone on stage. I've had to correct costume colors for my long-running shows to accommodate this. But you also can't just take for granted the new costumes can be taken on tour since some regional theaters may not have the same kind of lighting." These are the threads William ironically tugs at to prevent things from unraveling, a procedure made instinctual by his professionalism.

He explains his process, "I don't pick any colors until I see what the set looks like. And I only start sketching after I've made a spreadsheet of the production—a breakdown of the script by character, scene and song—so I can see the full scope." This can also identify what is required of the costumes and any complications that may arise.

"Here's a tip," he declares, "When in doubt, always take the most com-plicated thing you have to the oldest person in the room." And that's what he did every time he brought his designs to the Matera costume shop up until the day it was no more. When Matera was alive it was the locus of theatrical costumes from opera and dance to musicals and concerts. Of course there had been others. For a time Brooks Costume Company had 250 costume makers in its employ, but after several incarnations closed in 2015.

What always set Matera apart was Barbara herself who'd been mentored by the great Irene Sharaff (1910-1993) with whom she worked on the costumes for the William Wyler (1902-1981) motion picture version of "Funny Girl". Tirelessly creative and ingenious, Matera was beloved for being willful yet fair, showing the custodian the same respect she would a major designer. The dance projects and anything that involved beading were her favorites. At the requiem gathering of her friends and family, one that came up was the scintillating red and gold gown designed by Anthony Powell (1935-2021) and worn by Kate Capshaw in 1984's "Indiana Jones and the Temple of Doom". Steven Spielberg, who's always wanted to direct an MGM-style musical, opened this picture with Capshaw as songbird Willie Scott crooning "Anything Goes" backed by a tap dancing chorus in 1935 Shanghai. Beaded to within a centimeter of material, the dress has tiny dragon patterns (by Holly Hynes) along the mandarin collar that no one can possibly see, even in HD. Yet there it was. Brought on location to Sri Lanka, the gown was damaged when an elephant took a bite out of the back. A panicked overseas call from the production had the beaders at Matera scrambling to replace the missing section with whatever 1920s and 1930s seed pearls and assorted beads they had left. Powell had the unenviable responsibility of filling out the insurance claim with "eaten by elephant". Spielberg's wish, meanwhile, was granted finally in 2021 when he remade "West Side Story".

But years of attrition had taken its toll on one-stop custom and rental shops that, as William recounts, "delivered everything from soup to nuts." He says, "Experienced stitchers are becoming more difficult to find, much less the kind of drapers at Matera who know the best way around any fabric. The shop did everything from cutting patterns to sewing." Nowadays, producing everything in-house isn't possible. William has to shop for some items and outsource the bulk to various specialists like Vincent's, Parson-Meares, Eves, and Jennifer Love Costumes. But truly skilled stitchers, beaders or lace makers are a dying breed. "Making it even worse," he sighs, "Budgets are shrinking all the time."

There's also the question of the availability of specific fabrics. "That depends entirely on the fabric makers." If one needed chiffon, not a problem. If it has to be polyester crepe de chine, rub a lamp. And unfortunately it's a coveted material to substitute for silk, which stains darkly with sweat and tends to plaster on the body. "And, even if you found the right material, it may not come in the color you want so it still needs to be dyed." A couture gown is probably worn twice or thrice in a lifetime. A theatrical gown, says William, has to be made with the same technical guile, but has to be worn six nights a week and two matinees. "And if it has to be dry cleaned, those chemicals are going to be brutal on the material." Which takes William back to the challenge at hand—the not so simple task of coming up with the right material for the right dress in the right shade of yellow.

CHAPTER FIVE
Silk Degrees

New York City trudged toward the mid-1970s across a quagmire of drug trafficking, loan-sharking, and protection rackets masterminded by the Mafia. The crime families had a vise-like grip on the labor unions, ensuring control over municipal and commercial services from garbage collection to transportation and construction. Aggravating matters further, the mayor (from 1974 to 1977) Abraham Beame (1906-2001) was beset by a fiscal crisis he tried to attenuate by borrowing against city pension funds, running operational deficits on buses and subways, and threatening to lay off over ten thousand police officers. In retaliation, a coalition of various unions, the Council for Public Safety, circulated a horrific death's head-illustrated leaflet "Welcome To Fear City: A Survival Guide for Visitors to the City of New York", implying the city was already on the precipice, that an undermanned NYPD would transfigure it into a hellish wasteland. The New York Times, in June 1975, reported that a million copies of the scaremongering fliers had been printed; but shortly after, ran a follow-up that public outcry halted further distribution.

Regardless, there was little use denying that by 4pm of October 17, 1975, $453M of the city's debt was inescapably due. Mere two hours before default, however, an announcement was made that through gnashed teeth, the United Federation of Teachers (UFT) would use its pension funds to stave off a bankruptcy filing. Behind the scenes, Beame and New York governor Hugh Carey (1919-2011) continued their months-long efforts to wrangle for federal assistance. But a little over a week later, sitting president Gerald Ford (1913-2006) spoke before the National Press Club in Washington DC and said, "I can tell you, and tell you now, that I am prepared to veto any bill that has as its purpose a federal bailout of New York City." Next morning, the New York Daily News summed up the speech into the pithy headline: "Ford to City: Drop Dead". This, of course, only served to spur New York into really buckling down to tackle its runaway budget. And although Ford eventually did approve government aid, on election day, resentful New Yorkers backed Jimmy Carter for presidency instead.

Political posturing aside, New York truly was being held together by little more than spit and baling wire. This was the decade when a citywide power outage caused mass looting and vandalism, David Berkowitz aka "Son of Sam" went on a year-long killing spree, and six armed men drove into the Lufthansa cargo terminal at JFK and robbed its vault of $5M in cash and $875,000 in jewelry. Felony rates were up and street crimes an everyday occurance. Vacated storefronts dotted the city. With nearly a million residents scampering off to the suburbs, there were boroughs of abandoned buildings. Into the vacancies in Manhattan came society's misfits. Artists, writers, designers, photographers, musicians, actors, people of color, the gays claimed their downtown corners of Sodom-Upon-Hudson for dirt cheap rents. And it was exactly from such fertile grounds of chaos that wonderful things began to blossom.

In another place and time, these disparate groups may have remained insular in fabricating their own sets of habits and norms. But in the hothouse that was Manhattan, they fed off each other's creativity and not only produced works that propelled their own métiers but impacted the rest of the world. They would also come together and discover shared community and joy—when they danced. And many from that era will say they did so in the legendary SoHo nightspot—The Loft.

SoHo is an abbreviation of South of Houston (Street) that first appeared in a 1963 report by city planner Chester Raskin. The neighborhood's reputation as a dry goods and commercial center was sealed by stores like Tiffany & Company (first called Tiffany, Young and Ellis) that opened here on Broadway in 1837, and Lord & Taylor on Grand Street in 1853. Five hundred of its industrial buildings feature cast-iron façades that can span further than masonry, allowing more expansive floor space and larger windows. One prime example still there is the 12-story Little Singer building on 561 Broadway designed in 1902 (and built the following year) by Beaux Arts-trained New York architect Ernest Flagg (1857-1947) for the Singer Sewing Machine Company. The entire neighborhood was designated an historic district by the New York City Landmarks Preservation Commission in 1973.

From the late 1960s through the early 1970s, rents in SoHo were a steal. But the neighborhood was zoned for businesses. When people began to take residence in many of the vacancies, it did not go unnoticed. After being threatened with eviction, a coalition of artists campaigned to have the City Planning Commission permit over one thousand lofts reclassified for residential use in 1971. And at one such loft on 645-647 Broadway, the modern dance club came of age.

In 1970, David Mancuso (1944-2016) was short on the rent for his 1,850 square ft SoHo apartment. So he decided to throw a party. Rent parties are believed to have started in the 1920s when impoverished African Americans supplemented their meager incomes by raising donations from social gatherings they held at home with swing dancing and musicians. Mancuso's first rent party charged $2.50 to cover food, punch, and coat check. Sent out to friends were thirty-six invitations for Valentine's Day 1970, inscribed with the slogan "Love Saves the Day", the first letters of which is also the acronym for the drug lysergic acid diethylamide (LSD). Mancuso happened to be a devout follower of the Harvard University clinical psychologist and counterculture hero Timothy Leary (1920-1996), an advocate for the use of psychedelics in expanding consciousness. And Mancuso wanted the party to duplicate the experience of a drug induced mind altering journey. But to music and dancing.

Utilizing Koetsu turntable cartridges, custom Klipschorn speakers, and Mark Levinson amplifiers, Mancuso aimed for sonic purity as opposed to sheer volume (keeping levels to 100 decibels). He also eventually got sound engineers Alex Rosner and Richard Long (1933-1986) to help improve the equipment and optimize the acoustics. To the hundred or so people who went to the Valentine's party, the music was only there for atmosphere. Mancuso has even admitted an initial reluctance to manning the turntable, worried it would keep him from being the genial host. But a rapport was struck between Mancuso, the music, and the guests, one that deepened and grew stronger as he continued to host more parties.

Mentions of the Loft and Mancuso have the propensity of wandering into metaphysical territory. Anyone who had been there (especially in those early years) lapse into quasi-mystical jargon to describe dancing in a euphoric collective. It isn't entirely unheard of, after all, but perhaps not since days of yore and certainly not in the cynical ghettos of downtown Manhattan. People began requesting certain songs and Mancuso would more than oblige, sometimes anticipating what they wanted to hear. Soon, the music and the dancing became the primary reasons everyone kept coming back for more. And so it came to pass that the recurring reply of anyone being asked their plans for an evening? They were going to "The Loft".

That most of the guests were at least acquainted sustained the Loft's membership-only policy and the status of its events as 'private' parties. Becoming a member wasn't difficult. All that was required was being vouched for by someone who was already one. This kept things friendly, attaching an unspoken chain of responsibility should anyone misbehave. Mancuso's main objective, however, was for everyone to be embraced by the Loft. He wanted gay or straight identifying people, of diverse ethnicities, social and economic backgrounds to disregard their differences for a night, and simply revel in music and dancing.

Over on W. 43rd Street and Ninth (today the Off Broadway Westside Theatre), Sanctuary laid claim to a different but no less important breakthrough. Erected as a red brick and brownstone German Baptist church in 1889 by architect Henry Franklin Kilburn (1844-1905), the main floor has a capacity of four hundred but accommodated over a thousand during its years as the bacchanalian temple called Sanctuary. Here was where shaggy-haired Francis Grasso (1949-2001) perfected slip cueing records.

Stationed between a wall of organ pipes and a marble altar, Grasso would play a record on one turntable while listening solely via headphones to another playing simultaneously on a second turntable. Once he found a section that matched the one currently playing, he blasted it over the speakers precisely on the beat to sustain a continuous stream of music, setting a precedent for the following decades. He was also known for overlaying one song on another for minutes at a time. And even when Thorens turntables with speed controls became available, enabling Grasso to 'beatmatch' in tempo, his segues still required an excellent ear for music and extraordinary skill.

Sanctuary's notoriety gave director Alan Jay Pakula (1928-1998) the idea to shoot a scene there for his 1971 thriller "Klute". Grasso can be spotted in a few frames as Jane Fonda, in her Academy award-winning title role, wades through dancing men and women, totally fictitious as it happens. At this juncture, Sanctuary's lone straight man Grasso was sardined by banquetes of church pews with a gay congregation that demonstrated rapturous adoration by showering him with 400mg Quaalude capsules. Sanctuary closed in 1972. Grasso moved on.

Other clubs took up the slack. There was The Tenth Floor, immortalized as the fictional The Twelfth Floor in the classic Andrew Holleran (pen name of author Eric Garber) novel "Dancer from the Dance". The title comes from "How can we know the dancer from the dance"—a line in the William Butler Yeats (1865-1939) poem "Among School Children" (published in the poetry collection "The Tower", 1928). This ruminative phrase emphasizes how dancer and (literal and metaphorical) dancing are indivisible in Garber's febrile and Fitzgeraldesque accounting of life in the gay enclaves of New York and Fire Island. Another club, Nicky Siano's Gallery is historic as the training ground of not one but two Loft regulars who later joined the ranks of nightlife's most fabled DJs: Larry Levan (1954-1992) and Frankie Knuckles (1955-2014).

———————————————

Enter Disco. The word was taken from the name of the new jazz boîtes in 1940s Paris—*"discothèque"*—so-called because instead of live bands, music was provided via records. It's supposed to have been derived from "bibliotheque" or library, but instead of books these clubs were record repositories. As a music genre, disco is instantly recognizable today. Its earliest manifestations, however, are somewhat nebulous and often referred to as "proto-disco".

Actually, Mancuso's Loft playlists were eclectic—from classical and jazz to some obscure record he had unearthed. Blasé New Yorkers respected Mancuso's aptitude for taking them on sonic trips. And anything he played would either be something everyone already loved or suddenly be worth coveting. But no one could've really known disco lay just around the turn of the vinyl. In the moment, all that mattered was music that could worm its way through the ears and work down to the feet and arouse the rest of the body. To that end, the most obvious go-tos were Detroit-era Motown, Philly Soul, and danceable R & B (Rhythm and Blues), but the Loft was a haven, after all, for all sorts of outliers.

"Soul Makossa" by Cameroon musician Manu Dibango (1930-2020) was introduced in 1972 at the Loft by Mancuso. It is commonly cited among the first songs that can be classified as disco. In hindsight, basic elements that typify the genre include a 4/4 time signature, hi-hat sounds syncopated with the melody, repetitive basslines and vocal hooks. But for every rule, there also seems to be a song that breaks it. For instance, "Makossa" doesn't even have a melodic line. And while disco clocks in at around 120 beats per minute (BPM) on average, Silver Convention's "Fly, Robin, Fly" (1975) comes in just a hair over a hundred. Many other downtempo grooves would eventually comprise a sub-genre called Sleaze, played as a sort of envoi to an evening's set, which is to say during the couple of hours before everyone spilled out to the streets as sunlight crawled up the spires of a city stirring from its fitful slumber.

Other 'rules' were summarily discarded as disco amplified its scope and ambition. Soon disco incorporated latin percussions, hand claps, lush arrangements with crescendos and stentorian vocals, orchestral brass and strings, lilting flutes, shimmering harps and tambourines, mournful violins, along with a myriad of unusual sound effects. But what makes a piece of music disco can still be a bit confusing, primarily because the name itself has the generic patina of having been plucked by record industry executives from out of a hat. Any credible determination can only be made of music from the period, i.e. early 1970s to early 1980s. Even then, anyone daring to list quintessential disco classics will have to contend with the woefully inadequate qualifier "countless"—not to mention the chasm between those favored by the underground and those of the Top Forty-listening public.

Nevertheless, it would be remiss to overlook seminal works. Love Unlimited Orchestra's "Love's Theme" (1973), for example, is among the first records to sell well without the prerequisite radio airplay. Composed and arranged for a 41-piece orchestra by the Barry White (1944-2003, whose own "You're the First, the Last, My Everything" would chart the following year) it became a hit solely from having been heard at the clubs.

Music industry bible Billboard magazine (Est. 1894, charted songs from 1936) officially affirmed disco by listing the most often played songs at New York clubs in its October 26, 1974 issue. Taking the top spot for four consecutive weeks was the 18-minute seamless A-side of Gloria Gaynor's "Never Can Say Goodbye" album consisting of "Honey Bee", the title track, and "Reach Out I'll Be There". This was another first, the uncredited work of Tom Moulton, a former model and records promotions man, who would also rework MFSB's "Love is the Message" (composed in 1974 by Kenny Gamble and Leon Huff) into an 11-minute gem.

The impetus to produce longer music for dance predicated on the assumption that pop songs are 'radio-friendly' at around the three-minute mark while dance music was better without pausing to switch platters. Additionally, three to four minutes leave DJs little time for doing anything else for six hours at a stretch but keep their eyes on the turntable and their hands reaching for that next record. Moulton's foray into mixing began with tapes of continuous music he spliced together for The Sandpiper, the Fire Island restaurant that was converted into a dance club, and later redeveloped as the Pines Pavilion. But arguably his finest achievement was the 'accidental' invention of the 12" single.

He was finishing his mix of Al Downing's "I'll Be Holding On" (1974) when he learned that the studio was out of the seven-inch acetates customarily used for test pressings, and they had to settle for a ten-inch one instead. But he was unhappy with the way the dead wax (the blank space between grooves and center label) took up more space than the actual song. So he asked to have it recut with the grooves more spread out across the record's surface. Though warned that doing so would jack up both the volume and dynamic range, he went ahead with it. This resulted in a sound better suited in the cavernous space of a dance club and led to the first 12" acetate produced by Moulton for South Shore Commission's "Free Man" (1975). DJs loved the new format, which came with plain center stickers and became the standard more widely known as "white label", "promo only" records. An organized New York record pool was later founded by Mancuso with Steve D'Acquisto (1953–2001) and Paul Casella for official distribution of these pressings among accredited New York DJs.

Also in 1975, Van McCoy & the Soul City Symphony sold ten million copies of "The Hustle" with its earworm of a piccolo riff, name checking the dance most associated with disco. A reconfigured version of the Lindy Hop, the hustle is said to have originated in Spanish Harlem, spreading throughout the Puerto Rican, black and gay communities, and prompting the New York Times to announce on July 12, 1975: "The Hustle Restores Old Touch to Dancing" referring to its partnered steps. Preference for couples or solo dancing has been seesawing through the years and would continue to do so through the 1970s. Favor gradually tipped toward solo because skill in executing specific steps was unnecessary, thereby relegating couples dancing to professional performances and formal occasions.

Six months following the Times story, the epic 17-minute "Love to Love You Baby" heralded the arrival of Donna Summer and producer Giorgio Moroder. Originally recorded in Munich and released in the U.S. by Neil Bogart (1943–1982) under his Casablanca Records label, it was simply a tantalizing prelude to Summer's career. Her hits with Moroder included entire vinyl sides ("Try Me, I Know, We Can Make It", "McArthur Park Suite"), motion picture soundtrack cuts ("Down, Deep Inside" from "The Deep"), full-on concept albums ("Once Upon a Time", "Four Seasons of Love"), and a diva duet with Barbra Streisand ("No More Tears"). But bar none, their most influential smash is the first electronically engineered song using a Moog synthesizer—"I Feel Love"—an irresistible siren's call to dance music's future.

———————————————

Disco as cultural touchstone cannot be overstated, an all-encompassing presence in music, popular entertainment, arts, social interactions, and fashion. Today, people have simplistic, even caricaturesque, and therefore imprecise ideas of what fashion was like in the disco era. The more complex reality, however, sits at the intersection where fashion and disco's separate tangents finally crossed and began informing each other's respective developments.

Bohemian crochets, patchworks, and frilly peasant tops, so in demand during the hippie years, were now dreadfully outdated. And despite concerted efforts by brands and magazines to push maxi skirts, those were actually dead-on-arrival at retail. Fashion fumbled around for direction before disco finally led the way. This is why and when haute couture ceded its clout over to the more populist pret-a-porter, energized by its own growing number of runway shows. From a design perspective, however, this hardly meant blue collar.

Rock has always belonged to the proletariat—typified by the denim cut-offs of punk heroine Patti Smith. Disco, on the other hand, demanded high gloss, the suave disposition of upward mobility. A night out called for urbane garments that dazzled, glamour in motion everlasting. The dancefloor became a dais for individuality, the potential for self-actualization. And ironically, in nightlife's anonymity and shadows —everybody can be a star.

For women, disco was an overdue license to wear whatever they wanted. They gravitated toward slinky dresses or the more 'competitive' business attire of pantsuits. In footwear, unabashedly sexy yet torturous stilettos were just as favored as more comfortable wedges and platforms. The acquiescence of men to being objectified was confirmed by chest-baring shirts (some with buttons placed eight inches below the neckline) and posterior flattering pants. Yawning jacket lapels and flared trousers with creases sharp enough to slice across a packed club may seem flamboyant today but back then they were encased in tailoring of a more formal modernity. Suits in slim silhouettes signaled a new sobriety that was taking hold of fashion, a portent of the conservatism aborning on the horizon.

On May 6, 1975, the world's foremost fashion editors, reporters, photographers, and buyers were having a wretched day. Not a particularly patient cadre to begin with, they were already at their wit's end by the time they arrived at around 6pm on the southwest corner of Houston and Broadway. It was difficult enough trying to make it downtown at that hour on an average Tuesday. But the rain that had been steadily pouring over the city all day made the trek insufferable. Now that they were there, they found themselves drenched to the skin and staring at the entrance of a nondescript building. Surely it was the right address? Why yes, yes it was. Their increasing numbers soon bottlenecked the way up to the second floor where they crammed, chiseled cheek by haughty jowl, into a plain loft space with rows of white chairs neatly arranged facing the runway. They searched frantically for their assigned seats only to find them already occupied by young men they didn't recognize.

Amidst the frantic shoving and scuffling for seats, they muttered their frustration—"Why *here?*" Sure, Calvin Klein had a penchant for minimalism. But he could have arranged the same set up anywhere. Of all places, what possessed Klein to unveil his Fall 1975 collection here? Unbeknownst to most of the major department store buyers and the peevish masthead names of Vogue and Harper's Bazaar, every Saturday night from September to May, this venue on 599 Broadway became the underground disco called Flamingo. It was founded by former Broadway dancer Michael Fesco (1935-2019) and reputed to be the first disco that catered exclusively to New York's chi chi all-white gay men for a then rather exorbitant $600 annual membership fee. It was the birthplace of shirtless bartenders and the themed nights, those Black or White parties, that became hallmarks of the gay circuit events of the 1990s. And, for a time, this was Calvin Klein's favorite joint.

It's been speculated that Klein deified the all-American male here, in the company of beautiful young men whose days were spent in well compensated professions and nights in careless frolic. They served as the templates Klein would try to recreate over and over in his advertising campaigns and Bruce Weber-helmed fashion shoots. As club members, they knew about the show weeks in advance and were able to finagle invitations. They were the ones who'd commandeered seats, smug in their conviction that, after all, this was their turf. The fashion people were the interlopers.

More than half an hour past the appointed start of the show, some members of the press finally surrendered to their seething indignation and walked out. But their departure mattered not. The room was filled to the rafters, with even more people outside brandishing their invitations unable to get in. And the over three hundred-piece collection was an unqualified smash—sleek blouses tucked into high waisted, wide legged trousers, cinched with thin belts, rendered in Klein's signature ivories and accented with reds and browns. It won the designer, in June of that year, his third Coty Fashion Critics Award. Klein did deserve the applause. It was an assured collection and eminently sellable. Yet how much of the praise was ignited by the evening's frisson? Closer inspection reveals little of anything extraordinary beyond refined stylings that's been underway since Yves Saint Laurent's "Le Smoking" women's evening jacket came out ten years earlier. Other designers had also been experimenting on svelte looks with far more impactful results.

The Belgian-born designer Diane von Fürstenberg (an erstwhile princess by way of marriage to German nobleman Egon von Fürstenberg, 1946-2004) introduced, a year earlier, the silk jersey wrap dress. With long sleeves and a hemline falling just above the knee, it's basically a clever reimagining of traditional Chinese robes, the v-neckline feature accomplished by closing the right panel over the left and tying it securely on the side. Florentine-American designer Giorgio di Sant'Angelo (1933-1989), whose ethnic collection predates Saint Laurent's gypsy dresses by a year, was a pioneer in ravishing eveningwear that incorporated stretch material, making them all the better for dancing. And of course, there was Halston (1932-1990).

At the time of Klein's showing at Flamingo, Martha Graham needed a dress for an award ceremony at which she was to honor the British ballet conductor Robert Irving (1913-1991). One of her friends, the esteemed Leo Lerman (1914-1994), who had been an editor at Vogue as well as editor-in-chief of Vanity Fair, introduced her to Halston. The former milliner was at the peak of his powers and gifted Graham a dress, firmly declining her offer to pay for it. That same year, Graham worked for the first time with Nuryev (with a first billed but supporting Fonteyn) for a performance of "Lucifer" at the Uris Theatre (Est. 1972, now called Gershwin Theatre). For the project, Graham got Halston to create a bodysuit with a coiled snake headdress for Fonteyn and a gold jockstrap for Nuryev. Seeing his bodysuit on Fonteyn surely impressed Halston. In a couple of years, he reproduced it in cashmere, wool knit, and stretch satin, introducing them as Halston day or evening "body sweaters".

Halston's shirtwaist coats and dresses had already established several core trends of the times. Made of machine-washable ultrasuede—the fabric most linked with Halston—the garments were sumptuously soft while resistant to sagging, pilling, or shrinking. Structurally, they were modified versions of men's shirts: lean silhouettes and sleeves from smaller armholes, oversized set-in collars, yoke in back, front buttons that open from the breastbone instead of the neckline to affect a low décolletage, and matching wide belts. Their versatility made them as appropriate for evening, with the right accessories. But Halston's halter gowns, his Grecian one-shoulder himation and chiton confections, dynamic in bias-spiraling crepes, jerseys, hammered satins, and silk chiffons of fissured necklines? Those were meant for the habitués of Studio 54.

Commencing April 26, 1977 to the weeks and months thereafter, the din outside 254 W. 54th Street only grew insistently louder and more desperate. The ruckus was caused by an unlikely motley of socialites, young professionals, and bridge-and-tunnel people, all striving to get past the velvet rope separating them from the fool's paradise that was Studio 54. Constructed in 1927 as the Gallo Opera House by architect Eugene De Rosa (1894-1945), the building had changed hands several times over but retained some of its theater interiors even after it had been converted by Steve Rubell (1943-1989) and Ian Schrager into the hottest disco in town.

Now the stuff of legend, Studio 54 has been the topic of in-depth think pieces, tell-all books, coffee table photography compilations, art exhibitions, cautionary documentaries, and fictionalized films. Perpetuated in all of them are disclosures of debauchery unbridled —from the VIP basement to the "Rubber Room" balcony. In many ways, Studio 54 exemplified and magnified the arguable best and worst aspects of the disco phenomenon, catapulting it to mainstream visibility and thereby hastening its demise.

Guests entered through a mirrored foyer, aglow with red lights, into a 5,400 square-foot space (with a capacity of 2,500, though able to pack as many as 4,000 people on a good night) featuring chrome-plated bars, lounging areas, and a 50-ft wide domed ceiling over the main dance floor. A conversation-starting giant set piece was the backlit waning crescent moon with a human profile (by design firm Aerographics) which reeled into view against the center wall. Later, an equally enormous spoon was added, trailing from the right to meet the moon at midpoint. Then, lights would shoot up the moon's nose, a sledgehammer-to-the-head allusion to the permissive and rampant use of cocaine at the club.

Before Studio 54, Rubell and Schrager were a couple of nobodies who owned a moderately solvent establishment of little consequence in Queens. Sure, it was equipped with the latest bells, whistles, state-of-the-art light and sound, and fog machines. But it bore no signs the duo's foray into Manhattan could surpass their wildest imaginations. Studio 54 became a juggernaut by cultivating a cult of celebrity inside while administering a tyrannical admission policy outside.

They had their membership directory of course, as well as pages and pages of typed up celebrity lists. Club promoter Carmen D'Alessio lured personages like Diane von Fürstenberg, Lauren Hutton, Margaux Hemingway, Marissa Berenson, Robert Isabell, Mick and Bianca Jagger.

Marquee names like Farrah Fawcett, Liza Minelli, Grace Jones, and Freddie Mercury were also free to breeze right in as they pleased. Where the public was concerned? Determining who was worthy of coming in and who was turned away was a coin toss. Hoping to affect the outcome, the rabble lobbed either empty threats or monetary, sexual or pharmaceutical bribes at the doormen. Others resorted to more unorthodox means such as scaling down into the premises from the building next door. Schrager himself admitted to documentarian Matt Tyrnauer that a man (allegedly in black tie) was once found dead days after being stuck in the ventilation shaft in what appeared to have been a tragically botched incursion. The more the masses were kept at bay, the more fervent was their yearning to be a part of Studio 54, proof that there is none so potent an aphrodisiac as rejection.

The closest to any rhyme or reason came from Rubell, who sometimes manned the doors, when he once proclaimed he wouldn't let himself in. Glean from that a glimpse into Rubell's drug addled psyche. It helped to be beautiful. But that was subjective to whoever was the evening's designated gatekeeper. Being dressed well was a good start, but a genuinely outrageous outfit was definitely a plus. Eccentricity certainly made regulars out of the likes of 70something retired lawyer Sally Lipman a.k.a. "Disco Sally", and "Rollerena", putatively a stockbroker and former Vietnam Vet who always appeared in a frilly long dress, rhinestone glasses, and roller skates, waving a magic wand wherever he went.

Tabloid fodder of extravagant parties and salacious gossip kept the cash and coke flowing. In just the first year, the club grossed $7M, and Rubell and Schrager were also profiting from ancillary ventures. The Studio 54 logo (by graphic designer Gil Lesser, 1935-1990) appeared everywhere: from a Casablanca double album disco compilation to jeans designed by Norma Kamali (who was dating Schrager at the time) and made by denim manufacturer Landlubber. An ad for the jeans featured a naked man, photographed by Gordon Munro, slipping into a pair. Its droll tagline: "Now everybody can get into Studio 54" was courtesy of Peter Rogers, the man behind the lauded "What Becomes a Legend Most" campaign for furrier Blackglama.

Upmarketing something so working class as denim could really only have happened during the disco years. But the honor of coming up with the first designer jeans belongs to someone else, someone whose social cachet could raise denim above its undistinguished pedigree: Gloria Vanderbilt (1924-2019). The direct descendant of "The Commodore", she was the only child of Reginald Claypoole Vanderbilt (1880-1925) and second wife Gloria Morgan (née Maria Laura Mercedes Morgan, 1904-1965). At ten years old, she was caught in a custody battle between her mother and her aunt, Mrs. Harry Payne Whitney, ostensibly over control of the $5M trust fund she had inherited from her father. Throughout October and November 1934, supermarket rag headlines screamed with courtroom testimonies. At the end of the acrimonious trial, the Supreme Court of the State of New York awarded sole custody to Aunt Gertrude.

After having been consigned to the society pages, Vanderbilt was news again in 1976 after signing a denim deal with Murjani International. Its newly-appointed U.S. head, Warren Hirsch (1932-2016), asked Vanderbilt to find some use for the bales of denim languishing in their factories in Hong Kong and Macau. With the manufacturer's production capabilities, it was a quick turn around to roll out Gloria Vanderbilt jeans. It justified its $36 a pair retail price (expensive comparative to an average of just under $10 for a pair of Levi's) with a form-fitting cut, the elegant gold swan logo embroidered against the indigo color of the denim on the front, and the designer's longhand signature stitched on the back right pocket. Others jumped into the designer jeans market including older brands like Jordache and Fiorucci. Klein claims his line was suggested by a stranger he met at Studio 54.

———————————————

Halston, meanwhile, hadn't been simply idling in the VIP banquettes. His relocation to the Skidmore, Owings & Merrill-designed Olympic Tower was the talk of fashion people and ladies who brunched. They likened it to an ascension to Olympus itself, at least if the gods had a vertigo-inducing view of Saks and St. Patrick's across the way. At 641 Fifth Avenue, up to the 21st floor, and through an unmarked door, was the studio and showroom of Halston Enterprises. Surrounded on the outside by reflective dark glass, it was a U-shaped 12,000 square foot space covered with carpet the color of aged merlot, and walled with mirrors stretching up the 18 foot-high ceilings. Littering this sanctum were tastefully modern furniture, fragrant Rigaud candles, and a profusion of orchids in bloom. All of it was expensed to Norton Simon Inc (Est. 1968) which had acquired the Halston brand as a trophy, the sui generis among its mass market portfolio. And for a while both parties were gratified by the arrangement.

Showing the collections at Olympic Tower convened his friends—Minnelli, Graham and Rubell—on the front row, and his retinue of Halstonettes—Karen Bjornsen, Pat Cleveland—on the runway. Respected journalists like Marian Christy extolled the simplicity of his designs, "the voice of reason" in juxtaposition to the "nonsense" of French fashions. Unfortunately, in this business, it takes but a season or two for that same voice to grate. And whatever it was Halston wanted to say became unconvincing, slurred by copious cocaine. The longer his sunglasses stayed on, the more erratic his behavior became. His irrational outbursts, thundering from on high, sent his employees cowering.

One casualty was his friendship with Elsa Peretti who'd been his muse and part of his pre-fame clique (including designer Stephen Burrows and illustrator Joe Eula, 1925-2004). She had modeled for Halston and Helmut Newton (1920-2004) but was later recognized for designing sinuous jewelry at Tiffany & Co. and conceiving the Halston perfume flacon. Max Factor (Est. 1909) was producing the perfume and contracted Bernard Chant (1927-1987, of International Flavors and Fragrances) to formulate the original juice, anchored by an oakmoss base and lit by notes of marigold and melon. While everyone loved the scent, Max Factor was resistant to Peretti's irregularly shaped bottle. But Halston was so enamored that he put up $50,000 of his own money to have it made. The perfume was a bestseller. Halston celebrated privately at his E. 63rd Street townhouse and with a public launch at the San Francisco I. Magnin (Est. 1876) flagship where a five-course dinner was served with Dom Perignon 1962, while the department store's first floor counters were removed to make way for a dancefloor.

None of the people around them could explain why Halston and Peretti's friendship had curdled. But it did happen after she had designed the perfume bottle, for which she received a sable coat as remuneration. According to the Bob Colacello tome "Warhol's Exposures", Peretti later flung the coat into a fireplace during an altercation with Halston. Peretti herself confirmed this account for a July 2014 Vanity Fair profile. But mere months following the incinerated sable incident, another vituperative clash erupted when the two unexpectedly encountered each other in the celebrity basement of

Studio 54. After snarling vicious insults and accusations at each other, they parted ways for the last time.

Pity catfights in the basement were the least of Studio 54's problems. Like many others before him, Rubell was ill disposed to success. He overindulged. His ego grew in proportion to the hard cash they were stockpiling in garbage bags. And he impetuously mouthed off in public, once confiding on record to finance reporter Dan Dorfman (1931-2012) that there were things he didn't want the Internal Revenue Service (IRS) to know. On the morning of December 14, 1978, some thirty IRS agents raided Studio 54 and walked away with doctored accounting books and boxes of files. This swiftly led to more search-and-seizures, then formal charges. Two years later, Rubell and Schrager pled guilty to corporate tax evasion and sentenced by Federal Judge Richard Owen, who made a point to describe their crime as "one of tremendous arrogance." They were sent to a minimum security prison camp adjacent to Maxwell Air Force Base in Montgomery, Alabama and released after a little over a year. They were able to publicly reinvent themselves by conceiving the "boutique" hotel, opening Morgans, Royalton, and Paramount in New York. Rubell died of complications caused by AIDS in 1989. Schrager, on the other hand, became a well regarded hotelier, open-ing the Delano in Miami and the Mondrian in West Hollywood, both designed by industrial architect Philippe Starck. Studio 54 itself, meanwhile, passed on to the stuff of legend as the most phantasmago-rical incarnation of disco.

In the June 1976 issue of New York magazine, an article by British writer Nik Cohn—"Tribal Rites of the New Saturday Night"— detailed another side of the disco lifestyle, this time from within the parameters of lower middle class Bay Ridge, Brooklyn where the place to be was club 2001 Odyssey. A copy of the magazine somehow made its way to the desk of Australian-born music and film producer Robert Stigwood (1934-2016) who immediately bought the film rights. Stigwood first contracted Cohn to turn his article into a screen-play but the result wasn't quite satisfactory. He hired the more seasoned screenwriter Norman Wexler whose 149-page rewrite is what eventu-ally became the motion picture "Saturday Night Fever".

Misremembered details and revisionist accounts, intentional or otherwise, riddle what is known today about the making of the picture. Its star John Travolta, for one, sounds increasingly self-congrat-ulatory with each preposterous retelling. Still, there are particulars that may be corroborated, beginning with creative conflicts necessitating the replacement of original director John G. Avildsen (1935-2017) with John Badham. The troubled production also involved whiny doubts over the casting of a sitcom émigré, Travolta, for the lead. Then, because it wasn't quite a traditional musical, Badham and Travolta clashed over how the dance sequences were shot. The actor, who had tirelessly trained and rehearsed for five months, was apoplectic that the director had excised his footwork, going for medium to close up coverages. Stigwood broke the stalemate and insisted Badham relent to Travolta's wishes.

Budget restricted their options on many levels including having to shoot on locations where diegetic noise was an inconvenience. In another instance, the scene in a dance studio where the leads were practicing was filmed using a favorite at discos: Boz Scagg's first major hit "Lowdown". Unfortunately, Scaggs refused to grant rights to the music. So David

Shire, who was scoring the picture, substituted it with his own hastily composed but no less effective "Manhattan Skyline". Other happy outcomes came out of the lean and scrappy production. Costume designer Patrizia Von Brandenstein found the central white polyester two-button single-breasted suit with wide jacket lapels, a matching waistcoat, and a pair of 28-inch waist white flared trousers at a Brooklyn thrift shop.

"Saturday Night Fever" opened on December 16, 1977 in wide release at over seven hundred theaters nationwide, ultimately grossing around $237M in its first run. The critical acclaim it received can be attributed to its gritty depiction of a disaffected young man, stuck in a dead-end job, who lived for dancing at his local disco. It's a wonder no one has ever bothered to mention its parallels to the Karel Reiz (1926-2002) 1960 motion picture "Saturday Night, Sunday Morning" starring Albert Finney (1936-2019). Perhaps more troubling though is how people overlook the many reprehensible elements of the picture—not the least of which is having a main protagonist who's utterly narcissistic, misogynistic, homophobic, and racist. Although Cohn would later confess to having completely fabricated the source material, it may still be argued that the Tony Manero character Travolta played is a fair representation, within the narrative's intellectually and culturally stunted milieu. And for whatever it's worth, Manero sought, however unwittingly and not fully realized, absolution. So truly, the fondness with which "Saturday Night Fever" is still remembered rests on overlooking the plot for the sheer pleasure of its infectious music and dancing. For twenty-four weeks in 1978, the motion picture soundtrack held the top spot on Billboard's album charts. Strategically released before anyone had seen a single frame of the film, forty million copies sold worldwide and was (until being supplanted by 1992's "The Bodyguard") the number one bestselling soundtrack of all time—owed in no small part to the Bee Gees.

Anyone who may have heard of the Bee Gees in the early 1970s likely knew of them as the poor man's Beatles. The brothers Gibb—Barry, Robin (1949-2012), and Maurice (1949-2003)—had middling success with songs like their first number one in the U.S.—1971's "How Can You Mend a Broken Heart". But the group's folk-rock sound wasn't cutting it anymore. They camped out in Miami where it was hoped fresh inspiration would strike while they recorded at Criteria, the studios from where enormous hits by the Eagles, Aretha Franklin, and the Average White Band were produced. It worked.

The newly high pitched harmonies and funky soul sound of the brothers' 1975 album "Main Course" gave the Bee Gees a second U.S. number one single "Jive Talkin". The next album "Children of the World" was even bigger, earning them their third number one, "You Should Be Dancing". It also happened to be the first chart topper on Billboard's Disco Action Top 30 (issue dated August 28, 1976) when tracking was expanded from what was playing in the estimated 1,500 discos in just the New York area to include the thousands cropping up nationwide.

But "Saturday Night Fever" was the game changer. The trio was in Château d'Hérouville, the crumbling 18th century estate and storied recording studio outside of Paris, when they received a call from Stigwood (who was also their manager). He told them about the movie and asked them to contribute songs to the soundtrack. Together with co-producers Albhy Galuten and Karl Richardson, the brothers had been working on their next album and had a handful of ready cuts. They airmailed Stigwood five demos that would transform the trio into superstars and a picture of modest prospects into a veritable barnburner.

Barry's natural tenor gently ambles over the lush harmonies and string arrangement of "How Deep Is Your Love". The counterintuitive lead ballad was a Billboard number one on Christmas eve of 1977 and snowballed the popularity of both the picture and the brothers Gibb way into the following year. The second single off the soundtrack, "Stayin' Alive", was number one in February 1978, followed by "(Love Is) Thicker Than Water", the second for the youngest Gibb brother, Andy (1958-1988), who had an equally stellar solo career. The next two songs to take over the top spot were also Gibb productions and cuts from "Saturday Night Fever": "Night Fever" and the Yvonne Elliman-sung "If I Can't Have You". Later, the Bee Gees and Andy returned time and again to dominate the charts.

The Gibbs were on a roll. And crucial to that was their direct involvement with composing and producing because dance music has always been a producer's medium. Many were 'bands' cut out of whole cloth by enterprising producers from the merely mediocre to absolute geniuses. One prolific producer was Nile Rodgers who, together with bass guitarist Bernard Edwards (1952-1996), co-founded Chic with a 1977 self-titled breakthrough album (with drummer Tony Thompson, and vocalists Norma Jean Wright, Alfa Anderson, and Luci Martin). 1978's "C'est Chic" came with the single "Le Freak", which sold seven million copies. Wrongly relegated as a B-side, "Good Times" from the third album "Risqué" has since been ruthlessly sampled in at least a couple hundred tunes, most evidently in the Sugarhill Gang's 1979 "Rapper's Delight". Rodgers and Edwards were also responsible for producing "We Are Family", which updated the sound of Sister Sledge, the sibling quartet of Debbie, Joni, Kim, and Kathy. The universality of the title cut was malleable enough for use by everyone from the gay community to the Pittsburgh Pirates. The album's lead single, "He's the Greatest Dancer" was a slice of nightlife with a recitation of what a disco god would and should wear: "Halston, Gucci, Fiorucci".

Another production duo—Jacques Morali (1947-1991) and Henri Belolo (1936-2019)—begat another female-led act, the Ritchie Family. Morali and Belolo crafted the music, then cast Cheryl Jacks, Cassandra Wooten and Gwendolyn Oliver as vocalists. In 1977, the producers released the first Village People album with Victor Willis on lead vocals, backed by anonymous singers. But the need for an actual group to make public appearances prompted them to run an ad in the trades (accounts are unclear if it was Show Business or Backstage) for non-Equity performers, spelling out their priorities: "Macho Types Wanted: Must Dance And Have A Moustache".

By virtue of the album's cover and tracklist, it was quite clear that the Village People was gay ultra masculine fetish set to music. In fact, legend has it that Morali discovered the next member of the group, Felipe Rose, at the notorious W. 14th Street after-hours bondage and S&M dive The Anvil. Rose was doing double duty tending bar then dancing on top of it, barely dressed in Native American feathers and loin cloth. Morali filled out the rest of the group with other archetypes: construction worker David Hodo, leatherman Glenn Hughes, and cowboy Randy Jones. Yet surely even more remarkable than the Village People's worldwide hits was the general public's almost wilful disregard of the not at all subtle innuendos of their lyrics. To this day, there is no shortage of weddings where straight people unashamedly spell out "Y.M.C.A" with their arms while dancing in ignorant bliss.

In the two years between Newsweek's November 1976 cover story "The Disco Whirl" and the November 1978 Time magazine cover "Travolta Fever", disco had woven itself into the social fabric. And that the Time cover came out eleven months after 'Fever' hit cinemas attests to the power of disco. Other media tried to appraise it in good old dollars and cents. Life magazine ran its own feature that same month,

"The Delirium of Disco" in which writer Albert Goldman described disco as "the hottest business in the entertainment world". On network television, a CBS "60 Minutes" report by Dan Rather revealed that disco had become a $4B business. According to his research, some four hundred major and 'cash grab' record labels were releasing around 150,000 singles on the odds that one in ten was going to be a hit.

Already late to the party, radio finally tried to reclaim its role for steering record sales. In 1978, Manuel Francisco "Paco" Navarro (1937–2019) was an established radio personality on Spanish language WJIT New York when he crossed over to its English language sister station WKTU FM. To his astonishment, it was thrashing on pop programming that attracted less than one percent of the city's audience. He told management they had been ignoring what people wanted to hear and somehow convinced them to radically adopt an untested all-disco-all-the-time format. And for his new 6-10pm WKTU slot, Navarro modulated the rapid fire speech pattern he used at his former station to a honeyed Puerto Rican-accented spiel: "Paco's my name and disco's my game". This bumped up WKTU's reach forthwith to over 11% enabling them to break WABC's airwave dominance.

Overnight, disco was playing around the dial. It may be surmised that singers and bands known as pop or rock acts came out with disco records either from a sincere appreciation of the music or in order to remain relevant. Rod Stewart and the Rolling Stones led the charge in 1978 with "Da Ya Think I'm Sexy" and "Miss You" respectively. From a self-imposed hiatus that had kept him out of the charts since his mariachi-inflected Tijuana Brass days, jazz musician (and the record mogul behind A&M Records) Herb Alpert returned with his 1979 hit "Rise". During the recording, Alpert slowed down the proposed 120 to a sultrier 100 BPM, and agreed to the improv handclaps, surely contributing to making the instrumental a dancefloor favorite.

Much to the consternation of purists and fan bases, other artists colluded with disco producers. Pete Bellotte, from Donna Summer's team, produced Elton John's "Victim of Love", which drew complaints that John did not play piano or keyboard on the record, nor did he write any of the music. Bob Esty (1947-2019), who had worked with Summer and Barbra Steisand, composed (with writing partner Michele Aller) most of the material on Cher's "Take Me Home". In the meantime, the Electric Light Orchestra simply did it on their own with "Discovery", the album the band's keyboardist Richard Tandy called "disco very". It charted number one in the UK, top five in the U.S., and sold over 3M copies.

Other surprise disco hits of 1979 included Pink Floyd's "Another Brick on the Wall", Kiss' "I Was Made for Lovin' You", Paul McCartney and Wings' "Goodnight Tonight", Chicago's "Street Player", and Blondie's "Heart of Glass". Regrettably, when Newsweek ran its Donna Summer "Disco Takes Over" cover story on April 2, 1979, the scene was already awfully crowded. After Dracula himself (George Hamilton in "Love at First Bite") showed up at a disco, Big Band was discofied via A.J. Cervantes' Tuxedo Junction, and the oddity that was "The Ethel Merman Disco Album" arrived at record stores—how much more could the bandwagon bear? The wheels were about to come off.

CHAPTER SIX
No Jacket Required

Cash pouring in from "Saturday Night Fever" had Hollywood doing a jig. It only took a few months for rivals Motown and Casablanca to hammer out a détente and rush out "Thank God It's Friday", a meandering comedy set in an LA disco. Released on Casablanca, the soundtrack merged powerhouse artists from both labels, but the only clear winner was Donna Summer's "Last Dance", which picked up the Academy Award for Best Original Song. The picture more than tripled its $2M cost.

Peanuts compared to the $366M haul of the Paramount Pictures-Travolta 'Fever' follow up—"Grease", co-starring pop country singer Olivia Newton-John (1948-2022). Barely recognizable from the 1971 Jim Jacobs and Warren Casey stage musical on which it was based, the movie directed by Randal Kleiser isn't even disco at all. But it had catchy new John Farrar compositions, the Barry Gibb-penned and Frankie Valli-sung theme, along with choreography by Patricia Birch. Paramount didn't take much convincing to greenlight a sequel with a new cast. Birch returned to choreograph *and* direct. Robert DeMora (1934-2020) supplied costumes straddling the 1950s and 1960s, with some leather biker looks for good measure. Three years later, "Grease 2" came out a critical and financial disappointment. People carped that it just gender-flipped the same story.

This Michelle Pfeiffer and Maxwell Caulfield-headlined picture has since been positively reappraised, amassing a cult of advocates including director Michael Showalter, and actors Andrew Garfield and Drew Barrymore. Next generation writers and critics Louis Peitzman, Mat Whitehead, and Gwen Ihnat have written think pieces in Buzzfeed, Huffpost, and the A.V. Club respectively, while USA Today, Entertainment Weekly and the BBC have also weighed in with glowing assessments. Social awareness has helped. It's not quite as acceptable now to see Newton-John's character in the original drastically alter herself to win over a man. In "Grease 2", Pfeiffer's Stephanie doesn't compromise herself or her standards; it is Caulfield's Michael who has to convince her that he's worthy. Besides, the sequel's opener makes the first picture's intro look positively lazy. A brigade of dancers barrel through the credits to a ferocious original Four Tops song "Back to School" interjected with intros to the cast and their motivations. The six-minute number took a week to rehearse, then shot at Excelsior High School in LA.

Another picture, in the meantime, was set at a more pertinent institution of learning on W. 46th Street in New York: the High School of Performing Arts (Est. 1947, now Fiorello H. LaGuardia High School). There, "Fame", directed by Alan Parker (1944-2020) centered on the hormonal lives of singers, dancers, and actors, and raked in $42M. Two bits of trivia: designer Isaac Mizrahi, who went to school there appears briefly; and, because Michael Gore and Dean Pitchford's title song by Irene Cara had yet to be recorded, Donna Summer's "Hot Stuff" scorched the three day-shoot of the street dancing scene. The completed soundtrack was certified platinum in the U.S., Canada, and Australia.

More typical teenagers dancing were on syndicated programs: American Bandstand (on air since 1952) with Dick Clark (1929-2012) and Soul Train (since 1971) with Don Cornelius (1936-2012) in the U.S., Top of the Pops (since 1964) in the UK. The format was like broadcasted parties. In between appearances by a few guest artists lip synching their songs, teens danced to the latest hits. Disco 77, shot in Miami, went all out disco and aired thirteen episodes on CBS affiliates and was renamed Disco Magic for another thirteen episodes before being exported to 70 countries. Deney Terrio parlayed having trained Travolta into his fifteen minutes hosting Dance Fever, a competition formatted series.

All the while, a backlash was simmering. For several years, disco had been too omnipresent, diminishing in quality, aggravated no doubt by the breakneck speed with which records were getting shot put out the assembly line. Plus, rock fans felt alienated. The most discordant note shrieked out of a local radio station in Chicago. To hype a doubleheader game between the White Sox home team and the Detroit Tigers, Major League Baseball tapped one of WDAI FM's disgruntled shock jocks. He came up with the promo Disco Demolition Night offering discounted entrance tickets to anyone who showed up at Comiskey Park with a record, all of which were to be destroyed during the game as a ritualized rebuke of disco.

More than double projections, fifty thousand rowdy fans streamed into the stadium on July 12, 1979. Crates of vinyl were brought to center field and detonated to the chanting of "Disco sucks!" Questions were left unanswered. Were those indeed disco records? If so, why would these people own them in the first place? If these had only been bought for the event, wouldn't this actually have contributed to sales, thereby negating discounted tickets? Simply put, no one really was thinking.

The explosion was like the retort of a starting pistol. People mobbed the field, set fires, and tore at anything they could get their hands on: the grass, the bases, the batting cages. The second game was postponed and the White Sox had to forfeit to the Detroit Tigers. The end-of-the-year op-ed by Dave Marsh in Rolling Stone along with subsequent public comments made by Nile Rodgers and others denounced the stunt as racist and homophobic, pointing to its very specific target demo. The debacle may not have directly caused disco's undoing, but it was a signpost.

With buoyant orchestrations, anonymous session singers and musicians, the sub-genre called Italo Disco slogged on in Italian, German, and other European markets until *la vita* wasn't so *dolce* anymore. In the U.S., many radio stations stopped playing disco, resulting in sluggish sales. Disco's lullaby was the ten note synth riff of "Funkytown", a worldwide hit for Casablanca and producer Steven Greenberg's Lipps Inc. never to be repeated. Countless niche record companies flatlined. The careers most tarnished were disco's frontrunners. Donna Summer's 1980 album "The Wanderer" entered the top 20, but its singles struggled to chart. Going soft rock for their next outing yet failing to crack the top 40, the brothers Gibb made a prudent retreat into the studios, composing and producing hit albums for others like Barbra Streisand, "Guilty", and Dionne Warwick, "Heartbreaker". Nile Rodgers also made hit productions: "Diana" for Diana Ross, "Kookoo" for Deborah Harry, and "Let's Dance" for David Bowie (1947-2016).

Giorgio Moroder scored motion pictures for director Paul Schrader's 1980 "American Gigolo" and his 1982 "Cat People" remake, for Brian de Palma's 1983 "Scarface", and for Tony Scott's (1944-2012) "Top Gun" 1986.

———————————

Hopes were high for the next cinematic outing of Newton-John, who had two offers on the table. One from her "Grease" producer Alan Carr would have her play second fiddle to the Village People. She went for the other, playing the role of the Greek muse of dance—Terpsichore in "Xanadu". The great Gene Kelly joined her for what no one knew was going to be his last film role as, not coincidentally, the same Danny McBride character he played in "Cover Girl". The director, Robert Greenwald, better known for documentaries, was a gamble. But he was also, coincidentally, the nephew of Michael Kidd (1915-2007), the first choreographer ever to have won five Tony awards.

The Olivia Newton John-Electric Light Orchestra "Xanadu" soundtrack generated six singles and sold two million units in the U.S. alone. The motion picture, alas, got slaughtered by critics and shunned by movie goers. Second only to a frivolous script, its most unfortunate blunder may have been lacing up in roller skates. "Skatetown USA" from William A. Levey crashed and burned. And profits made by Mark L. Lester's "Roller Boogie" were due to having been made for chump change. Still, during the filming of all three, roller disco was huge. Kids, bankers, bistro waiters, Olympic athletes, and celebrities, almost everyone from coast to coast was on skates. But the fad skidded to a stop.

Somehow, a black-tied Kelly roller skated with dignity intact through the "Xanadu" finale. Choreographed with giddy frenzy by

Kenny Ortega, it was a composite of set pieces with grouped dancers performing different things simultaneously. There were mimes juggling bowling pins, new wave waitresses, and men in striped zoot suits. "We shot that scene at Zoetrope, the old Desilu studios (Est. 1919 as General Service Studios, today Sunset Las Palmas)," recalls dancer Larry Blum, who is captured for posterity over Newton-John's right shoulder when she makes her entrance. He was among those backing the star on the center platform. The men wore dress trousers, white shirts and ties under v-neck cropped velour jackets in garnet, taupe, gray and purple. The women were in belted dresses or blouse-and-skirt sets with high heels. "We must've spent a couple of months on that," admits Larry. "They were long, long days. But Olivia was very sweet. Whenever there were breaks, she sat and chatted with us. So we spent hours getting to know each other."

More impressive than the number of celebrities Larry has gotten to know throughout a long career is how he's kept his sunny disposition. He doesn't particularly mind being one of Hollywood's background performers. At the 2011 Hollywood Fringe Festival, he was admirably sanguine, sharing his escapades via his dishy autobiographical show "Blink & You Might Miss Me". He says, "I've been on the road with Lily Tomlin on one of her national comedy tours. I've danced on variety specials of Bob Hope, Barry Manilow, and Carol Burnett. As an actor, I've been in episodes of the Golden Girls, as well as multiple day-time serials from General Hospital to Days of Our Lives. I got to work on a sitcom with a then unknown George Clooney."

The Bronx native was 22 years old with a degree in education when he fell into a different vocation hanging out with a gaggle of pro-fessional dancers in Manhattan. He went along to their classes and open-call audition grind of dancing, singing, and finally reading for

a part. He supported himself by manning a newsstand on the weekends. Eventually, he picked up equity and summer or winter stock gigs
before inheriting the role of Greg (originated by Michael Stuart) for
the touring company of "A Chorus Line". Larry reveals, "Most of that
character was based on the life of a good friend of mine Christopher
Chadman (1948-1995)." But, the production reneged on the promise
that he would get the Broadway spot once the nineteen-month tour
was over. He returned home to his very supportive parents (who had
driven or flown to every one of his opening nights). Months later, he
decided on a fresh start, loading all his belongings into a Honda Civic
and driving off to tinseltown.

"I was nervous as hell when I got to LA without a job," he admits.
Good thing his Broadway credentials got him noticed by Tony
Charmoli (1921-2020) who had started on stage but had moved on
to directing and choreographing for television. He booked Larry for a
People's Choice Awards number fronted by Dick Van Dyke. Larry says
the actor was "so nice when we met him", but he never came to any
of the rehearsals. "During the actual show, he couldn't keep up with
the routine, whenever we moved left, he moved right," he laughs.
"Either no one noticed or everyone thought that was a gag." Sure his
brushes with A-listers make for amusing Kaffeeklatsch tidbits, but for
people of a certain age, the guaranteed icebreaker is—Larry was a
pioneer Solid Gold dancer.

"Solid Gold" was another chart countdown (compiled by trade paper
Radio & Records) television show with musical guests. But it was
differentiated from the others by swapping out eager amateur dancers
for actual pros. And in spite of pop star hosts like Marilyn McCoo
and Rex Smith, the series (that ran until 1988) is more fondly
remembered for the Solid Gold dancers. Wardrobe department head

Rickie A. Hansen (1923-2010) wrapped skintight neon getups around the dancers who gyrated to the pealing of Anita Ward's "Ring My Bell" or the guitar riffs of Robert Palmer's (1949-2003) "Bad Case of Lovin' You". In hindsight, Larry says, "I think many of our outfits were repurposed from scifi TV shows." He had been recruited by choreographer Kevin Carlisle (1935-2022) to do the pilot and the first batch of episodes. "We did twenty eight numbers over several days around Christmas and it was exhausting!" But when the call came for Larry to do a new season, he was recuperating from a minor knee surgery and couldn't return. The show continued to shine with changing rosters of Solid Gold dancers.

Larry had recuperated when he joined the 1984 Summer Olympics dance corps in Los Angeles. "But at that point," he avers, "I was ready for a change." It came after he was doing stand-in duties for an awards show tech rehearsal. "Dick Clark, who produced a lot of the awards shows, thought when the ladies had to accept their awards, a gentleman should escort them." And so Larry became part of a new kind of supporting player who inconspicuously walked actresses at these ceremonies. "I've since done all of them. I've offered my arm to the biggest stars from Helen Mirren to Julianne Moore."

Conservatism snatched cultural dominance away from progressives in the 1980s. Suddenly, corporate mergers and stock options were sexy. Obscene wealth became the mise en scène of family sagas in paperback bestsellers and glossy primetime serials. Yuppies (short for young urban professionals) were protagonists on small and wide screens (often played by Michael J. Fox). Fashion responded with fine Giorgio Armani or Hugo Boss single or double-breasted jackets, cut wide, paired with pleated trousers. Weekends called for sweaters slung over Polos with upturned collars, flannel pants, and deck shoes. Yacht optional.

Proclaiming their right to head boardrooms, women donned domineering ensembles in an upended triangle silhouette, reminiscent of those with "quarterback" shoulder pads from Hollywood designer Adrian (1903-1959). But without disco as the fulcrum from which the spokes of fashion, dance, and entertainment turned, the wheel had to be reinvented. It was, sorta, by a renegade cable channel that went on air in 1981: MTV.

Music videos have been around since the 1940s, known as "Soundies" which played on video jukebox contraptions called the Panoram. But it was a fad that came and went. While some artists and music acts were filmed in the succeeding decades, hardly anyone noticed because there wasn't a regular platform on which to watch them. In 1978, some videos were sporadically airing on USA cable networks' "Video Concert Hall" but only as two-hours of air filler and on constantly changing schedules. In contrast, MTV was on all the time. Its problem was a dearth of fresh content. Exacerbating matters, management seemed determined to cater to a miniscule, white, straight male, rock leaning demo. It was not a winning formula. Record companies were eager to exploit a medium that, with the added promotional value of having visuals, could very well surpass radio. Staring down meager cable subscribers, scarcer videos, and pressure from labels to feature a wider array of artists, MTV finally gave in.

Prince (1958-2016) was wrapping up rehearsals for the upcoming tour of his album "1999" when award-winning director Bruce Gowers (1940-2023) shot footage of his live performance of the title song. MTV reluctantly aired this video timed to its release as lead single.

Despite being recommended in Billboard's Top Singles Pick —"the Apocalypse never sounded this danceable before"—on page 63 of its October 9, 1982 issue, "1999" faltered at number 44 on the charts. The first time around. The following year, "Little Red Corvette" crashed through the guard rails all the way to number six and went into heavy rotation at MTV. Almost immediately Warner Brothers reissued "1999" to radio stations. And just like that Prince went from cult artist to bonafide pop star. Only a month later, CBS came knocking with a little Steve Barron-directed video for Michael Jackson's new single "Billie Jean". And just like that MTV went from an obscure channel some cable service providers didn't even carry to the most important music platform for an entire generation.

Undoubtedly, "Billie Jean" was supercharged by Jackson's performance of it with the backslide, otherwise known as the Moonwalk, during the televised anniversary special "Motown 25". But where the dance comes from is a bit of a muddle. It's been alleged that Jackson saw Jeffrey Daniel, one third of dance music trio Shalamar, perform it during their "A Night to Remember" number on Top of the Pops. But it's also been part of the act of street dance pioneers The Lockers since the 1970s. Others have noted that Jackson's Moonwalk with the glove and the hat is a near frame-by-frame recreation of Fosse's performance as the Snake in Stanley Donen's 1974 picture "The Little Prince". Scuttlebutt even has it that the singer begged Fosse to direct the "Thriller" video. In any case, the move had been part of Jackson's mythos ever since.

The Moonwalk was seen again in the Walter Hill 1984 picture "Streets of Fire" executed with equal panache by Stoney Jackson (no relation, but coincidentally also a dancer on the "Beat It" music video) while lip synching to "I Can Dream About You" sung by Winston Ford

(1951–2007). And just for added complication, the song is by Dan
Hartman (1950–1994, one of few artists who transitioned from disco
to pop) whose original version is what's on the picture's soundtrack.
In Hartman's video for the song, he plays a barkeep singing along to a
clip of the movie. By the time the video aired on MTV, the cable channel was already airing a torrent of videos that made instant superstars
of Duran Duran, Jody Watley, the Eurythmics, Spandau Ballet, Human
League, and some brazen little hussy from Detroit called Madonna.

But before this generation of artists weighted their careers with
ever more experimental videos, the old guard wasn't quite done yet.
Newton-John, for one, toyed with an edgier sound for her "Totally
Hot" album, her first platinum seller. Upping the ante, she imitated
her "Grease" character and jettisoned her squeaky clean image and
saccharine country pop sound for 1981's "Physical", which sold ten
million copies. The titular single alienated her older fans and she was
dropped from the playlists of many adult contemporary radio stations.
But, it won over a younger pop audience, especially after the innuen-
do-laden music video aired on MTV. Beyond the fashion stir caused
by Newton-John's headband, the clip of her romping in a gym full of
brawny gay men heralded a behemoth industry on the horizon.

For decades, bodybuilding seemed stuck as a fringe avocation that
divided genders: men bulked up at the gym with barbells, while
women went to dance studios to lose weight. The kind of exclusive
dance and exercise classes at Elizabeth Arden for women of means,
touted by both Vogue and Harper's Bazaar in the 1930s, were becoming more common. In the 1980s women strove to slim down at home
with "Dancercize" from Carol Hensel, the first exercise album to ever

chart in pop roundups. Vintage Record Company reissued it a year later as "Carol Hensel's Exercise and Dance Program". By the 2nd and 3rd volumes, music including the Cars' "Shake It Up" and the J. Geils Band's "Freeze Frame" was packaged with illustrated instructions. But the floodgates truly broke when Jane Fonda released video home system (VHS) cassettes of "Workout". Named after the aerobics studio Fonda co-founded with Leni Cazden, the stretch-and-dance program combined prismatic nylon and spandex workout wear, sweatbands and leg warmers with the language of music videos to sell millions of copies.

Music videos had other sweeping effects on popular culture and how it was being consumed. Editing film or television shows to music wasn't necessarily unheard of, but not to the extent of emulating music videos and becoming the standard it became in the 1980s. Filmed images that held for up to eight seconds in the 1970s, could now only last up to 4 seconds before quick cutting to another shot. Then, without warning, montages with pop songs got embedded into any drama, comedy or action film. It was like having a music video inside every movie.

Hollywood churned out dance pictures again. A female welder by day and stripper by night (played by Jennifer Beals) yearns to attend a prestigious dance academy in Adrian Lyne's "Flashdance" (1983), $90M in domestic grosses. A city boy (Kevin Bacon) fights to hold a dance in a small town where it's outlawed in "Footloose" (1984) from Herbert Ross (1927-2001), $80M. A young woman (Jennifer Grey) comes of age in a Catskills summer camp in "Dirty Dancing" (1987) from Emile Ardolino, $60M.

While 'Dirty' had Grey and formally trained Patrick Swayze (1952-2009) do their own moves, Bacon and Beals were doubled for their dance sequences respectively by Peter Tramm (1957-1991) and his wife Marine Jahan. Because these pictures were relatively cheap to produce, they kept coming out. Some, like "Girls Just Want to Have Fun" (1985), were inoffensive. Joel Silberg's "Breakin'" (1984) at least touted the new breakdancing craze. Taylor Hackford aimed for dramatic tension with "White Nights" (1985) in which Baryshnikov and Gregory Hines, choreographed by Twyla Tharp, tap in the deadly crosshairs of the KGB. John Waters' "Hairspray" (1988) discoursed on race and body image. Broadway musicals with dance were translated into celluloid: "The Best Little Whorehouse in Texas" (1982) and "Annie" (1984).

On top of the box office, the soundtracks from these movies practically gave studios and record companies license to mint money. And the cross promotional benefit was pure win-win: soundtracks promoted the picture, the artists, and their individual albums. And everyone, including MTV, got bonus mileage out of videos. Sometimes, original material was composed. But more often, music supervisors would license a song, or even an outtake from someone's album, that could tenuously color a scene or evoke a mood in the picture and voila. These soundtrack compilations dovetailed neatly with giving anyone ownership of their favorites via blank cassettes. Coupled with the introduction of the Sony Walkman, personalized playlists gave portability and resulted in many declarations of affection through mixtapes and later mixed CDs.

———————————

There's a not altogether unbelievable yet probably apocryphal story that "Miami Vice" exists because NBC entertainment head Brandon Tartikoff (1949-1997) gave writer Anthony Yerkovich marching orders to whip up a television series with "MTV cops". True or not, that's what viewers got in 1984 when they tuned in at 10pm every Friday.

Outfitted in pastel T-shirts under sharkskin jackets with rolled-up sleeves, Don Johnson and Philip Michael Thomas waged war on drug lords against the candy colored art deco architecture of South Beach. While dancing never became a plot element, the neo noir actioner was like an hour long music video.

Dance did figure prominently in an episode of ABC's witty smash "Moonlighting". When the two-hour pilot aired in the Spring of 1985, it seemed like any other weekly procedural, but with a conceit built squarely on Cybil Shepherd and Bruce Willis' chemistry. She played ex-cover model Maddie Hayes who owned the Blue Moon detective agency and slammed doors better than anyone. He was incorrigible gumshoe David Addison who could wisecrack his way out of any jam. Defying every known rule of episodic television, it wowed critics and audiences with overlapping snappy banter, fourth-wall breaking inside jokes, and increasingly inventive set ups. The monochromatic "The Dream Sequence Always Rings Twice", for example, presented opposing solutions to an unsolved murder in the form of two separate dreams by Maddie and David. Cleverer still, her reverie was presented in a Warner Brothers-style potboiler while his looked more like an MGM glamour picture.

One day, "Moonlighting" showrunner Glenn Gordon Caron received a call from music producer Phil Ramone (1934-2013), who was wrapping up Billy Joel's tenth studio album "The Bridge". Ramone told Caron that the piano man had written a song that might work for the series. On November 18, 1986 the episode "Big Man on Mulberry Street" was highlighted by a six-minute dance sequence scored to the title tune from Joel, choreographed by Bill and Jacqui Landrum (1943-2008) and directed by Stanley Donen of "Singin' in the Rain" fame.

Shot just a month prior in a soundstage at 20th Century Fox Studios, the segment opens in a West Village basement dive with David bartending to dancers (including coming-into-their-prime Vince Paterson and Jerry Mitchell) dressed as 1960s beat poets. The camera then tracks a pair of high-heeled legs crossing a row of street level windows before the doors to the bar bursts open to reveal dancer Sandahl Bergman (who was incidentally also one of the Greek muses in "Xanadu"). David and Bergman's unnamed character dances to the song, then fades to closing time later with a second walk through and dramatic entrance by Shepherd who takes her turn dancing with Willis. The episode snagged the Landrums an Emmy nomination for outstanding achievement in choreography.

From the cannonade of video images, fans cherrypicked their looks. Stepping out no longer meant just dressing up, more like donning costumes identified with artists or music genres: gender-bending getups of Culture Club's Boy George, parachute pants of MC Hammer, frilly shirts of the new romantics, the tracksuits, sneakers. and bold colors of nascent hip hop artists. Kid Creole and the Coconuts brought back the zoot suit courtesy of costume designer Adriana Kaegi. Synth pop bands donned tailored ensembles. On the debonair end stood Robert Palmer, Bryan Ferry, and the Rolling Stones' Charlie Watts (1941-2021). Palmer was partial to Italian: Gianfranco Ferre, Barba Napoli, and Armani. Savile Row was favored by Ferry (Anderson & Sheppard) and Watts (Tommy Nutter, 1943-1992 and Chittleborough & Morgan).

Just outside of general purview, designers Issey Miyake (1938-2022), Yohji Yamamoto, and Rei Kawakubo of Comme des Garçons beguiled the denizens of fashion and nightlife. But their simultaneous rise and sublime aesthetics became a double-edged katana, which made them a readily marketable "movement" while being painted with a broadly racial brush. Despite yellow peril baiting feature headlines like "The Japanese Invasion", the appreciation was sincere. The minimalist shapes, the neutral palette and ingenious ways fabric wrapped around the body instead of being directed by stitching—these informed what aficionados wore to clubs, fashion and art gallery events. The same concepts were diffused to the masses as oversized, square cut tops, elastic-waist pants, and eventually the loose sweats that followed. There are no rational explanations, whatsoever, for acid wash jeans.

Black youth, on the other hand, had their own heroes. Rap and hip-hop gave them a voice with which to convey their exultations and frustrations. The formalwear of the 1960s soul groups were discarded for "B-boy (or girl)" fashions (B for dancing on the drum "break")—track suits, Lee trousers, Clarks shoes or Puma sneakers, caps or hats. From an adherence to wearing their 'Sunday Best' for church, fashion has always been an important component of African American culture. Modern streetwear of baggy jeans, color blockings, and logos on everything was conceived in their neighborhoods. But while dance was part of the scene, it eventually receded as the music, the spoken word rhythms, and epic poetry became their end all and B all.

———————————

Yet unrealized by anyone, the course corrections dance music and MTV made led to their providential collision. Because dance was, in reality, quite a popular category, record companies and artists simply recalibrated away from the "disco" classification and pulled from different genres. Those that sold records and played on top forty radio were synth pop, good old R&B, and to an extent, (danceable) rock.

The labels then marketed them by inverting the lengths of album cuts and the singles. In the past, the song as it appears on an album is the longer full-length cut while the single was shorter, edited down to three minutes and change for radio airplay. Somewhere along the way, the album cuts got shorter while "extended versions" were packaged as 12-inch singles, with sales officially reported by Billboard from 1985 on. But while everyone loved Rick Astley's "Never Gonna Give You Up", it couldn't have been more different from another dance hit "Break 4 Love" by Raze. In the splintering of dance music, hardcore nightlifers were determined to get their fix from less populist fare.

And content in their self-absorption, Gothamites cared not a whit about what some midwest shock jock and his fans thought. They still had places to go, like one of the disco holdouts: the mythic Paradise Garage with former Loftie Larry Levan at the decks. Partly funded by pre-opening 'construction' parties, the club had an inauspicious opening night during a blizzard. No liquor, a loosely enforced members-only policy, great music, and dancing, plenty of dancing. On Saturdays, a couple of thousand mostly gay, mostly Latino and black men, a smattering of women and white gay and straight men encircled the block of King Street. Filing through a garage door entrance, up a long ramp, and into a 5,000 square-foot dancefloor, they then pressed against Keith Haring (1958-1990) murals and were engulfed by strobes and Levan's smooth soul and funk sounds. His appeal was an idiosyncratic flair for playing winners as often as head scratching acapellas or seconds of dead air. Part of Garage lore was the night an unknown track, Taana Gardner's "Heartbeat", emptied the floor. Determined to batter the room into submission, Levan played it again, and again, and thrice more after that.

Between showstoppers, people relaxed on the rooftop, or in the lounges where movies were played or Levan's mother could be seen doling out fruit punch. And because some nights lasted well into noon of the following day, people wore comfortable T's, shorts and sneakers. Costumes were worn sparingly, for themed nights like the skimpy swimsuits worn by hunky 'lifeguards' who manned wooden stations around the floor at one summer Beach Party night. That event 'closed' with revelers being whisked away by chartered buses, then ferried over from Sayville to Fire Island. At 4pm Levan resumed the party at the Ice Palace.

Another New York club of note was Limelight, the former Church of Holy Communion that eye-patched entrepreneur Peter Gatien converted into a wanton wonderland with an upper level dancefloor designed by Swiss artist H.R. Giger. It closed down after Gatien's tax evasion arrest, and the gruesome death of Club Kid Angel Melendez. Those who preferred their murders from the literary school of 'more arsenic with your tea, vicar?' went instead to Sound Factory, or Danceteria, of which Henry Post waxed poetic (New York magazine May 1982): "a dreamworld of mysterious souls, sidelong glances, and the perfume of ruin."

Meanwhile, another Loft graduate Frankie Knuckles (who'd been a textile design student at the Fashion Institute of Technology, Est. 1944), was fronting a club in Chicago called Warehouse and evolving the new sound of dance. His sets were enhanced by his personalized mixing of songs with pulsing drums and elegant piano flourishes. Knuckles fans invariably showed up at record stores asking for what they had heard at the club the night before, eventually truncating what they called "Warehouse music" to just plain "house".

The insistent, compelling thumps Moroder and Summer laid down in "I Feel Love" decades ago catapulted house music, along with the cult of the DJ, to a whole new summit. A succession of drum machines—the Roland TR-808 Rhythm Composer, the 909, then the 707—circumvented the expense of live musicians. And when granted access to the stems (the separate components of a completed track), producers were able to let loose their own vision for a song. At first, they were hesitant—looping instrumentals to pad length, giving them cheeky subtitles, and hiding behind sobriquets. But shrewd club goers quickly caught on to who was responsible for the new versions. Soon, they audaciously gutted the original productions, inserted samples, altered the arrangements, sometimes retaining only the vocals, a hook or melodic line, and created something altogether new: the remix. Permutations added mileage to a single and multiplied the ways a DJ could integrate them into their sets. Thus was born the superstar DJ—whose rabid followers could recognize the signature sound of a remix if it were being transmitted at the frequency of a dog whistle.

In club event posters and postcard fliers, promoters John Blair, Marc Berkley, and Jeffrey Sanker top billed Masters at Work (Louie Vega and Kenny Gonzalez), Murk (Ralph Falcón and Oscar Gaetan), Abel Aguilera, Ralphi Rosario, Hex Hector, Victor Calderone, Danny Tenaglia, and Francois Kevorkian. Others earned stature beyond their home bases: Joe Gauthreaux (New Orleans), Alex Lauterstein (New York), Mark Picchiotti (Chicago), Pete Heller and Terry Farley (Brighton), Stephan Grondin (Montreal), Steve Lawler (London), Chus and Pablo Ceballos (Madrid). Sander Kleinenberg (the Netherlands), Paulo Gois and Manny Lehman (Los Angeles). To be clear, there were remixers. There were DJs. Some were both. Austrian-born New Yorker Peter Rauhofer (1965-2013) was fearless in pursuing opportunities as remixer, resident and touring DJ, Grammy-winner, and founder of his own record label—*69.

Reprising the disco years, mom-and-pop record labels like Masterbeat, Tommy Boy, Defected, Trax, Perfecto, Global Underground, Nervous, and *69 dropped a slew of (less costly) CD singles and full-length DJ sessions every Tuesday at big box outlets like Tower and Virgin Records. The in-the-know went to small retailers like Disc-O-Rama and ransacked the curated stacks at David Shebiro's beloved and lamented West Village store Rebel Rebel.

Because there were fewer parties for straight or mixed crowds, the Spanish island of Ibiza cornered that market and sold 24/7 nightlife to the world. Its international reputation grew from being an unofficial annex of the British rave scene. Tens of thousands make the pilgrimage to its cluster of clubs like the once 18th century country house that's now Amnesia, Cafe del Mar, and Pacha, which celebrates its 50th year in 2023. Surrounded by pristine Mediterranean waters, it's the native land of Balearic house music quivering to the beat of white curtains flapping in the wind, gurgling fountains, orange sunsets, and swaying palms. Between sets, people took in the breathtaking sheer drop views from Es Vedrà, the rock that juts up the southwestern seaboard.

Concurrent to Ibiza's popularity to straight people was the so-called gay circuit. No one agrees on how or why the word "circuit" came to be. Did it refer to the weekend-long run from party to after-party to the next day's party? Or the city-to-city travel to event hubs: White Party (Miami and Palm Springs), Black Party (New York), 4th of July (Provincetown), Southern Decadence (New Orleans), Fireball (Chicago), Hotlanta (Atlanta), Black and Blue Festival (Montreal), Rapido (Amsterdam), Circuit (Barcelona)? Regardless, thousands upon thousands of men participated in all of them. Apparently those weren't enough. There were local parties as well. Sinful Sundays boasted equal-opportunity go-go boys and go-go girls at West Hollywood's

House of Blues. At Chelsea's gay Roxy Saturdays Rauhofer held residency and was best-loved among the turntable pied pipers who enticed legions of men to 515 W. 18th Street.

Within this milieu there emerged a new gay male archetype, not seen since the 1970s "clone" of lean build, pornstache, tank top, jeans, and the convoluted back pocket handkerchief code system. In the 1990s, it was all about being well-groomed and tightly muscled, a romanticized masculine look straight (as it were) out of Calvin Klein ads, Abercrombie & Fitch and International Male catalogs. Style was equally clean—designer T's or tank tops, denim by Diesel, 7 for All Mankind, Citizens of Humanity, or True Religion, and Doc Martens boots. The most important part, however, occurred at around 1am when shirts inevitably came off until the club was one heaving, bare chested mass of pulchritudinous flesh.

This coincided with the nascent lifestyle of a steady diet of Pure Protein S'mores bars and daily workouts at neighborhood gyms like American Fitness in New York, and The Sports Connection and the Athletic Club in LA. Before long, gyms and Starbucks were trying to outnumber each other. As of 2020, research estimates over ten thousand coed gyms, independent or under parent brands like Ballys and Crunch, operate in the U.S. and earn over $4B in revenues.

For men, striving to gain mass and its attendant, homogenized hunky ideal further tied to the physical and psychological reaction to HIV-AIDS. In the race for a cure, individuals, politicians, federal and local agencies, big pharma, and the medical and gay communities had manifold, and often conflicting, agendas, which expedited stab-in-the-dark hypotheses and short term work-arounds. One, the use of steroids to combat "wasting" (the severe loss of muscle mass caused by the virus) led many to thereby equate beefy physiques with good health.

And what better way to bring attention to those muscles than by getting them inked? By the early aughts, panthers, dragons, esoteric symbols, and Chinese characters were tattooed across toned bodies. But for the dedicated clubber, the preferred signifier was tribal. Sure, some had personal reasons for getting them, but patterns culled from African, Polynesian, and Samoan cultures on the arms, chests, or backs of gay men were prevalent at the clubs. It may also be assumed that these were representational of the "tribal" dance music preferred by these men. Truth is, however, there's never been an official consensus on the definitions of dance music variations. People will identify the same mix differently—house, deep house, acid, progressive, tech, trance, tribal, etc. There was even a time "freestyle" was used for both music and dance.

Still, clubs could be navigated by sonic differences. Haçienda, the U.K. rave capital, specialized in music buttressed by rage and melancholy, ie. New Order, Depeche Mode. Heaven was less angsty, think Erasure, or brighter but no less subversive tunes from the Pet Shop Boys discography. Ministry of Sound tried copying Paradise Garage by bringing in American DJs, who were still smart enough to play to their audience since most Europeans were partisan to pop-y Trevor Horn, Ian Levine, or Stock-Aitken-Waterman productions. On the other side of the Atlantic, club goers, especially the gays, had a penchant for sounds raw and robust.

———————————

An important port of call for clubbing in the colonies was Miami during the renaissance of South Beach, unimaginable back in the 1970s when its population had stagnated into Cubans, criminals, and little old Jewish ladies. The row of Art Deco and Streamline Moderne buildings facing virgin white sands and effervescent blue waters were mostly dilapidated and vacant. But before decade's end, a Bloomingdale's window display designer called Leonard Horowitz and a woman called Barbara Baer Capitman rescued them from being torn down by unscrupulous developers. Aside from getting a mile of ocean front property into the National Register of Historic Places, Horowitz recommended painting the buildings in tropical pastels to attract younger residents.

Gradually, the area evinced signs of rebounding. In 1985, over two dozen male and female models spent a week on the roof of the Breakwater doing a Bruce Weber shoot for a Calvin Klein Obsession perfume ad. After the tear sheets came out, fashion people stampeded South to do their own shoots. By the 1990s there was so much work, the town was overrun by pretty young things. At the Clevelander, models were given a special rate of $75 a week to liven up the joint. Poolside at the hotel looked like a GQ or Sports Illustrated layout. After the sun had called it a day, everyone congregated at trendy new bars like the Spot or Whisky, ran mostly by a gaggle of legit or dodgy New York operators. From there, things just got wilder.

Fashion was exploding into the popular consciousness like never before. Peter Lindbergh (1944-2019) packed the powderkeg. George Michael (1963-2016) with an assist from MTV braided the fuse. Gianni Versace lit it. And perched on top were the supermodels who blew up with a bang all the way to the bank. The inexorable chain of events went like this: Liz Tilberis (1947-1999) ordered Lindbergh to come up with a cover for the January 1990 issue of British Vogue. The lensman, already known for images antithetical to the immaculate fashion photos of the past, submitted naturally lit and unretouched proofs of Naomi Campbell, Linda Evangelista, Tatjana Patitz (1966-2023), Christy Turlington, and Cindy Crawford. The resulting black and white cover of the quintet in jeans and Giorgio di Sant'angelo tops was seen by Michael, who cast them in his "Freedom '90!" video. Since the song was the pop star's disavowal of his public persona, he didn't want to be in the video. That was relegated to the women, shot front and center on 35mm film, and mouthing the lyrics along with male models John Pearson, Scott Benoit, Peter Formby, Todo Segalla, and (later photog) Mario Sorrenti. Versace saw it and cast Campbell, Evangelista, Turlington, and Crawford in his Fall 1991 ready-to-wear showing, unusual since runway and magazine editorial models were believed to be twains that never shall meet. His showing climaxed with the four strutting arm-in-arm, again singing along to "Freedom 90!", and securing the designer a permanent place in the fashion firmament.

Across fashion, media and the court of public opinion, the verdict was unanimous. These women, along with a few others, were anointed the goddesses of the era. They graced glossy covers, cosmetics and fragrance ads, and principally, the runways. Paparazzi and media chronicled their slightest gesticulations. Designers swaddled them in mountains of free clothes and accessories. And because a collection showing without them would lack attention and luster, their stipulated rates shot up to prohibitively astronomical heights. Arguably, the supermodels were worth every penny. Any runway they deigned to walk, every garment they wore was made electric, more vivid by their personalities. But, adjacent to the number of zeros on those checks they were cashing was the concern of designers over whether the press was focused on the fashions or the models. Probably both, because without question the models were an irrefutable part of why those designs were being more widely seen.

The runways used to be a sectarian rostrum for designers, fashion editors, buyers, a few clients, and photographers. In the 1990s, they were being covered by every news outlet including CNN (by Elsa Klensch, 1930-2022), CBC's Fashion File (with Tim Blanks) and MTV (House of Style by Crawford herself). It was then the runway became theater and walking it performative, choreographed to the attitude of the collection or the theme of its presentation. In this, some were supreme. Arrogance was a Campbell trademark. Yasmeen Ghauri's rolling gait from the hips was inimitable. Shalom Harlow, of the second generation supermodels, projected palpable drama, and she had trained in ballet and tap. Unavoidably, dance music became popular on the runways. RuPaul entered pop culture via dance hit "Supermodel". At Isaac Mizrahi's Fall 1994 show (documented in "Unzipped" by filmmaker Douglas Keeve) Crawford, Campbell, and Evangelista (and presumably everyone else) sang along to the Shem McCauley and Simon Rogers mix of Boy George's "Miss Me Blind" blaring inside the white tents temporarily installed in Bryant Park for New York Fashion Week.

That was the same year antiques dealer Richard Claycomb relocated to South Beach. For him, the needle may have dropped back in his hometown of Grand Rapids, Michigan, but the dance started in earnest in Chicago. At his new job in the Second City, he was rhetorically asked if his transfer had been motivated by the better career opportunities there. Richard punctured the middle management vanities of his supervisor by replying he came because the gay clubs in Michigan only stayed open until 2am while those in Chicago lasted until 5 in the morning.

When he got to Miami, the town was already in full swing. Recalling the places to be, he lists, "The Paragon, which brought in guest DJs, Warsaw Ballroom, and Twist, although that was more a neighborhood bar with a small dance floor. Score, formerly Kremlin. Then after Paragon closed, Salvation was great for a while." On Washington Avenue, Brooklyn mafioso Chris Pacielo opened the fashionable, mostly straight club Liquid using insurance money he'd collected on another club he owned called Risk (rumored to have been financed by Pacielo's share of a bank heist back in Bensonhurst) after it burnt to the ground 'accidentally'.

Around this time, Versace was in town, strolling along Ocean Drive when he noticed the kneeling Aphrodite bronze on the front terrace of the old Amsterdam Palace. Looking up and around, he fell in love with the Mediterranean revival built in 1930 by Alden Freeman, a member of the Mayflower Descendants and heir to a fortune father Joel made as treasurer at Standard Oil. Versace's decision to make this his new home had symmetry since records abound supporting the supposition that Freeman and Versace's lurid aesthetic would've been simpatico.

The designer forked out $2.5M for the decrepit property, $3.7M for the Revere Hotel (Est. 1950) next door, which was bulldozed to make way for a garden and pool, and another $32M for a total overhaul. In 1993, Versace greeted everyone from his new abode he called Casa Casuarina, around which whorled a helix of celebrity friends and models with cheekbones that could cut diamonds, and even better carved physiques. It was a housewarming that didn't quite know when to end. But on a pleasant July 1997 morning, Versace, in black shirt, checked shorts and sandals, was returning from News Café with a brown paper bag containing his just purchased copies of Vogue, New Yorker, Entertainment Weekly, People, and the Spanish edition of Newsweek, when a lunatic ended it all with two shots from a pistol.

The murder of Versace was a shockwave felt around the world, and a portent of fashion's desertion of South Beach. Richard says, "Parties went on. After Liquid closed, we went to Crobar at the Cameo Theatre. When the lights went up, we'd make our way to Cactus, an after-hours dance club on Biscayne Boulevard with a small dance floor and an outdoor pool for lounging." He elaborates, "Most of the dance clubs in South Beach were initially gay. The straights tagged along until Prince gave them their own mega dance club Glam Slam (a satellite of the one in Minneapolis), which had its Friday gay nights." And that, relates Richard, was when everything went downhill. "The Miami Beach police had intel that drugs were being sold there during straight nights." But as was the proud tradition of police departments, they pounced on the club on gay night. "Men were marched out to waiting TV crews who'd been tipped off. Word went around fast that going to Glam Slam could get you on the nightly news as part of a raid on illegal drugs at a gay event." Bad optics took down the club and the rest of South Beach with it. Clubbers moved on to more hospitable cities.

What time to go to a club also made a difference. Gospel-grade "anthems" by Robin S, Martha Wash, and Ultra Naté, and guaranteed floorfillers from Kristine W, Billie Ray Martin, or Suzanne Palmer played during peak hours until 1am. This was also when people reacquainted themselves with mainstream artists aiming to widen their fan base or revitalize their careers. Mariah Carey's five octave range powered David Morales' mix of "Dreamlover" (the first time she made a habit of actually re-recording her vocals especially for remixes). Whitney Houston songs were played, sure, like her take on Chaka Khan's "I'm Every Woman" remixed by Robert Clivillés and David Cole (1962–1995). But it was the Thunderpuss (Chris Cox and Barry Harris) mixes of "It's Not Right (But It's Okay) that gave her real club cred. Then, had Todd Terry not made a banger out of "Missing",

Everything But the Girl would've stayed a mid-tier duo (one half of which, Ben Watt, later also DJed, and remixed Sade's "By Your Side"). And, while the public thinks "Believe" was Cher's ticket to the comeback trail, she had actually hitched a ride out of adult contemporary purgatory two years prior on the Junior Vasquez mix of her "One by One".

The closer it gets to early morning, however, the darker and more abstract the sound becomes, almost devoid of vocals and melody. Propulsive dubs and beats raise nightlife's denizens to primal, hands-in-the-air states of abandon. The (usually) older set, who will have already gone home by then anyway, disparagingly referred to it as the "pots and pans" sound. Another criticism leveled at this scene was the recalcitrant promiscuity and drug use. True, many can coast all night on the stifling mix of adrenaline and testosterone. But more relied on synthetics to boost natural dopamine and endorphin rushes. The "happy" high of Ecstasy gave the sensation of being in communion with the crowd. But the overproduction of serotonin causes the body to compensate the day after and effect depression. Crystal meth jacked up energy levels but was addictive and chronic use came with a host of dangerous side effects. The parties' propensity for fine specimens of manhood resulted in more opprobrium: discrimination and the propagation of unrealistic physical standards. The circuit scene has been gradually phased out in the last decade for more racially and socially integrated clubs and music festivals, all playing the frothier, autotuned buzz of EDM.

———————————

Music of a different sort accompanied the methodical bustling at the Barbara Matera shop. Past sibilant steam irons and whirring sewing machines, William led Deborah Yates into one of its many work rooms. Steeled with trepidation, she stood patiently while he flung out bolt after bolt of fabric like a magician flicking cards from his tailored sleeves. "Because she was blonde, she was skeptical about how she would look in yellow." But after eyeing an array of materials against Yates' face, William settled on a handful that had potential. At least visually.

"I made the first one, a warm lemon, in chiffon, which we used for promotional images that ended up on the posters and the Playbill cover," he says. "Well, that didn't work on stage because it washed out under the lights." And so William made a new dress from a different material. But each succeeding version solved one problem only for another to arise. One easily ripped. Another's glass beads cut into Seán's palms everytime he lowered Yates from a lift. William was undaunted. "I learned a long time ago the quicker you give up on something that doesn't work, the sooner you can get to a solution." Ninth time was the charm. "The material is called 'cracked ice', I call the color a greeny goldenrod." It lit well and moved splendidly. But that wasn't the end of it because the hem length was next. William started at mid thigh, but kept inching lower with each new dress until the day he was hemming the latest version and Yates herself stopped him, "That's it!" William stepped back for a look. "Deborah, you're absolutely right."

Trust the dancer is another axiom William works by. "I've learned so much from them," he says. "If something doesn't work, they'll tell you. Nothing fazes dancers. They're natural problem solvers." Stro agrees, but she points out that his costumes add a lot more to the equation, "I actually see the whole persona of young dancers change because of William. They carry that sophistication onto the stage and then out into real life." Because in truth, the title costume designer is hardly adequate to cover everything that William actually does. Beyond designing looks compatible to a story, he makes a conscious effort of hewing to the performer's personality.

William strives for a fusion of actor and character. "I like coming to rehearsals because what they have on tells you who they are and what they are comfortable in for dancing. Different performers need different things," he points out. "For example, when Charlotte (d'Amboise) took over from Karen (Ziemba), I added sleeves to the housewife's floral dress because she wasn't comfortable with exposed arms." While both actresses are superb, slight differences in their skirts also play to their skills: d'Amboise's has an hourglass silhouette of layered underpinnings that gently billows on descent; Ziemba's is wispier and shorter by a sliver so that it radiates higher to a perfect circle when she twirls.

On many of the company's outfits, William implanted velcros and camouflaged snaps for requisite quick changes. Another shortcut is barely visible up close: the maître d's vest is immobile, gapping only at the very top front, probably fastened to the shirt as an easy-to-strip single piece. For the off-the-rack jackets, gussets inserted below the cap of the sleeves and stretch in the side seams allowed dancers to throw their arms up without the shoulders hunching and the rest of the garment pulling along. The three-piece Ermenegildo Zegna suit purchased for the two left-footed Gaines, however, was mostly spared from this indignity, serving more as the character's figurative armor, a disguise even. And having Gaines peel the jacket off is the shedding of restraint, his assent to the invitation to dance.

Squeezing into tights, tutus, and pointe shoes in the hurry from dressing room to the wings is a commotion all too familiar for dancers. Yet, there is something different here. Making last minute adjustments to their false eyelashes and wigs while doing leg extensions and waiting for their cue—are these not men? Better. They are Les Ballets Trockadero de Monte Carlo.

The company's genesis was from a Ridiculous Theatrical Company shtick poking good natured fun at the 1970s mania for Russian ballet. Conceived by Larry Ree and Richard Goldberger, the satire pirouetted around pretend prima ballerina Madame Ekathrina Sobechanskaya (played by Ree). Some in the dozen or so of the troupe, however, chafed at merely backing one central drag persona. Peter Anastos, Natch Taylor, and Anthony Bassae consequently quit and formed Les Ballets Trockadero de Monte Carlo. "Its inception was in September 1974 at the building on Ninth Avenue just across the Apple store in the Meatpacking District," Tory Dobrin, current artistic director, points out. It used to be the West Side Discussion

Group (WSDG) headquarters where weekly Wednesday night socials were held on the second floor. Tory says Eugene McDougle, then WSDG coordinator, leased the space to the fledgling dance company and later "was really responsible for organizing the group and served as general director until he died some five, six years ago."

Endearingly called the "Trocks", they proved to be more than a one-note gimmick. Though their actions are heightened to excess, these dancers clearly have the training needed to carry out and send up ballets properly. And, while they embody feminine archetypes, they don't technically impersonate women. Beneath the makeup and tutus, no efforts are made to hide beards, chest hair, thickset arms, and stocky legs. There's also the stage names. In the 1930s–1950s, any ballet of consequence had to be Russian. Dancers—British, American or otherwise—assumed Russian monikers in order to align themselves to everything they connoted. Alexandra Denisova, for instance, was born Patricia Meyers, while Alicia Markova was formerly Lillian Marks. The Trocks adopted the practice with an extra twist: the argot of drag. Their stage names are puns or inside jokes—Nina Enimenimynimova, Nadia Doumiafeyva, Ida Nevasayneva, Marina Plezegetovstageskaya, and Tatiana Youbetyabooktskaya. Some honor ballet greats: Jacques D'aniels is for Jacques d'Amboise (1934–2021, also Charlotte's father), while Mikhail Mudkin is for Mikhail Mordkin (1880–1944).

Then there's the wit of the routines. These aren't cheap pratfalls but clever slapstick that sometimes rely on the audience having a rudimentary understanding of ballet idiom. Tory insists, "We're not aiming to be randomly mugging onstage." Their most uproarious bit is hands down the Dying Swan solo, adapted from the 1905 Fokine choreography for Pavlova. It's a spellbinding piece of extended bourrées, upper body and waving arms, which inevitably gets viewers howling in uncontrollable laughter when the "swan" begins "molting", feathers fluttering down from her tutu and sprinkling like snow on the boards.

The Trocks gained recognition for its absurdist sensibility after a New Yorker magazine October 14, 1974 review by noted dance critic Arlene Croce declared it "dead on target and hilarious". Not that there haven't been serious hurdles. The increased visibility of the Trocks fomented resentment in the dance community, especially from the ballet contingent, over what was perceived as disrespect for the craft. Worse, that dancers were being made the object of public ridicule. And so, they closed ranks. "Before I even joined," says Tory, "my friends kept warning me that I would be destroying my career." He asserts that the Trocks were suspiciously locked out of receiving arts funding and had to subsist solely on ticket receipts.

They were thrown a crucial lifeline by Betty Connors (1917-2009), head of the Committee for Arts and Lectures at the University of California, Berkeley, who scheduled the Trocks to appear at Zellerbach Hall in 1976. Tory explains that in the dance world, UC Berkeley is among the important theaters that can confer official status to a company. "By including the Trocks in her series, Betty opened doors for the company," he says. In subsequent years, the troupe embarked on a North American tour and guested (alongside legends Jimmy Stewart, 1908-1997 and Orson Welles, 1915-1985) in the hour-long, nationally-televised 1977 Shirley MacLaine CBS variety special "Where Do We Go from Here."

For Tory that question took years to answer. Born and raised in California, it was an earthquake registering 6.6 on the Richter Scale that shook him to his feet. The damage done to his school entailed the reassignment of students to Fairfax High where he was still required to attend Phys Ed daily even though the boys class was already full. Hearing of his dilemma, a teacher tersely responded, "Go take dance!" He recounts, "So I took the class of this New York beatnik type modern dance teacher who really encouraged us to express through improvisations." Then, during his college freshman year in Paris he met a student at the school founded by Étienne Decroux (1898-1991) whose proteges included French actor Marcel Marceau (1923-2007) and American actress Jessica Lange. Decroux is known for mime corporel, creating dramaturgy using only the human body and its physics. Tory gave it a try. He didn't really take to mime, but the experience did awaken his calling. "I realized then I wanted a career in dance," he says, describing himself returning to the U.S. an "obsessed dance person". He continues, "I studied with different people and all the ballet teachers in Los Angeles." He went on to the Houston Ballet Academy (Est. 1955) and joined the Dallas Ballet for a season.

All that, however, did not a true believer make. He says, "In the seventies through the eighties, many young people viewed ballet as outdated. And at 26, I had this somewhat arrogant modern dance attitude." He admits, "I didn't even really get into ballet until after I was already a Trock. I heard from a friend of mine that they needed dancers for a nine-week tour through South America. My aunt, who coincidentally had done publicity for them, had been telling me for years that I should audition for the Trocks. I went. I spent an intense two weeks learning pointe work and nine ballets." What finally sold him? "The educational station CUNY (City University of New York) TV was airing these old taped performances of the Kirov and the Bolshoi," he says, "and I had never been exposed to those ballets. I remember watching Alla Sizova (1939-2014) doing 'Sleeping Beauty' and Maya Plisetskaya (1925-2015) in 'The Fountain of

Bakhchisarai' and thinking: what the hell is that? I got hooked. At the time, you just didn't see that kind of dancing at ABT or New York City Ballet. So intense and full of life, very ornate and bizarre. And exactly what we aspire to at Trocadero."

Tory recounts, "On my first tour with them, we went to São Paulo, Rio De Janeiro, Belo Horizonte, Curitiba, and Santiago, among others. For the most part, audiences were very welcoming, boisterous and fun, although some were probably unaware of what they were in for when they came to see us. But, throughout South America, the locals used our presence as a form of protest against their military governments. Then, in Córdoba, two of our dancers—one Puerto Rican, the other Mexican—were picked up and arrested, simply because they stuck out, speaking in their versions of Spanish and being, well, gay. We did clear all that up but it just added this awareness of the repression in some of these regimes."

Unfortunately, the late 1980s visited misfortune upon the Trocks. The frequency of HIV-related deaths and their cumulative grief ravaged the theater and fashion communities. "And the company itself," adds Tory, "was imploding." Two of the founders were long gone (Bassae left in 1976, followed by Anastos in 1978). And the ballet mistress resigned. The National Endowment for the Arts was under pressure to cut support for anything out of the conservative wheelhouse, leaving the Trocks' finances in shambles. All the stress bred conflict between the general director and the artistic director, prompting the former to fire the latter. "Meanwhile, our booking agent at Sheldon Soffer Management was quitting. But he still had things to tie up and since we weren't getting much work, I offered my services as his assistant," Tory says. Founded in 1960 by Sheldon Soffer (1927-2021) and closed after his retirement in 1999, the agency represented major dance acts including the Trocks, Pilobolus, MOMIX, Twyla Tharp, and Mark Morris. It was excellent training ground for Tory who helped with correspondences and reviewed contracts, while learning how to negotiate and land bookings.

"Hearing first hand what venue operators needed to sell tickets, things they would never tell the artist or anyone else switched my perspective," he says. "It was plain to see that everyone wanted the same thing—to make a show happen. And the agent has to find solutions of compromise. When presenters ask for things, they have legitimate reasons for doing so. And generally speaking, these are reasonable asks. The presenter, the management, the agency, the company, we're all in this together so we can put on a good show that will make the audience happy and come back." When the agent finally left, Soffer offered Tory the job. He laughs, "That was actually stupid. I've had only about a month's training, but I was cheap. I accepted." Simultaneously, he was still with the Trocks and things were looking dire. "By the early 1990s, we weren't working very much at all. We were flat broke. One day, I said to Eugene—why don't we pare it down to a chamber company, to just say, six or seven dancers? We'll start pulling ourselves together." Luckily, the general director shrugged, "Sure, why not?" Tory adds, "And since I was also serving as the booking agent, I was able to get the Trocks into some venues. Slowly but surely, we recovered."

A contributing factor to the Trocks' ability to weather lean years is their abstinence from impermanent trends. Their repertoire cleaves close to the classics or familiar works of illustrious choreographers including Paul Taylor, Graham, Robbins, and Balanchine. Through the years, additions to the repertoire have been intermittent, though it often came down to the ineluctable matter of cost.

With a spartan overhead, there's a misperception of the Trocks being a lean, mean, money-making machine. Tory bluntly refutes it, "We don't have any money." Public record tax filings reveal this non-profit organization to be invariably in the red, and thus dependent on grants and the ticket-buying public. "We're very frugal and pretty open about our finances. We have nothing in the way of infrastructure. We have a storage unit for our costumes and often need an inexpensive place to rehearse. We would love to do contemporary ballets, but if we have to pay for rights, we can't do it."

Instead, Tory actively seeks out classics ripe for parody. "We uncover some great pieces through our frequent collaborations with Elena Kunikova," who hails from the Vaganova Ballet Academy in St. Petersburg, and teaches technique classes and academic courses at various New York institutions. Elena was instrumental in the Trocks winning the Company Prize for Outstanding Repertoire in the Classical category at the Critics' Circle National Dance Awards for 2006. "We started working with Elena almost thirty years ago," recounts Tory. "I was thinking of us doing the 'Pas de Trois des Odalisques' from 'Corsaire' and someone suggested I check out Elena. I took a class she was teaching at Steps (On Broadway, Est. 1979) and we clicked."

He enthuses, "She has a really wonderful sense of humor. She comes in totally prepared with the knowledge about how it's supposed to look, and she keeps at it until it's just right." And as she does for every Trocks project, what Kunikova strove to get 'just right' is authenticity of technique. "Sure, there must be others who have the knowledge but what makes Elena exceptional is her way of articulating these movements and drawing them out of someone," says Tory. And fully understanding the piece permits the comedy to surface. "We shape the material by keeping things relaxed since the guys tend to be natural comedians."

Because getting laughs is the goal, Tory guides, edits, and keeps tabs on all the jokes. He says, "We don't allow improvising during the actual performance. I log which Trock does which role in which city." Because any dancer can contribute, each Swan Queen might have a different take on the role. "The camaraderie comes from everyone here getting a fair chance to be a soloist. It keeps us focused and on friendly terms," adding, "and we don't use the same jokes every time. So whoever's seen our Swan Lake twice already will still see fresh material. We even put in things that happen in rehearsal like when the whole line of dancers fell over in 'Paquita', and the bit when one of the guys who drops the ballerina then does a couple of push-ups. But, a petite dancer struggling with someone statuesque can only work once," he says. "What always works? A tutu, wig, eyelash, pointe shoes." Such is the unassailable import of costume, inextricable to being a Trock as ballet.

One Trock, who had passed but still very much present in his creations for the company, was costume designer emeritus Mike Gonzales (who was also Tory's partner). His costumes are the ellipses that let the audience connect to the original ballets or the characters from which a particular segment was derived. "Mike joined as a wardrobe person and designed all the costumes but he danced with the company too. That was a great time in my life," he says. "We broke up in 1990, but eventually became really close friends until he died in 1996. The memory of his performances and the beauty of his costume designs in so many pieces, in archives, and souvenir books will make him a presence in our lives for a long, long time."

To keep the expense of making new ones minimal, many of Gonzales' original designs are still in use, and under the care of the wardrobe supervisor. For a while, this position was held by Jeff Sturdivant, who wasn't daunted by joining an itinerant company since his family, in his youth, had moved around quite a lot for his father's profession. But, he admits, "I hadn't worked in dance before." Fortunately, he was a quick study and straight away picked up on ways tradecraft helped garments function effectively. Says Jeff, "Of all the costumes for theater, those for dance can be the most challenging. It's very physical. You have to be mindful of wear and tear. We inspect each outfit carefully so a dancer doesn't put on something that has seams that are ready to break." He adds, "Because every dancer we have can dance any role, adjustments and alterations are often made. And, if we have a corps of eight, we make sure to have at least ten costumes ready—in different sizes and shapes. Because that's another aspect that's unique to the Trocks—we celebrate multiple body types to make that one line."

Trust is integral to working in the unpredictability of live performances. When things go sideways, and they often do, it can mean the difference between bringing a show to a premature stop or proceeding without anyone noticing anything has gone awry. "Once", relates Jeff, "we were in Bogota. Because of the high altitude, we had an oxygen tank at the side of the stage, just in case someone had trouble breathing. But one night, the dancer playing the Prince fainted before he could get to it. Across the other wing, our Swan Queen saw what was happening and stalled by extending his solo. Without a single word being exchanged by anybody, we rushed to the fallen prince, quickly undressed him, and took him to the dressing rooms to recuperate, while another dancer changed into the prince's costume and resumed the show. No one in the audience was any the wiser!"

He explains that the budget makes the diligent care and maintenance of existing costumes even more imperative. "For example, the dying swan costume with the molting feathers. In theater, we have this expression of 'relative white', meaning anything closest to white will look white against a black backdrop. So we need and have real 'relative white' feathers to make the number's effect happen. Those feathers are precious to us. After a performance, they are carefully gathered off the floor where they will have picked up dust and dirt. We then put them in a mesh laundry bag and shake them out gently to dislodge any of the accumulation.

"Whenever we traveled for a show, another part of what I did was pack what we needed into some 15 to 20 boxes and make sure they get to where we're headed," he explains. "Then, after we arrived at our destination, I unpacked everything and checked if each costume was in perfect condition." Being in another country presents its own difficulties. He recalls the three weeks they had spent in Singapore, Thailand, and Hong Kong. "At the time, the humidity in those cities was so high that after two weeks the garments simply wouldn't dry. We tried everything from fans to hair dryers. Nothing worked. The dancers had to go onstage with wet costumes for several shows." Sometimes, Jeff says, someone local to each city was hired to help with dressing and keep track of everything. "Language barriers can be a problem," he admits. "And, they just aren't." Jeff recalls, "We once had a show in China where this woman, who had worked with us before, had already retired. But she came out of retirement because she was so fond of the Trocks. I don't speak a word of Mandarin or Cantonese, while she couldn't converse in English. But you know what? We understood each other perfectly well. All we had to do was look at each other and we knew what had to be done."

Although Jeff is no longer with the company, he has only the happiest memories. He says, "During my entire tenure with them, not one dancer ever lost a headpiece. But, oddly enough, wigs flew off! We've tried securing them with hair pins, tape, or glue, but sometimes they still came off. Lucky for us whenever it happened, people just assumed it was part of the act. And it would end up being the highlight of the evening!" Jeff insists, "I will always be a Trock. The friendships and bond that you establish lasts over a lifetime. And if I learned anything from working there, it's that with imagination anything is possible."

If there are borders to that imagination, they only continue to be crossed. The Trocks have traveled to practically every city on the planet: Athens, Bangkok, Barcelona, Beijing, Brisbane, Caracas, Cologne, Dusseldorf, Glasgow, Johannesburg, Leipzig, Lisbon, Madrid, Melbourne, Moscow, Rome, Sydney, and many more. That the Trocks' popularity shows no signs of waning is aided by Tory's vigilance in seeking the same equilibrium that the three original founders grappled with: Anastos was the one who wanted choreography for laughs, Bassae believed in letting the audience find humor in dancing with dead serious integrity, while Taylor fretted over expenses. Tory tends to understate his contributions but is fairly confident they have stayed true to their mission. "All I've done is keep the company in a good place. I do worry that I operate from a restricted mind frame caused by financial stresses and concerns. But we are doing well and when the day comes when I see that it's not, that will be the time to change. Right now, it seems to be in a good place."

Accounts of people wearing apparel primarily identified with the opposite sex go back to the furthermost reaches of recorded history.

Cross-dressing is rooted in centuries of antecedents and laden by complex impulses from temporary use as disguise to acts of social insubordination. Onstage, female impersonation became necessary because patriarchy had decided it immodest for women to draw attention to themselves, thereby excluding them from participating in theater. It was customary for boys and men in ancient Greek and English renaissance times to take on female roles, a practice maintained through to the amateur antics of Harvard University's Hasty Pudding Club (Est. 1795) and Princeton University's The Princeton Triangle Club (Est. 1891).

In the seraglios of 1800s Turkey, dozens of *köçek* (boys who danced as women) in embroidered velvet jackets, skirts, and bejeweled hats performed for the sultan and the aristocracy. By 1805 there were hundreds of them in Istanbul and taverns across the Ottoman empire where their acclaim unfailingly caused violent altercations among spectators vying over their favors.

The onnagata male cabaret dancer emerged earlier still during Japan's Edo period of the 1600s. To impose oversight on the burgeoning array of licentious amusements, the ruling Tokugawa shogunate corralled them all to licensed 'pleasure quarters' such as the Shimabara in Kyoto or Yoshiwara in Tokyo. Once walled off and perimetered by a moat, the Shimabara came to be known as a "floating world" that provided anyone, whatever their class, respite from daily worries. It was here Kabuki (derived from the word *"kabuku"* meaning something outlandish or extraordinary) was created for the merchant class as a mawkish alternative to the dignified Muromachi Period-conceived Noh theater of masks and austere gestures. Although supposedly originated by a female dancer called Izumo no Okuni, Kabuki became exclusively male in the 1620s when women were prohibited from being onstage. Onnagata dancers assumed all the female roles in painted faces, 25-pound wigs, and kimonos with vasiform skirts, which forced them to dance with their backbones and minimal use of legs.

Because it was presumed that well-bred women (always shielded from sunlight by parasols) had pale complexions, the onnagata substituted the masks used in Noh with stark white makeup (mixed from wax and rice powder) accentuated by crimson lips, dots on the cheeks and over shaved brows. Wigs (or natural, waist-length hair) sculpted with pommades were ornamented with dangling trinkets, flowers and pins. The dancers attracted such admiration that their porcelain doll-like-ness became the standard of Japanese feminine beauty—later appropriated by courtesans and immortalized by the geisha.

It was at these pleasure quarters the male geisha appeared in 1730, followed a couple of decades later by their female counterparts who completely took over the profession by 1780. Around this time, Chinese opera—a fusion of music, song and dance, martial arts, acrobatics, costume and make-up—featured men called *nándàn* who played all the female or "Dan" roles because women were also banned from the stage during the Qing Dynasty.

The geisha, as artists, was among the lowest social classes. But she still wielded considerably more autonomy and power than housewives. To obtain an affluent patron, soothe or amuse customers, the geisha had to be outstanding in dance, fashion, music, and conversation, skills that took years to hone. Apprentices, called *maiko* (dancing child), start as young as seven years old, attending daily classes on how to dance, play the shamisen, and conduct tea ceremonies. Unlike those worn by the average Japanese woman, the kimonos of the geisha have neck-lines noticeably lower in the back since exposing the nape of the neck is thought to be very sensual. They also featured extended (about 200 centimeters longer on average) hems that are supposed to trail along the floor as a sign of grace and prestige.

Outside formal settings, the geisha may wear traditional kimonos. Woven from the finest silks, *awase* kimonos worn during the cooler months are lined and embroidered with seasonal motifs such as pine trees, bamboo, and cherry blossoms. During the warmer months, the lighter and unlined *hitoe* kimonos are likely to have prints of dragonflies, cranes, hydrangeas, and reeds. The finishing touch for any kimono is the *obi* that has its own variations and conventions. But for the geisha, this silk sash is usually four-meters long and thirty-centimeters wide, tied low around the waist, and always knotted in back.

———————————

Crossdressing advanced through the artifice of theater. Its colloquial term "drag" was derived from stage slang for male actors assigned women's roles and don skirts that would "drag" on the floor. Opera called them *travesti,* and in reverse there were "breeches roles" for women (usually taken by mezzo sopranos) who performed the parts of prepubescent males such as Siebel in "Faust" by Charles Gounod (1818-1893) or Cherubino in *"Le nozze di Figaro"* by Mozart.

Born enslaved to a tobacco plantation owner called Ann Murray in Hancock, Maryland, William Dorsey Swann (1858-1925) is the first person who professed himself "queen of drag". In his twenties, he brought together other formerly enslaved individuals into the "House of Swann" for underground balls where they could wear elegant dresses and dance. In 1888, the Washington Post reported:

"Negro Dive Raided. Thirteen Black Men Dressed as Women Surprised at Supper and Arrested." The story detailed the fracas on L Street where Swann, attired in a cream satin dress, was taken into custody for female impersonation. But it was his open resistance that inspired many others to fight back against the system. In confronting the policeman arresting him, Swann declared, "You is no gentleman!"

1900s vaudeville was more acclamatory of drag. And none was more fabulous than self-titled "female illusionist" Julian Eltinge (1881-1941) who never played drag for laughs. He sang and danced through role and costume changes as a woman, only delivering the twist reveal of removing his wig at the end of the act. He earned more plaudits in silent pictures, his command performance for Bertie (King Edward VII), and for the publication of "Julian Eltinge's Magazine of Beauty Hints and Tips" promoting his own line of women's cosmetics, corsets and shoes. Even in comedic scenarios, not once did his impersonations veer in the slightest toward farce. And he kept a stubbornly cryptic aura. Each time he was pressed about his personal life, he invariably replied, "I am not gay, I just like pearls."

Drag itself, however, remains vulnerable to fickle societal disposition. Even after (what is it now, the hundredth season of) RuPaul's Drag Race, it still has to evade prejudices by toggling between earnestness and humor. But along the fringes, drag sought its own legitimacy through 'beauty pageants' in the 1960s. A behind-the-scenes snapshot of the Miss All-America Camp Beauty Pageant was shown in Frank Simon's documentary "The Queen", which premiered at the Cannes Film Festival in 1968 and restored by art house film distribution company Kino Lorber in 2019. The film overall is revealing of the audacity it took to have been a drag queen Pre-Stonewall. But time has granted added relevance to the coronation scene, which appears again in the 1991 Jenny Livingston documentary "Paris is Burning". In it, third runner-up Crystal LaBeija storms off the stage, ranting that the pageant's outcome was rigged. She delivers a fiery diatribe about how systemic racial bias prevented black and hispanic drag queens from taking the crown.

A few years later, the first pageant dedicated to people of color was announced: "Crystal & Lottie LaBeija presents the first annual House of Labeija Ball" at W115th Street. Drag 'houses'—such as Paris and Burger Dupree's House of Dupree, Angie Xtravaganza and Hector Crespo's House of Xtravaganza—formed surrogate family units to shelter marginalized queer and trans 'children'. The Harlem balls became the podiums on which these houses competed in discursive categories patterned from fashion locution, which yielded the grandiloquent posing they called "Vogue" after the magazine. It was seen outside the balls for the first time when voguer Willi Ninja appeared in the Malcolm McLaren (1946-2010) music video for "Deep in Vogue" in 1989. The following year, the dance would shine under a global spotlight like no other.

———————————

In LA's San Fernando Valley, the Wizarding World of Harry Potter theme park materialized over land once cradling the Universal Ampitheatre, the setting of great concerts by Toto, Bette Midler, Sting, and Donna Summer whose show was recorded for her 1978 double album "Live and More". But on September 6, 1990, no one in the filled-to-capacity venue could have guessed they would witness one of the most memorable performances in all of pop music history.

It was the night of the seventh annual MTV Video Music Awards. Reporters, pop superstars, and music industry moguls had been there for hours, grandstanding for the pre-show hoopla and yawning through interminable acceptance speeches. Still, the air was heavy with anticipation. Closing out the ceremonies was the year's most nominated artist. It had to be worth the wait, right? It was.

The stage was revealed to be a replica of an 18th century French salon while a familiar spacey intro with high toms echoed from the speakers. Through enthusiastic cheers, Madonna made her entrance in a resplendent *robe à la française,* a sky-scraping wig, and multi-strand pearl choker. She paused on her mark, curtsied, then launched into the biggest dance hit of 1990—"Vogue". Despite the enormous dimensions and weight of the dress, Madonna intrepidly glided across the set, flanked by back-up singers (Donna de Lory and Niki Harris) and a coterie of dancers (all of whom were in the corresponding video directed by then in ascendance auteur David Fincher). So taut was the choreography—a curiously congruous blend of the minuet, vogueing, and raunchy humor—every move followed the music's progression. The TR-909 beat drop of kick, snare, and hi-hat cued Madonna to snap open a folded hand fan like she was cracking a whip just before uttering the song title. At another point she fanned herself in profile to the music's vibration.

For the past six months, "Vogue" had been ruling the airwaves, clubs, and charts in over thirty countries. It debuted in March via WQHT 97.1 FM radio in New York, was certified double platinum by the Recording Industry Association of America (RIAA) in June, and has since sold upwards of six million copies worldwide. From a budget of the most threadbare of shoestrings, Shep Pettibone and Madonna composed and produced it as the B-side to her next single, "Keep It Together", at the behest of Warner Brothers head of dance music Craig Kostich.

A prolific producer and remixer, Pettibone was ubiquitous from the 1980s to the 1990s, remixing singles for pop headliners and innumerable lesser known dance music artists. Pettibone and Madonna collaborated on several other singles and albums—most significantly "You Can Dance" (1987), "The Immaculate Collection" (1990) and the criminally underrated "Erotica" (1992)—up until he eventually retired from the industry altogether. "Vogue" was recorded at a makeshift 24-track basement studio on W. 56th Street where, Pettibone said, Madonna delivered her track and chorus vocals from a closet that had been converted into an audio booth. To the best of his recollection, it was a fairly quick process since the singer had always been a "one-take" artist, and he never needed to punch up her phrasing or correct tonal problems. The insertion of the oft-chanted middle eight, naming Old Hollywood celebrities, was decided and written on the spot. Upon hearing the final cut—an infectious 116 BPM house music masterpiece—Warner Brothers executives instantly agreed this was too good for a B-side.

It was released as a standalone and shoehorned into her 1990 "I'm Breathless" album to support the motion picture "Dick Tracy" in which she starred with Warren Beatty and Al Pacino. The choreography for the tour was by Vincent Paterson. But the voguing itself is attributed to dancers who brought authenticity to the proceedings—José Gutiérrez and Luis Camacho Xtravaganza, both of the House of Extravaganza. Still, its stance as a paean to ball culture and defiance of the anguish brought on by the AIDS epidemic is sometimes overlooked. The song actually opens in abject bleakness telling listeners that heartache is everywhere and proposing the dancefloor as an escape. Its rallying cry of "life's a ball" alludes to a party as well as the Harlem balls. Her MTV performance is even pointedly lip synched in the manner of drag.

In the lead up to the awards night, Madonna's team was convinced it was an occasion to push the upcoming "Keep It Together". The prevailing sense was that "Vogue" had already been done to death—live in front of close to two million fans in eleven countries during her just concluded world tour, and in the nonstop rotation of its black-and-white music video on MTV. Here's where things get murky. The tour's choreographer and co-director Paterson says the 'Marie Antoinette' performance had been his idea. A different anecdote contends that sometime during the Nice leg of the tour, Madonna latched on to the concept during a game of charades between her and her troupe when the film "Dangerous Liaisons" came up.

A searing tale of the amoral and treacherous schemes of the French aristocracy, the 1988 Stephen Frears motion picture starring Glenn Close, Michelle Pfeiffer, and John Malkovich was translated for the screen by Christopher Hampton from his own 1985 play *"Les liaisons dangereuses",* itself an adaptation of a 1782 French novel of the same name by Pierre Choderlos de Laclos (1741-1803). Among its many laurels was an Academy Award for Best Costume Design for James Acheson. It must be mentioned however that he had taken creative license in rolling the look back by twenty years to the 1760s. Fashions had drastically changed to more relaxed silhouettes by the story's original time frame. But Acheson rightfully argued that structured gowns are far more befitting aristocratic bearing than the looser chemises of the later era. Given how lush the costumes were in design and construction, few quibbled.

The outfit Madonna selected for her MTV awards appearance was pulled from the Warner Brothers costume department, previously worn by Close as the malevolent Marquise Isabelle de Merteuil. The front of a *robe à la française* doesn't (and isn't meant to) close entirely, rather, pinned to a stomacher as lavishly embroidered as the petticoat, which is supported underneath by wide panniers. Its narrow elbow-length sleeves are trimmed with ribbons and lace. Acheson's design is also rather uncommon since such a gown in this shade of ivory would have called for more color contrast in the embroidery and details. Existing examples of these dresses are of rare 1700s Chinese silk with a damask pattern, accomplished by reversing the weave structure so both the warp and weft floats are visible on the same surface. Though European in appearance, the weight and selvedge-to-selvedge width of these fabrics betray them as imported from China, undoubtedly via the East India companies operating out of England, France, and Holland.

Meanwhile, Madonna's number reverberated in the succeeding years. In 2013, Sal Cinquemani at Slant magazine placed it at the top of his list of "The 20 Greatest MTV Video Music Awards Performances of All Time". Mackenzie Dunn at Best Life Online in 2019 ranked it second in "The 25 Most Memorable MTV VMA Performances of All Time" (bested only by Madonna's "Like a Virgin" debut in 1984). As late as 2021, it took first place in E Entertainment's "The Most OMG VMA Performances We're Still Talking About", and was included in Nylon magazine's list of moments that "changed pop music forever", by Stefanee Wang.

The particulars of Madonna's rise and conquest of all she surveyed have been inexhaustible media fodder since she proclaimed her mission statement to "rule the world" on TV's American Bandstand in January 1984. Every song, album, outfit, every night on the town or morning jog in the park with fitness trainer Rob Parr was news. Any present day doubts over the irrational hysteria surrounding the artist may be allayed by a reminder that media outlets deployed a squadron of helicopters to Malibu in attempts to secure footage of her wedding to first husband actor Sean Penn in 1985.

Earlier that same year, Jack Skow (1932-2021) wrote a cover feature for the May issue of Time magazine in which he coined the term "Wanna-Be's" describing the legions of girls and young women who copied her looks. Shortly after, a "Madonna Look Alike Contest" launched "Madonnaland", the Macy's in-store boutique shilling cropped sweaters and accessories like crucifix earrings and rubber bangles at around $4. An only-in-New-York aside, Andy Warhol (1928-1987) was a judge in the contest. By the following decade, many articles purported that Madonna's stranglehold on pop culture was "over", contradicted by the regularity with which the assertion was being made and that ink and air time were being spent to do so.

Wherever Madonna was, controversy was mere steps behind. She elicits fervent admiration and vitriol, the former of which can sometimes be backhanded, and the latter often inordinately misogynistic (and of late, smacks of ageism). In over a century of Forbes, she was the first female entrepreneur to be plastered on the cover (October 1990). Appended to the main caption— "America's Smartest Business Woman?"—the question mark is a précis of the establishment's (and yes, even the public's) feelings of what to make of this human firestorm. Some of the pushback was fueled by her persistent provocations. Her incendiary music and videos kept inflating moral indignation while stoking the flames of fascination with a poker aimed squarely at America's most sensi-tive triggers: sex, religion, and race. And those sparks erupted into conflagrations that would've consumed lesser mortals.

Fashion and dance are truly the most powerful artillery in Madonna's considerable arsenal. Her early training as a dancer was the sturdy foundation on which her singular brand was built. At age 15, she started late at the Rochester School of Ballet where openly gay owner and teacher Christopher Flynn (1931-1990), a former naval officer, became a supportive mentor. With his help, Madonna earned a four-year dance scholarship to the University of Michigan (Est. 1817), which required her to attend an hour and a half technique class twice daily along with rehearsals. Some time later, she auditioned for and won a spot for six dancers (out of three hundred aspirants) to participate in an American Dance Festival workshop in Durham. She was spotted there by dance legend and Martha Graham protege Pearl Lang (1921-2009), who took her on as a student. It wasn't long before Flynn was urging Madonna to "stop wasting your time in the sticks" and hightail it to New York.

For a 1985 interview, Flynn said the young Madonna had "a wonderful dancer's figure, slender, shapely and long in the leg." Reciprocally, she has mentioned Flynn whenever asked about those impressionable Michigan years. On several instances, she has publicly credited him for more than the building blocks of her skills. It was Fynn, she said, who broadened her worldview, cultivating her appreciation for art, classical music, literature, and opera. But of greater import was his imbuing her with self-worth. She said, "He was the first human being who made me feel good about myself. He brought me to my first gay club, a place where I finally felt at home."

David Bowie, before her, inarguably created the template of the morphing pop star. But it may be reckoned Madonna had a cannier handle on the zeitgeist, gender politics, fashion, art, imagery and performance. And recklessly dosed with the taboo and the profane her oeuvre can't ever be matched in any foreseeable future. In the beginning, her East Village thrift store style was congruent to the downtown vibe of her eponymous first album. But for the "Material Girl" video, she and director Mary Lambert commuted her look uptown by recreating the Marilyn Monroe (1926-1962) "Diamonds Are a Girl's Best Friend" number choreographed by Jack Cole (1911-1974) for Howard Hawks' (1896-1977) motion picture version of "Gentlemen Prefer Blondes" (1953, previously a 1949 stage musical). The Kenny Ortega-modified number unveiled a film star Madonna in a duplicate of the pink gown worn in the picture by Monroe. The original designer, Travilla (1920-1990), was reportedly miffed over not being consulted.

But it was her live concerts where Madonna achieved the finest blending of dance and fashion. Per Billboard's Boxscore chart that sums up concert tour and live entertainment attendance and gate receipts, Madonna is the highest-grossing solo touring artist of all time. Concerts used to be fairly predictable, with rare exceptions like Bowie's "Glass Spider" and Pink Floyd's "A Momentary Lapse of Reason", both 1987. For a couple of hours, an artist or band just warbled their hits as recorded. Seasoned musicians may vary, extend, or shorten sections of their songs live, but audiences pretty much just got what they expected. And at the very pinnacle of her fame (or even way after), hordes would've shown up to watch Madonna do just that. Instead, with "Blond Ambition" she transfigured the pop concert into full blown theatrical spectacles. She planted the seeds of transgression in the use of the masculine form "Blond" and they germinated during the empowering "Express Yourself" boss look of monocle and Jean Paul Gaultier men's pinstripe suit. But on the jacket, two chest-level vertical slits partially reveal what's underneath. Taking it off, the now iconic Gaultier corset with conical bra is displayed, her shot across the bow on prosaic notions of gender conformity and male superiority.

Artistic explorations of androgyny and bondage is the nexus between Madonna and Gaultier. Their propensity for going against the grain strengthened it. The singer had already been seen twice in Gaultier: a black knee-length dress over leggings at the January 1985 American Music Awards, then in March of the same year, a white version for the premiere of "Desperately Seeking Susan", the motion picture she starred in with Rosanna Arquette, directed by Susan Seidelman. Two months later, Madonna reappeared in both for Rolling Stone magazine: white on the cover, black for an inside spread entitled "Boys of Summer", shot by Herb Ritts (1952-2002). She did get around to asking the designer to create the costumes for the tour and Gaultier was only too thrilled to do so. Two conical bra corsets were made: one in salmon, another in gold. Fashionistas were already well acquainted with the design (an exaggeration of lingerie label Maidenform's Chansonette bra 1940s-1950s) since the *enfant terrible* had introduced it back in 1982 and incorporated the look in dresses for his Fall/Winter 1984-1985 Barbès collection.

Another clever bit in the tour's costuming were the bowler hats, black corsets, harnesses, and biker shorts in "Keep It Together", seen by many as a nod to Milena Canonero's design for the Stanley Kubrick (1928-1999) thriller "A Clockwork Orange" (1972). But the choreography suggests a closer affinity to Fosse. Even the Windsor chairs are out of his playbook (those have also popped up in "Open Your Heart", for both video and live in the "Who's That Girl" world tour 1987, as well as in "Bye Bye Baby" at "The Girlie Show" world tour 1993).

Since the seminal Blond Ambition, critics and fans have equated Madonna's live tours as masterclasses in showmanship. And other artists thereafter could only hope to come close to her ever more elaborate thematic acts, complex dance routines, multiple set and costume changes, special effects, not to mention those plethora of fashion, dance, and art references. And her costumes, often overseen by stylist Arianne Phillips, have only become more high fashion. For just one number—"Justify My Love"—in "The Girlie Show", lavish black-and-white Edwardian costumes were adapted from the "Ascot Gavotte" scene in George Cukor's (1899-1983) "My Fair Lady". To accomplish that, MGM lent Madonna the originals by Sir Cecil Beaton (1904-1980) who had created them for the stage and film versions, winning a Tony in 1957, then an Academy Award in 1964.

Also for that tour (inspired by the 1941 Edward Hopper, 1882-1967, oil-on-canvas "Girlie Show") Madonna sported tails, top hat, and walking stick à la Marlene Dietrich (1901-1992) from the 1930 Josef von Sternberg (1894-1969) motion picture "Morocco" while also evoking the emcee character from "Cabaret" when she announces, "Ladies and gentlemen, step right up. The greatest show on earth is about to begin. We have dancing girls. We have dancing boys". She followed that number in a striped shirt reminiscent of Gene Kelly's "Anchors Aweigh" look.

For 2008's "Sticky & Sweet Tour", ravishing outfits were provided by Tom Ford, Riccardo Tisci for Givenchy Haute Couture, Roberto Cavalli, with assorted footwear and accessories from Chanel, Stella McCartney, Yves Saint Laurent, Miu Miu, and Dior Homme. For "Rebel Heart" 2015, there were coats by Prada, bandolier vests and masks by Nicolas Jebran, custom J. Brand jeans, a flapper dress by Jeremy Scott for Moschino, and a matador outfit by Fausto Puglisi. The lace and jacquard bodysuit under a multi-tiered crepe de Chine skirt, fringed silk shawl and flamenco hat were by Alessandro Michele for Gucci.

"Vogue" itself would figure in fresh musical and sartorial takes throughout Madonna's tours—notably during 2004's "Re-Invention Tour" for which Christian Lacroix reinterpreted the "Dangerous Liaisons" look with a bejeweled bustier and a one-arm gauntlet, fishnet stockings, and knee-high boots. In the 2012 "MDNA" tour, she was in an update of Gautier's corset and suit: a metallic silver and patent leather coiled bra and torso cage framing a crisp white shirt and tie, and opera-length black gloves. To date, "Vogue" has lost none of its potency. As of 2020, it has surpassed 100 million streams on Spotify, while its official video has been viewed over 150 million times on YouTube.

Goaded into being auctioned off to a roomful of squealing women, Adam Garcia as Kevin O'Donnell slowly stripteases to INXS's "I Need You Tonight" in the 2000 picture "Coyote Ugly". But the spin and knee slide across the bar was only choreographed by Travis Payne on the day of the shoot, after director David McNally belatedly learned that Adam was a trained dancer. And it could've been done with less panache. "After one take, I was directed to tone it down because it looked too professional," chuckles Adam. Of course it did. The playful charm was all Adam. The swagger? That came from eight shows a week of having portrayed Tony Manero in the West End musical iteration of "Saturday Night Fever".

At that point Adam, the son of a Colombian father and an Australian mother, had barely been off his feet since he tripped into ballet classes at age six. He'd tagged along with his best friend, whose interest waned while Adam's had just begun. "I wanted to continue with the classes, but the studio was a bit too far away," he recalls. So he went to one closer to home in the outskirts of Sydney—the Dumbrell Academy (renamed Capital Performance Studios). Mulling over his youthful exploits, he admits, "I never thought of making it a career. I danced for fun," made more enjoyable after he learned tap from Dein Perry. Ballet had bestowed Adam with technique and discipline while tap gave his moves dimension until he was "the very instrument for making noise, improvising beats."

His first paid gig was tap dancing in front of Sydney town hall for director Baz Luhrman. From there he picked up more work to earn cash even after he was already at university. But it was Perry, "a real father figure and mentor to me," who gave him a major break. "I grew up with him and we've been very good friends ever since. We'd done a few things together, so when he said, 'Wanna do a tap show?' I agreed because I was crap at university anyway. I was just playing pool, basically." Perry brought Adam into the Australian musical "Hot Shoe Shuffle", which was exported to the West End in 1994. Despite performing in one of the world's theater capitals, Adam was unmindful of seriously pursuing a career. "The show was just a six-month deferment from university," he says. "But a year and a half later, I was still in London." Believing there were already many other actors and dancers vying for the same roles, he was sure he'd end up back-packing through Europe before going back to Australia. Instead, one show kept leading to another, until another happened to be "Saturday Night Fever".

But landing the part was no strut down the footpath. "I think I auditioned seven or eight times," confides Adam. There was dissension over who should take on the white polyester mantle of Tony Manero, whether they should find a 'name' actor-dancer or go with an unknown. Director and choreographer Arlene Phillips fought for Adam.

At one of the call backs, a producer intimated the role was practically his. Except not quite. Because another producer kept holding more auditions. Of course, the part did go to Adam. "I really owe Arlene a lot for taking a chance on me," he says, repaying her by strutting head on into the part. But that also meant learning a different way of dancing. He says, "It took a while for me to master the hustle." Since partnered dancing wasn't exactly his forte, he thought he would never get it. The songs too, originally composed for a higher pitch, took extra vocal coaching. And because he had to sing, dance, and be onstage for every scene, Adam needed moments to pause else he might run out of steam or throw up halfway through the show.

It didn't help that their biggest set piece—an enormous facsimile of the Verrazano Narrows Bridge—experienced typical technical glitches. It broke down, twice. "When that happened during the bench scene where the Tony and Stephanie characters are having a heart-to-heart talk, we ad libbed until the bridge finally moved completely in place," laughs Adam. Costumes by Andy Edwards were more dependable, designed to look like 'real' clothes, reminiscent enough of the disco era without being outmoded. Edwards used materials with Lycra, viscose, and hydrocarbon for flexibility and the constitution to absorb sweat. The shoes had reinforced heels to withstand nightly abuse. Of the iconic white suit, Adam says "We had four made, one of which I got to keep and is now in my mum's house in Australia." Box office receipts were brisk. After opening in 1998 at the London Palladium (Est. 1910), reviews were as mixed as those for the motion picture. Variety acknowledged Adam's "indefatigable athleticism", while James Whitaker of the Daily Mirror wrote that the show had "some of the best dancing ever seen on West End". More impressively, Adam was nominated for the year's Laurence Olivier Award for Best Actor in a Musical. And, his single of "Night Fever" was a U.K. smash.

After the fever subsided, acting parts came his way. But dance has always been a constant. In the mystery series "Agatha Christie's Marple", he played Raymond Starr, gigolo and dance instructor. In 2000, he strapped on his industrial strength Blundstones for "Bootmen", a film directed by Perry. They re-teamed again for an Australian and U.K. tour of "Tap Dogs", a display of virtuoso tap in eighty minutes. Five years later, he was in the English National Opera's version of "On the Town". In 2009, Adam was empaneled to judge "Got to Dance", one of the many televised amateur dance competitions mushrooming everywhere (such as "Dancing with the Stars", "So You Think You Can Dance", and "America's Best Dance Crew").

A year later, he stepped into Gene Kelly's shoes for a stage revival tour of "Singin' in the Rain" across Australia. "It was an exciting time. I just got married (to Nathalia Chubin) with a baby (Arya Storm Diana) on the way, and I was doing this amazing show." The country was hyped over the return of the prodigal son, as well as the novelty of thousands of liters of water spraying onstage to simulate rain. Back in 1985 when splashy special effects were scarce, there was a West End musical practically identical to the motion picture, save minor tweaks. The Arthur Freed (1894-1973) and Nacio Herb Brown (1896-1964) standard "You Were Meant for Me", composed in 1929, was used in the picture for the step ladder scene, but excised from the musical. It was reinstated in the revival, and as Don Lockwood, Adam was in the middle of it when disaster struck. "I was taking a gliding step behind the ladder when this feeling like an electric shock shot up my left leg!" he recalls. The subsequent medical evaluation showed he had sustained a "Grade two muscle tear, twelve centimeters, along my calf," says Adam. The doctors gave him a window of recovery of six to twelve weeks with 70% chance of recurrence. He had no choice but to withdraw during the Melbourne run.

This year, for Jonathan Church's new "42nd Street" (choreographed by Bill Deamer), Adam tapped through the character of imperious director Julian Marsh who pressures an ingénue into becoming a star. But for Adam, "A dancer is really 'watchable' when he gives in to how the music is making him feel, just letting go, and conveying that through movement." He says a sense of musicality is vital, "not only in the sense of keeping time and doing the choreography, but feeling the music and where the moves should be. I think that the rhythm, tone, style, and nuance of a piece of music are why we have different dances. People hear, feel, and express music differently."

———————————

Creative bankruptcy is often blamed for the revivals, remakes, reboots, franchise films and series clogging streaming services and cineplexes. Another suspected culprit is precarious economic conditions. After all, why willingly risk millions if one can invest in familiar intellectual properties? But, that this is a 21st century issue, or even in any way unusual, are somewhat misapprehensions.

All art is loomed from precedents. Consider the 2023 "42nd Street" Adam was in. That's a revival of the fabulous 1980 musical (about a musical), the victorious final act by director and choreographer Gower Champion before he expired the day the show opened. It was based on the 1933 Lloyd Beacon motion picture, itself adapted from the Bradford Ropes (1905-1966) novel (1932). Songs for the musical not only came from the film's soundtrack by Harry Warren (1893-1981) and Al Dubin (1891-1945) but some composed for other films. Hollywood, Broadway, and the West End, literature, dance and fashion have been plundering their own vaults and riffing off each other for years. Their annals are eidetic images in a dizzying, seemingly endless hall of mirrors.

A look at West End's 2005 "Billy Elliot: The Musical" (from which actor Tom Holland came) bounces back to the 2000 picture (directed by Stephen Daldry, starring Jamie Bell at thirteen) then back further to a reading of a play by Lee Hall called "Dancer". Hall drafted his own experience of growing up an outsider, but conceded his struggle to become a writer wouldn't be visually compelling. It was when he had, "this vision of a little kid running down a back lane wearing a tutu" that he came up with the tale of a boy yearning to become a ballet dancer against the backdrop of a hard scrabble pit village. The film's epilogue of an adult Billy (played by Adam Cooper) in a performance attended by his father and brother is yet again a refraction. In the picture, the show Cooper as Billy is doing is the very real production of Matthew Bourne's gender-swapped and slightly rearranged "Swan Lake". That show had hugely popular runs on the West End, Broadway, and in several European and Asian countries.

Way before Sam Rockwell laced up in Bob Fosse's La Ray footwear in the "Fosse/Verdon" series, Fosse directed 1979's "All that Jazz" and laid bare some of his own sins—narcissism not least of them. Via his simulacrum Roy Scheider (1932-2008) (with his girlfriend Ann Reinking basically playing herself), Fosse strung together sequences resembling his life, structured like Fellini's own exercise in self-analysis "8½". It opens with the title song over a stage rehearsal, borrowed from (and rumored to have been Fosse's effort to out-Chorus Line) Michael Bennett. That rehearsal scene was appropriated yet again by Sylvester Stallone to open "Staying Alive" his critically-reviled 1983 "Saturday Night Fever" sequel, in which Travolta's Tony Manero is upgraded by choreographers Dennon and Sayhber Rawles from weekend to working dancer in a fictional musical with costumes by Bob Mackie.

Fosse's legacy endures. The 1989 music video of Paula Abdul's "Cold Hearted" (directed by David Fincher) recreated a scene from "All That Jazz". Panoplies of his choreography never fail to entertain. The 3-act revue "Fosse" ran from 1999 to 2001. Then, his "Dancin'" was revived in 2023 by original cast member Wayne Cliento (who was also in "A Chorus Line"), costumes by Reid Bartelme and Harriet Jung. Originally choreographed by Fosse in 1978 (except the "Yankee Doodle Disco" number by Christopher Chadman), the new production of this unvarnished dance spectacle was generally well-received, though Jesse Green called it both "thrilling" and "frustrating" in his New York Times review this year "…a Wiggle is Worth a Thousand Words".

As for "A Chorus Line"? An uninspired film version was directed by Richard Attenborough (1923-2014) in 1985, which at least added flashbacks and the scene of hundreds of hopeful dancers queuing into the theater. Making his way toward backstage, headshot in hand, Matt West as Bobby asks someone who'd been cut, "What's he (the director) looking for?" To which the exiting young man quips, "Baryshnikov." A revival in 2006 was directed by (the original's co-choreographer) Bob Avian, with (original cast member) Baayork Lee recreating Bennett's routines. After it closed two years later, a making of the revival documentary, "Every Little Step" mimics the 1985 film's opening of thousands of dancers anxiously lining the street for the open-call audition, fretfully chewing their lower lips, and no doubt wishing, "I hope I get it."

Today's preponderance of media platforms, abbreviated attention spans, and fractured fandoms have made it imperative to keep making content programmed to pander. If it doesn't have meta callbacks, easter eggs, and a post credit cliffhanger or two, why bother? Sex says it sells. Nostalgia retorts hold its beer.

The sweetest music to the ears of potential theater investors has to be the nostalgia frontloaded "jukebox musical". In 1999, Phyllida Lloyd directed and Anthony Van Laast choreographed "Mamma Mia!" the flimsiest of excuses to revisit the Abba catalog. It nonetheless roused every full house to the 1976 disco classic "Dancing Queen" from the West End to Broadway to a movie adaptation in 2008. Two decades worth of memories from Billy Joel's discography was utilized to brilliant effect by Twyla Tharp in 2002's "Movin' Out". With a "piano man" Joel avatar singing from overhead, dancers on stage perform as 'characters' from the pop singer's songs strung together as a single narrative. Soon, a cavalcade of similar crowd pleasers based on popular music had everyone dancing in the aisles: "Jersey Boys" (2005, featuring the songs of Frankie Valli and The Four Seasons), "On Your Feet!" (2015, Gloria Estefan), "Head Over Heels" (2015, the Go-Gos), "Summer: The Donna Summer Musical" (2017), "MJ The Musical" (2022, Michael Jackson), and so many others. Unfortunately, the biggest of hits aren't guaranteed to fill seats. Tharp tried to repeat "Movin' Out" with Frank Sinatra songs for "Come Fly with Me", but it didn't quite take off. And despite having absolute stompers like "September", "Fantasy", and "Boogie Wonderland" by Earth, Wind & Fire, "Hot Feet" the 2006 musical conceived, directed, and choreographed by Maurice Hines got the cold shoulder.

Too many intangibles obscure the view of any direct path to a surefire hit, which doesn't prevent people from trying to find one. But in the trying, a show may be regarded, fairly or not, as artificial, even exploitative. Independent companies are more likely to incubate fresh ideas under creatively authentic circumstances. Exempting soloists, amateur collectives, Broadway, touring, amusement parks, cruises or industrial shows, there are over a thousand dance companies in New York. Of these, The Bang Group, forged on the professional rapport of David Parker and Jeff Kazin, has thrived on consistently clever and entertaining work since 1995.

Not that it's been smooth sailing for either of them. David was discouraged by his parents from wanting to be a dancer. "I made do by taping coins to the bottoms of my school shoes and improvised with my own idea of tap dancing," he recalls. "When I was fifteen, I saw dances from MGM musicals and it was as if they were personally beckoning me. I spent every weekend in revival movie houses paying rapt attention to golden age Hollywood musicals and imitating them at home as closely as I could. As soon as I got my driver's license I secretly went to a studio I found in the Yellow Pages and started learning tap and ballet. I never thereafter thought about doing anything else." But in 1980, a Tharp show opened David's eyes to doing more. He says, "I realized then that merging various dance forms could break out of musicals, that it could become a whole theatrical language ancient yet modern, smart yet hilarious. The next year, I studied with her company and resolved to be both dancer and choreographer."

Jeff, ironically enough, found his footing after giving up on his dream. "Since age six I wanted to dance on Broadway. I spent three years auditioning for every show that would see me and was cast exactly twice in a couple of awful productions." He was at a particularly low point when David broached the topic of working together. Jeff admits, "Migrating from musical theater dancing to the contemporary concert stage was difficult, but destined." David continues, "I found Jeff to be a highly charismatic dancer. And after he saw some of my choreography, it was clear he understood what I was doing—rhythm as the organizing force and underlying motor. Our dances don't need tap shoes to exist, it's visual as well as aural. If you don't hear it, you can see it. I like it both ways."

An essential piece, "Slapstuck" typifies the layered levels of their repertoire: a wordless dialogue of attraction, rejection, struggle for dominance, and surrender; an adept visual excursion across different dances; and an unforced sense of humor. Fundamental too are the kinetic sounds of footwork and punctuations by the contact and ripping apart of the inventive, velcroed costumes by Jeroen Teunissen.

David recalls reaching out to Teunissen (who was then half of Dutch label Rozema/Teunissen) when his Transient collection for the Fashion Institute Arnhem (Est. 1998) was featured in an issue of The New Yorker. "We were looking for costumes that would be essential to the creation of a work and not just clothing for it." Jeff adds, "I don't think Jeroen ever created costumes for dance before, but his use of social behavior as the foundation of his designs was synonymous to what we had in mind, this coming together of disparate elements. But there was a learning curve. The Velcro outfits were genius but required a lot of trial runs—more strength needed here, flexibility there, what material gives a modicum of ventilation, etc. He and David will discuss the concept for something we're working on and very often Jeroen creates something that works right out of the gate."

The complex rhythmic exchange of body slamming, attachments and separations, lifts and inversions that became "Slapstuck" has been widely seen in different countries, and to the delight of the culturati in Philadelphia, San Francisco, New York, and other cities nationwide. In 2011, the Institute of Contemporary Art Boston (Est. 1936) invited The Bang Group to stage an interactive version where bubble wrap was handed out to the kids in the audience so they could participate in the noise making. Everyone had a blast.

Closing in on its thirtieth year, the company's seven full-time dancers (up to twenty for bigger shows like its annual holiday offering "Nut/Cracked") continue, says Jeff, "our purposeful mixing of tap, jazz, ballet, disco, flamenco, and modern to dispel any preconceived notions of what dance is or what it can do." Needless to say, a sequel to "Slapstuck" is forthcoming.

———————————

Repeatedly extracting from the same sources may yield uneven results but remakes and revivals are still seen as, at least, hedged bets. And some productions do aim high. After being hailed an art house darling for his 2017 picture "Call Me By Your Name", director Luca Guadagnino undertook a redo of Dario Argento's 1977 cult classic "Suspiria". The horror-giallo amalgam's setting of a supposedly prestigious Freiburg ballet academy was so negligible that Guadagnino thought he could put it (and the Cold War era of the original's release) to better use. Alongside some psychological malarkey were themes of religion, motherhood, and female power. But the real humdingers were the dancing and the costumes.

Particularly intriguing is how dance isn't used to reveal internal emotional states, rather an outward expression of will. Here dance is literally magic, the very means by which the academy's coven of witches cast their spells. Belgian–French choreographer Damien Jalet was commissioned for those scenes because of his 2013 *parkour nocturne* at the Louvre—*"Les médusées"*. Referencing both the mythological gorgon as well as the French verb for being stunned into paralysis, it was performed by thirty dancers amid the statues of the museum's sculpture rooms as a meditation on motion and stasis. Jalet said Argento's "Suspiria" was an inspiration for *"Les médusées",* which he subsequently used as the basis of his six-minute witches' sabbath "Volk" for the remake's blood-soaked finale.

According to press statements for the picture, he and Guadagnino wanted to bring an elegance to the "technical, mathematical" ways the body contorted. He said, screenwriter David Kajganich (who'd cited German expressionist dancers Mary Wigman, 1886-1973, and Pina Bausch, 1940-2009) described it in the script as being "very chaotic", but Jalet added touches of Indonesian dance to make it "ritualized," a staccato of abrupt stops and starts, and an arm styling that is both "intimate and harshly linear." Most of the actresses were professional dancers, except Dakota Johnson and Mia Goth, both of whom went through daily eight-hour rehearsals. Johnson, whose character is supposed to be a newbie, also trained a full year prior.

For her research, costume designer Giulia Piersanti perused back issues of German magazine Sibylle (Est. 1956) and old Rainer Werner Fassbinder (1945-1982) pictures. She also studied the art of Louise Bourgeois (1911-2010) and came up with fresh prints for custom-made blouses, dresses, and scarves, as well as actress Tilda Swinton's body-skimming floral caftan. The opening scene in a Midwest American farm was dressed in pastel jackets, sweaters, and skirts before traveling to a 1970s Germany of somber yet intense hues. Piersanti's corded costumes in crimson for the frightening climax insinuates the use of knots in the occult as well as the visual suggestion of dripping blood. Unfortunately that bright shot at the end may have arrived too late. While no one really knew what to expect, the original's stunning visuals and super saturated colors were always going to be a problem for the remake. Damned if you copy, damned if you don't. Guadagnino didn't. It underperformed at the box office, deemed too ponderous to be scary. Of its shortcomings, the lack of vision was not among them.

Another common tactic is marrying an already well-liked piece with a star name. While there are a few genuine thespians—Laura Linney, Angela Lansbury (1925-2022)—who've had no problem shuttling from stage to screen, some try to gain respectability that can only be attained in the theater. To wit, Daniel Radcliffe, who's spent a portion of his career refusing to be stereotyped, immersed himself in the role of J. Pierrepont Finch to demonstrate "How to Succeed in Business Without Really Trying". But for the business of show, Radcliffe tried. And try hard he did. Radcliffe signed on to the revival in 2011 from director-choreographer Rob Ashford. It was a fiftieth anniversary commemoration of Frank Loesser's (1910-1969) musical (1961), inspired by the satiric Shepherd Mead (1914-1994) book of the same name, subtitled "The Dastard's Guide to Fame and Fortune" from 1952, and adapted into a 1967 film featuring many of the stage cast.

Even while filming the Harry Potter franchise's last installment, Radcliffe was already taking brutal dance and vocal coaching. When the fruits of his labors were displayed in full at the Al Hirschfeld theater (formerly Martin Beck, Est. 1924) it became clear he brought a couple more important things to the show. In essaying the conniving Pierrepont-Finch, Radcliffe's endearing interpretation is a departure from previous nakedly amoral portrayals. And, his star power drew a crush of young fans who may not have otherwise ever gone to a musical.

The dapper yet pliant men's suits and pretty women's dresses were designed by Catherine Zuber to inhabit a 1960s corporate setting. But what fixed everyone's attention was the lead's peacock blue bow tie, visible from the nosebleed sections, and throughout his adventures scaling up from lowly window washer to vice president of advertising. That it was because of an ad agency this accessory was there in the first place is one of those serendipitous flukes that's now Broadway lore. It had been part of Radcliffe's wardrobe, art directed by Serino/Coyne, for the show's sharply colored posters. Everyone thought it was so striking Radcliffe should wear it on the show. It ended up being the memento Radcliffe put up for bid to benefit the annual Broadway Cares/Equity Fights AIDS' Easter Bonnet fundraiser. By the time Darren Criss took over for Radcliffe, the bow tie had taken on a life of its own. They gave Criss one in purple. Nick Jonas followed in the role and got one in jade.

Also that year, the Jeff Calhoun-directed and Christopher Gattelli-choreographed "Newsies" had its out-of-town tryout at the Paper Mill Playhouse (Est. 1934). It was an adaptation of the 1992 directorial debut of choreographer Kenny Ortega for Disney. In both, when a phalanx of news boys (led by Christian Bale on film, Jeremy Jordan on stage) burst into a number while on a work strike, the *a priori* knowledge of song and dance being endemic to musicals is needed to suspend disbelief. That's less an issue in the next Bale fronted picture, "Swing Kids" because dance itself is the plot.

Shows about dance competitions in situ have a tinge of verisimilitude that make excellent gateways for the uninitiated, especially since these often center on an underdog with whom the audience can identify. From that subgenre came the Baz Lurhmann-directed (from his own 1984 play) "Strictly Ballroom" in which classically trained Paul Mercurio played a man dead set on winning the Pan-Pacific Grand Prix Dancing Championship, but finds his maverick style at odds with the standards of the Australian Dancing Federation. A new mix of John Paul Young's 1977 disco hit "Love Is in the Air" is used for the obligatory last dance. Divided critics didn't hamper its earning $11M.

Overkill is an understatement when it comes to Luhrmann's 2001 "Moulin Rouge", abundant as it was with costumes (designed by the director's wife Catherine Martin, and Angus Strathie), dancing (choreographed by John O'Connell), pop and classical music, high and low brow references, and more besides. Yet Luhrmann threw the bathroom and kitchen sinks in anyway. And it may as well have been edited with a Cuisinart. At its core are the bohemians of the Montmartre, with Nicole Kidman and Ewan McGregor giving nuance to their stock characters, courtesan with a heart of gold and impecunious poet. Not enough? Oh by the way, she's dying of consumption. So remote is this farrago from any plane of reality that objective scrutiny is to miss the point and just be trivial.

To the British Film Institute (Est. 1933), Luhrmann said the idea of "Moulin Rouge" came to him after witnessing a typically bonkers Bollywood musical in a picture palace in India. He recalled not understanding a word of dialogue yet being bowled over and sharing in the visceral reaction of the thousands around him. Luhrmann homaged Bollywood tropes with several scenes in his movie, and in the sampling of "Chamma Chamma" into the nonsensically titled "Hindi Sad Diamonds" number. From that high, the picture dips to despairing depths with "El Tango de Roxanne" (the Police's 1978 "Roxanne" filtered through "Tanguera", the 1958 composition of Mariano Mores, 1918-2016), guitar by José Feliciano, sung by McGreggor and Jacek Koman.

Like "Saturday Night Fever", however, "Moulin Rouge" works mostly as spectacle. If the pastiche of music and blitzkrieg of images don't cause epileptic seizures, they garble the picture's questionable aspects: a heroine with zero agency, degradation of women, sexual assault, cultural appropriation without representation, overacting. In 2018, the Boston tryout of "Moulin Rouge! The Musical" from Sydney-based Global Creatures promised to make it to New York, come what may. It did and there it still is.

At the 75th Festival de Cannes, Luhrmann premiered his biopic of Elvis Presley (1935-1977). At his peak, the baritone with the warm vocal register sold four million records on a paradoxical persona of wholesome boy-next-door and sexy rock-and-roll star. Critics had initially been dismissive of the Nashville upstart, wary of his country-pop sound and revolted by what the New York Daily News described as his "grunt and grind antics". To side step controversy, his now fabled 1956 appearance on The Ed Sullivan Show is said to have been deliberately shot from the waist up. The estimated sixty million Americans who tuned in and the wailing in-studio audience propelled advanced sales of "Love Me Tender" to the tune of a million copies.

For "Elvis", the duty of re-enacting the singer's pelvic exertions and famous sneer went to Austin Butler, while costuming him (along with thousands of extras) fell again to Martin. To custom craft many of the decades-spanning and requisite leather and rhinestone outfits, Martin reunited with fashion designer Miuccia Prada, who'd previously worked with Luhrmann and Martin on their 2013 "The Great Gatsby".

It's always been odd, this partnership between the unbridled
Luhrmann and the sedate Prada, whose cerebral wares were in kinship
with those by Helmut Lang and Jil Sander in the 1990s. On celluloid,
however, the director and the designer arrive at an accord over which
the glitterati gushed. Shoe designer Manolo Blahnik, who created
footwear for "Moulin Rouge", also contributed pieces here including a pair of two tone calf leather lace ups and toggle chukka boots,
which ruefully, wasn't in blue but cappuccino suede.

In footwear, it was undoubtedly 1948's Michael Powell (1905-1990)
and Emeric Pressburger (1902-1988) picture "The Red Shoes"
that prompted a million dancers to strap on pointe shoes. It defies
conventional categorization since it's fantasy, it's horror, it's a musical.
Except when it isn't. Meta before meta was a thing, it has multiple
realities collapsing into itself. It's based on the Hans Christian Andersen
(1805-1875) fairy tale, with a performance of "The Ballet of the Red
Shoes" within the movie. It stars Moira Shearer (1926-2006), a principal at Sadler's Wells Ballet. The Boris Lermontov character is alleged to
be a proxy for Diaghilev (Powell and Pressburger insisted he was based
on filmmaker Alexander Korda,1893-1956); while Massine himself is
in the cast as the maker of the titular footwear.

With straight-faced lines like—"Why do you want to dance?" to
which Shearer's character ripostes "Why do you want to live?" and a
poster that reads "Dance she must"—it's easy to see how it resonates
with those who are called to this life. Reams of learned theories have
been postulated on its themes and their supposed meanings. There is
a scene of Shearer leaving her hotel in a tiered and pleated azure blue
Jacques Fath (1912-1954) ball gown (the ballet costumes were by

Hein Heckroth, 1901–1970). She's wearing a crown. Not a tiara. A crown. She is driven along the scenic Moyenne Corniche to a villa where she ascends stone steps to meet Lermontov. Was this meant to symbolize her rise, only to be bookended later by her fall as punishment for her, a woman's, ambitions? About the only thing certain? That gown was spectacular.

Another pair of red flats made cinematic history in the Roger Vadim (1928–2000) picture *"Et Dieu…créa la femme"* (1956). To accent the wardrobe designed by Pierre Balmain (1914–1982), its star Brigitte Bardot, a trained ballerina, entreated shoemaker Rose Repetto to make them for her. Since 1947 dancers the world over have treasured the footwear in black boxes imprinted with the Repetto name in silver foil that came from a shop tucked away on rue de la Paix. Its proximity to Palais Garnier was convenient for performers, the same way Maison Clairvoy (Est. 1945) is preferred by the dancers at Moulin Rouge in Montmartre. In the UK, Freed produces custom pointe shoes worn by ballerinas everywhere. Now under Japanese fashion giant Onward Kashiyama, Freed began making shoes out of a Covent Garden basement in 1929, branching out to dance apparel in 1985.

Stateside, Gaynor Minden (Est 1993) treaded its own path by using polymer to mold its flats, which recover their shape after being slipped off. On Broadway, theater people rely on Times Square cobblers T.O. Dey. It had been in the business of orthopedic shoes in the 1920s, was acquired by Angelo Bifulco in the 1970s, then passed on to his sons Thomas and Gino. The next decade, the family concern ventured onto the stage with corrective, comfortable, and meticulously constructed footwear. Despite only having under twenty artisans on staff, custom shoes in the thousands are made for shows, celebrities on both coasts, and individuals with orthopedic problems.

Red also became a banner color for T.O. Dey after handcrafting designs by Gregg Barnes for the "Kinky Boots" musical (2012 tryout, 2013 on Broadway), directed and choreographed by Jerry Mitchell. With music by pop singer Cyndi Lauper and book by Harvey Fierstein, it was adapted from the 2005 British film comedy based on the true story of struggling Northamptonshire shoe factory W.J. Brooks Ltd, which avoided closure by marketing women's style shoes to men instead. Barnes credits the production of most (around 150 in all) of the shoes to T.O. Dey with some pieces by another Broadway footwear stalwart, Phil LaDuca.

As one might imagine, getting six inch stilettos to balance and tolerate the weight of male dancers while they're doing somersaults and splits was the conundrum. The thigh-high pair of the title was done in three leathers piped with black to make the red appear brighter—one that was foiled, another in crocodile, and a third in patent. After a couple of times heels broke during tryouts, a five and a half-inch steel shank was added, up the heel and bending down toward the ball of the foot, while the interiors were padded with high impact foam. Barnes has publicly admitted to extensive experimentation with materials and styles to get it right because as he's said, "Costumes should be built like iron maidens, but move like butterflies."

Making garments for dance can be irresistible to accomplished fashion designers. Gaultier has conceived over three hundred costumes for Régine Chopinot since they first met in 1983. A hundred thirty suits, gowns, and jaunty hip-huggers by *il maestro* Giorgio Armani lent a serene aesthetic to "Bernstein Dances", a dance revue based on the music of Leonard Bernstein by Hamburg Ballet's director John Neumeier. Fashion returned the compliment with the Comme des Garçons 2005 Printemps Collection from Rei Kawakubo who drew parallels to the strength of ballerinas and motorcycles in incongruently paired neoprene and saddle-stitched leather jackets with pink and white tutus. In 2006, Marc Jacobs created costumes for "Amoveo", the 35-minute ballet by Benjamin Millepied. Francisco Costa, creative director at Calvin Klein from 2003-2016, designed paneled pants and dresses in neutrals for fellow Brazilian Elisa Monte's "Slope of Enlightenment" in 2007. Isaac Mizrahi has contributed to many works by Tharp and Mark Morris. For the latter's 2022 Burt Bacharach and Hal David song-and-dance tribute "The Look of Love", he came up with close-to-the-body separates in a joyous medley of green, purple, pink, and ochre.

A correlation may be discerned between the clamoring to relive the past and the collective anxieties of the present. The internet was well on its way in dismantling revered institutions. The smart-phone was a bullhorn into which people vented their every emotional outburst in real time. Politics had everyone at each other's throats. A runaway virus effectively shut the world down. And life was becoming little more than a fusillade of Instagram posts.

Forty years had elapsed since radio decreed an end to disco, time enough to wash away the illusory and unjust stigma it had been bearing. Its banishment from the airwaves did cause record sales to plummet and many an artist's career to evaporate. But Gloria Gaynor could've told them that public perception and dated category name notwithstanding, disco survived.

David Mancuso had kept hosting his Loft parties through the early 2000s. He'd even presided over one in London, organized by keeper-of-the-flame Tim Lawrence (with Colleen Murphy, Nikki Lucas and Jeremy Gilbert). As was his custom, Mancuso manned the deck and played each song in its entirety, his unspoken opinion that this is how the songs are meant to be heard. A couple of things had changed, however. People in the crowd were either too old to be partying or too young to know which version of "Turn the Beat Around" was playing. Also, the event started on a Sunday afternoon and ended before midnight. So basically a tea dance.

By then, the disco tea dance had gone the way of traditions as sacred as Halloween at gay outposts from Mykonos and Key West to the Blue Whale on Fire Island. During Cape Cod's tourist season, people from all over the world descend into the Boat Slip in Provincetown. At this glorified motel astride the coastline, people cram into a tiny dancefloor with low ceilings, and overflow out to the poolside deck for daily tea dances. Conducting these events is cherished resident DJ Maryalice, a former Governor Bradford restaurant waitress, who's been spinning for thirty years now. Programming around themes, she seldom changes the playlists, usually consisting of songs every regular knows like the backs of each other's designer summer shorts. Then, like a demented choir, the revelers will overpower the music with full-throated sing-alongs to Dead or Alive's "You Spin Me Round (Like a Record)" or Thelma Houston's "Don't Leave Me This Way". But knowing the tea dances themed around Madonna or Solid Gold will finish with the same songs won't dampen their enthusiasm. When those finales play, they will go insane. Every single time.

———————————

In 2017, a retrospective on the designer of the disco era, "Halston Style" was mounted at the Nassau County Museum of Art (Est. 1969). It wasn't the first. The learned Costume Institute curator Richard Martin (1946-1999) organized "Halston—Absolute Modernism" at the Met in 1991. The institution's "Charles James: Beyond Fashion" exhibition didn't happen until 2014 (from pieces Homer Layne had accumulated since the designer's passing). James' (and William's) old home—the Chelsea continued to welcome illustrious personalities from photographer Robert Mapplethorpe to bestselling authors Nick Bienes and Rhea Gallaher, the couple who wrote under the pseudonym Judith Gould, and lived for a decade on James' floor after the 1982 publication of their breakthrough novel "Sins" (which became a 1986 Joan Collins, Nielsen's ratings bonanza). The couple penned six more bestsellers while at the Chelsea.

For years, New York's Lincoln Center has been hosting al fresco swing dancing. But lately it's added the Silent Disco series to the Summer for the City events lineup. Participants don wireless headphones and dance in the outdoor space it calls "The Oasis" topped by a ten-foot and thirteen hundred-pound rotating disco ball. At the same time, there's been a resurgence of roller disco with enthusiasts (who couldn't have been there at the first go around) flocking to RollerJam USA in Staten Island, Dreamland Roller Rink in Prospect Park, and to that skaters' paradise Skate Circle just north of Sheep Meadow in Central Park.

At the not too distant Wollman Rink, in the summer of 2022, Nile Rodgers celebrated a reunion with Madonna at his DiscOasis rollerskating event. In private, it was a chance to reminisce about working together on her "Like a Virgin" album. In public, it was the launch of the singer's "Finally Enough Love: 50 Number Ones" the four vinyl compilation of her number one hits on the U.S. Billboard Dance Club Songs chart, the most number ones of any artist on any Billboard chart, ever. And that doesn't even count the almost weres (nor the non-dance singles that reached number one on the Billboard Hot 100 chart). No matter how many hit ballads she's notched, Madonna's dance music has always been the best received by critics and her fan base. It's the most conspicuous through-line of her massive body of work, her sovereignty unassailable. And she paid tribute to her roots with the 2005 smash "Hung Up". Not just with its Abba sample, but with a "Saturday Night Fever" referenced video. The Guinness World Records certified that her songs have been remixed and sampled more than any other artist, 324 as of March 2018. How many more have been produced in the last five years?

———————————

Voguing for trophies is also still a thing, spreading out from its Harlem setting to warehouses in (appropriately enough) Queens, and in the swankier, better-lit television studios of the internationally franchised Drag Race. Today, these reality show drag contests have mainstreamed their lingo like "shade" and "werk", while phrases such as "Village People Eleganza Extravaganza" and "CEO Platinum Card Executive Realness" have become understandable to the masses. Praises for the recently concluded FX series "Pose" was warranted by its frank look at the ballroom culture of the 1980s and 1990s (albeit fictionalized) and having LGBTQ+ people of color as the stars, in the writers room, production, and as consultants.

Analogous progress has been made to open doors to non binary dancers at venerable companies such as Pacific Northwest Ballet in Seattle and Béjart Ballet Lausanne, Switzerland. Of course, there was also the historic appointment of Misty Copeland as a principal at ABT, the first African American to do so at an international institution. From a speculative yet chillingly plausible slant, Franklin Ritch's debut picture "The Artifice Girl" questions the demarcation of humanity and artificial intelligence with trenchant conversations on sentience and self awareness. It is topical, and indeed telling, that Ritch ends his film with the titular AI meeting, perhaps answering, those intriguing points by dancing.

Aware of the prominence of his role in the opening segment of "Contact", Seán went through his fitting realizing he was up against formidable competition. Two of them. "Have you seen Stephanie's…?" he asks rhetorically. "They are magnificent!" William was having Seán's partner in the scene Stephanie Michels trussed up in a gorgeous confection that places a couple of her finest assets front and center. "No one is going to notice me!" By way of a rejoinder? He decided he'd have to put his own on the line and went commando in skin tight sea-foam suede britches.

Other adjustments took place during rehearsals. "I think we've been on too many raised rectangular stages that dancing on the circular ¾ thrust stage at floor level took getting used to," according to Seán, "It was great for the feeling of the club. But, especially in the smaller Newhouse, orienting to the audience hemmed in around us felt odd." Then there was the swing. "Timing the swaying to match sections of the music was difficult. For a while we couldn't get the count to line up. The music is four beats to the bar. But the basic trajectory of the swing was seven beats of the song. We needed to manipulate the speed several sways in advance to get it and us on it downstage on the one at the start of the bridge. Usually, after you've learned a routine, it all becomes part of natural muscle memory. But initially, I kept thinking to myself, 'okay, here's the bridge, now I have to do the handstand'. Thankfully, we were finally able to make it all look seamless."

Those who've had the pleasure of working with Stro witness an inimitable alchemy occurring when she gathers her ingredients and stirs. Performances are coaxed out of some, nudged from others. At once creator and catalyst, she makes everyone feel comfortable enough to offer ideas so long as they serve the story. She is always taking stock, keeping measure, brooding over what could use leavening or do with more weight. William explains, "Filmmakers have their cameras to control what people see. We in the theater are not granted the same means. Never knowing what the audience is looking at, we need to be always aware of the panorama."

This was made evident, he says, "During the first dress rehearsal, a frantic Stro calls to tell me the black costumes were causing the dancers in the club scene to fade into the background!" William hurriedly glazed some pieces with reflective sheen so that even in gloom they stood out like obsidian. Others he recreated in browns, blues, or purples. He had the dancers refitted with new costumes that were good to go. With just days till preview, showtime was almost upon them.

CHAPTER NINE
A Love Trilogy

"Contact" (in previews from September and opened October 1999) raised the Mitzi Newhouse Theatre curtains on a replica of the 1767 oil painting *"Les hasards heureux de l'escarpolette"* by Jean-Honoré Fragonard (1732-1806). It depicts a young woman wearing a voluminous vermilion frock, seated on a cushioned swing in ascent, and bathed in sunlight slashing down through a canopy of trees. Her left leg flung high, dislodged and suspended her shoe in mid air, flared her skirts and revealed her undergarments to the delight of a gentleman watching from below.

Several other elements in the painting augment this already erotically charged scenario. The background indicates this to be a private, secluded garden. Draped in shadows is an onlooking older gentleman who is manipulating the swing with ropes. And finally, it is being witnessed by two marble cherubs in back, one sheepishly bowed, and more pointedly another (a rendering of *"L'amour menaçant"*, the Etienne Maurice Falconet, 1716-1791 sculpture housed in the Louvre, Est. 1793) conspiratorially hushing everyone with a finger to his lips.

Alternately known as *"L'Escarpolette"*, "The Happy Accidents of the Swing" or simply "The Swing", the painting is regarded as the quintessentially Rococo crowning achievement of the French artist. Today, the original is on view at the Wallace Collection national museum (Est. 1900) in London. "I've always loved that painting," says Stro. "I've seen it many times and that cupid made me wonder what was really going on." The angelic figure must have intrigued Stro enough she set it on a pedestal as an easter egg across all three vignettes of "Contact".

This first recreates the painting onstage as a *tableau vivant,* but only just. It's been elaborated as a bucolic picnic, and the older gentleman working the swing from behind has been replaced by a young, virile manservant (played by Seán). In due course, Stro allows the motion to propel this segment called "Swinging". She says, "Moving back and forth like a giant spellbinding pendulum, the swing almost hypno-tizes the audience and removes any misconception that this is a chaste encounter." The scene throbs with innuendo and echoes the heaving bosom beneath the corsetry. As the lady's garments unfurl with revela-tion, so too does the tale. The aristocratically dressed man (Scott Taylor) on the ground departs to retrieve another bottle of champagne, giving the manservant impunity to join the lady (Stephanie Michels) on the swing. Together they ride that swing through gymnastic contortions of entangled limbs, each thrust and parry escalating in velocity and sultry abandon.

Stro says, "The movement is athletic. The choreography on the moving swing is death defying—what risks one would bravely take for love or the affection of another." It, uh, climaxes with a twist. The manservant is the lady's aristocratic lover after all! It is disclosed by the simple yet powerfully emblematic power of fashion: the presumed nobleman takes off an elegantly embroidered cutaway coat and replaces it onto its rightful owner. "All three characters are happily role playing and have no problem making contact whatsoever."

On the drawing board, the next story was to pick up two centuries later in 'swinging' 1960s Las Vegas where destinies were decided on the roll of the dice. But Stro and Weidman prudently traded glitz for something a bit more contemplative. "Did You Move" transpires instead in a 1954 Queens neighborhood where a couple dines at an Italian restaurant. With but a smattering of brief exchanges, the tension between them is laid bare. He is hostile and volatile. She is servile and skittish. The excruciating rigor with which Karen Ziemba plays the wife is something to behold. She chatters to fill in the emptiness of his indifference. Her brittle smile contains the futility of salving the wounds of a million such slowly dying marriages. And that makes what comes next all the more joyful and heartrending.

Each time the husband (Jason Antoon) leaves the table, he warns her not to move, and she defers. Stro says, "She recoils in fear. If someone spoke to you that way, I wondered what the most extreme movement would be to counteract such a brutal, violent order?" Her response? "Classical ballet!" The second he is out of sight, she escapes into her imagination where she can move as much as she pleases. "She fantasizes about getting away from her abusive spouse by dancing." And so she gleefully flits about the room, pushed on a rolling food cart by hairnetted busser Uncle Vinnie (Seán), and partnering with the maitre'd (David MacGillivray). It is an unspoken soliloquy of kinetic eloquence. Sadly, the segment closes as it began, when reality intrudes, her husband returns, and once again her light fades into dark stillness.

The titular vignette concerns fortysomething advertising executive Michael Wiley (Gaines) and his fated meeting with the baffling

Girl in the Yellow Dress (Yates). Wiley has just snagged presumably not his first but latest Clio (Est. 1959), the most distinguished award in advertising, commercial design, and communications. By outward appearances, Wiley is accomplished and respected by his peers. He should be happy. But he's not. And getting this award somehow pushes him over the edge. It isn't made clear how long he's harbored suicidal ideations, but back at his highrise apartment he decides to act on them.

As Wiley teeters from the noose of a tasseled curtain cord, his dark night of the soul unspools in time displaced sequences. What happens next may be inferred as the figment of an oxygen deprived brain. Ad exec walks into a bar and the woman of his dreams wafts through the fog of his wishful delirium. Spurred on by the bartender, Wiley fortifies himself with liquid courage and makes several clumsy attempts at trying to meet her. But inebriation doesn't really change the fact that he can't dance, and cutting in are several men who are able, and only too willing.

For the rest of the night, Wiley staggers, not just on the dancefloor but in the clash of objective reality's meaninglessness against man's insatiable search for meaning. It's the kind of quandary Albert Camus (1913-1960) essays in 1942's *"Le mythe de Sisyphe"*. In it, Camus compares man's repetitive tasks to the Greek myth of Sisyphus who was cursed by Zeus to keep pushing the same boulder up a mountain and have it roll down again each day for all eternity. He also posits that while suicide is a solution, this can only serve as an evasion since there is no more meaning in death than in life. Camus' alternate 'solutions' are taking a leap of faith or Absurdism, the willingness to accept the struggle as being "enough to fill a man's heart". Wiley chooses hope in the guise of the Girl in the Yellow Dress, subverting the bleakness of one of this segment's inspirations, "An Occurrence at Owl Creek Bridge" (1890) by Ambrose Bierce (1842-1914).

That the music is integral goes without saying. Stro and Weidman deliberated over having the show scored with original material or pre-existing music. She explains, "John and I imagined how someone on the verge of killing himself would see life pass before his eyes, and he wouldn't be hearing a new Broadway score." They agreed it made more sense to go diegetic. "Everyone has at one time or another been transported back by a certain tune to the first time they heard it. It could make us deliriously happy or desperately sad. It had to be music that meant something to Wiley during his lifetime." With infallible instincts for stagecraft, she and Weidman came up with an eclectic mix that unerringly paces the choreography while emotionally centering the characters. And, for those who recognize the music there's an added component of surprise in the context of their use.

The Rodgers and Hart standard "My Heart Stood Still" startles when it plays over the 18th century setting of the first vignette. Yet, the version by jazz violinist Stéphane Grappelli (1908-1997) (originally from his 1975 "Violinspiration" album) gives it sensual urgency. Then, classical pieces by the New York Philharmonic Orchestra, recorded in the 1970s under the baton of Leonard Bernstein, contrasts flights of fancy from the despair of a 1950s housewife. Assorted songs underline the final segment: "Do You Wanna Dance" (the 1965 version from the Beach Boys), and "Beyond the Sea" (an English-language version of "La Mer" originally by Charles Trenet, 1913-2001, here a lesser known cover by Royal Crown Revue from their 1996 pulp fiction concept album "Mugzy's Move"). They ebb and flow through Wiley's bungling efforts to dance. And Gaines, it must be said, very deftly trips all over the place even as he conveys pathos and longing. Also, the show's album swaps out Dean Martin's (1917-1995) 1960 hit used in the scene with Gaines' rendition of "You're Nobody Till Somebody Loves You" (originally from 1946 sung by one of its composers Russ Morgan, 1904-1969).

Meanwhile, with "Simply Irresistible" by Robert Palmer (from his 1988 "Heavy Nova" album), Yates endows her "girl in the yellow dress" a flinty film noir façade worthy of the Catherine Tramells and Matty Walkers of the silver screen. Yet, at the eleventh hour rug pull, she evinces genuine warmth and vulnerability to become Wiley's flesh and blood redemption.

One of the show's many truly astonishing feats was how Stro and Weidman's authorship, aided by William's costumes, and brought home by the choreography and the performances, delineated every single personality onstage. It's especially commendable for Weidman, a writer, to abstain from verbiage and rely instead on a glance, a wince, or a perfectly timed pirouette. So fully lived-in are the characters that had the audience paid but cursory notice, everyone in the corps still registered. Over there is a couple who just got engaged. On the other side of the room is an expectant mother. This is because, Seán confirms, "We were given clues and space to imagine our back stories. In the restaurant segment, Stro told me 'Go and push that food cart across the stage', then 'Do it slowly'. I don't do anything slowly in real life, so I hunched over and shuffled like an old man. I brought in the black horn-rimmed glasses with band-aid keeping the stems attached, and Uncle Vinnie was born."

Public reception and critical notices for everyone on and backstage were overwhelmingly ecstatic. The New York Times's Ben Brantley said "a dream ensemble of dancing actors and acting dancers has created the unthinkable: a new musical throbbing with wit, sex appeal, and a perfectionist's polish. Brimming with a sophistication untainted by cynicism…It's a sustained endorphin rush of an evening, that rare entertainment that has you floating all the way home." For Time magazine, Terry Teachout called it "magical…(a) trio of exquisitely tooled, MGM-style production numbers, but updated and given emotional weight. Each playlet is peopled with lonely hearts longing to reach out to someone, and when they finally touch, your own heart will do all the singing necessary."

In the flurry of approbations heaped upon "Contact" no mention was ever made of its semblance to the Gene Kelly-directed 1956 dance anthology "Invitation to the Dance". But that's understandable. There was more than enough about "Contact" and everyone behind it to write about. And, being a fairly obscure motion picture, 'Invitation' has not been cited by either Stro or Weidman as an inspiration. Nevertheless, it ought not be entirely overlooked as Kelly's valiant attempt to foster an appreciation of dance as an art form. But that was a hard sell to the MGM bean counters who put up roadblocks on the production.

First, there were delays. Then, contrary to his plan of being in only one segment, the studio stipulated that Kelly appear in all three. An extra segment called "Dance Me a Song" was shot but discarded on the cutting room floor. The ones that made it into the final cut were "Circus" in which a woman is caught in a love triangle between an acrobat and an ill-fated clown (who, incidentally, appeared in Madonna's "Girlie Show Tour" in 1993); "Ring Around the Rosy", about a gold bracelet passed from one person to another; and "Sinbad the Sailor" where Kelly, against a green screen, dances with animated Hanna-Barbera characters years before Julie Andrews and Dick Van Dyke did in Disney's "Mary Poppins". The picture flopped. Apparently, America wasn't ready for ingenious structure, a lineup of fine international performers, and consummate dancing. Until "Contact".

Seán recounts, "We were sold out before we opened. The night after, we were already told we were being moved (from the 299-seating Newhouse) upstairs to the Vivian Beaumont (1114 seats, making it an official Broadway show)." During the run, Seán met someone he didn't know would later play a larger role in his life. Back in Australia, Seán's mother was an actress who'd worked and became friends with Deborra-Lee Furness, the wife of another Australian actor known primarily for the X-Men film franchise. And so the Hugh Jackmans went to a performance and after curtain Seán heard a thunderous voice call out backstage, "Seán Hingston! Your mother said to say hello!"

There was worry the show would lose its intimacy with the transfer to the Beaumont, but this proved unfounded when Charles Isherwood rhapsodized in Variety magazine: "Once upon a time 'Contact' delighted; now it dazzles. Once it touched the heart; now it nearly breaks it." The Times also admitted it "deserved the larger audiences and the Tony nominations," which it got. Out of multiple categories, it won four—Best Featured Actor for Gaines, Best Featured Actress for Ziemba, Best Choreography for Stro, and Best Musical (which it also won from Drama Desk and Outer Critics Circle). Notably, Yates was also up for best featured actress, and up against Ann Hampton Callaway and Laura Benanti who were in another dance musical called "Swing!"

That votes for Stro in the director category may have been split between her nominations for "Contact" and her other show "The Music Man", also in contention that year, is not an unreasonable con-jecture. Losing that award to Michael Blakemore for "Kiss Me Kate", however, didn't diminish what she had accomplished in her first double duty as choreographer and director, joining the ranks of Bennett, Robbins, Fosse, and Agnes de Mille (1905-1993), whose choreography for the 1943 musical "Oklahoma" directed by Rouben Mamoulian (1897-1987) Stro reworked for the West End revival in 1998.

"Contact" went on a four month national tour ending in Los Angeles September 1, 2001, while its Broadway run tallied 1,010 performances until September 1, 2002. Its final show was broadcast over PBS' Live from Lincoln Center and filmed with two mid-orchestra cameras, another on a track in front, and one more in the rear orchestra from a platform with a 25-foot boom. The broadcast won the Primetime Emmy for Outstanding Classical Music-Dance Program. The show opened the following year on the West End for a limited engagement at the Queen's Theatre (Est. 1907, rechristened the Stephen Sondheim Theatre in 2019). Later, it was produced in Budapest (2009), Shanghai (2014), and Seoul (2017). The "Simply Irresistible" segment was reproduced (along with pieces by Robbins and Fosse) in 2012 by the American Dance Machine for the 21st Century (Est. 1976) at New York City Center.

———————————

The new millennium brought into Seán's life another blessing. He and his partner television producer Brad Hurtado flew to San Antonio, TX for the birth of their daughter Grace. The couple had met six years prior. Seán and pal Filion were coming from Sunday brunch when they passed Hurtado in front of Fairway on Broadway in the Upper East Side. After locking eyes, Seán and Hurtado have been together ever since, tying the knot in Hawaii on their twentieth anniversary of having met.

In 2010, the same year Seán joined the cast of the Bacharach-David musical "Promises, Promises", the Hingston-Hurtados bought a three-story 1881 fixer upper in Brooklyn with plans to renovate and convert parts of it as rentals. It took them another ten years to get the financing in place. But when they were finally ready to start, covid hit the brakes on construction and put the entire world on pause. Seán recalls Hurtado while away the days watching TikTok and thinking they could log their renovation in one-minute shorts. "After our contractor finally returned, we posted our first video," he says. "What I didn't know was Brad had snuck in a shot of me doing a triple pirouette at the worksite. He's convinced that's what put us over the top." In 48 hours the video had almost a million views and their TikTok account "Back to the Studs" had gained 150,000 subscribers. This was followed by an invitation to provide content to streamer Smart Healthy Green Living. Since then over thirty companies have collaborated with the couple and their TikTok videos have more than half a million followers and counting.

And all this time, their baby girl was growing up. Grace Hingston-Hurtado was juggling retail and college. And when covid restrictions were lifted, she started to seriously date one Oscar Jackman, the son Hugh and Deb had adopted the same year as Grace was. The Jackmans and Hingston-Hurtados had gotten closer since the kids were twelve and attended the same middle school. Seán and Hurtado attended the Invited Dress Rehearsal for Jackman's 2022 "The Music Man" revival directed by Jerry Zaks and choreographed by Warren Carlyle.

After "Contact", William's portfolio continued to grow, some in collaboration with Stro: "The Music Man" (2000 revival), "The Producers" (on Broadway, as well as the 2005 motion picture directed by Stro), "Big Fish" (2013), and "Bullets Over Broadway" (2014). In 2004, he designed for Stro's ode to silent films "Double Feature", the first full-length New York City Ballet choreographed by a woman. Ten years later, they went further afield of the Rialto. At the Eisenhower Theater of the John F. Kennedy Center for the Performing Arts (Est. 1971) in DC, Stro directed and choreographed her conceptual brainchild "Little Dancer", after having seen one of the bronze casts of Degas' *"La petite danseuse de quatorze ans"*. The artist exhibited his scaled down original at the sixth Impressionist exhibition of 1881 held at the five-room, red-walled studio of the French photographer called Nadar (Gaspard-Félix Tournachon, 1820-1910) at 35 Boulevard des Capucines. Degas' wax sculpture of a young dancer posed in ballet's fourth position was an unusual piece of mixed media incorporating hair, silk ribbon, linen bodice, muslin tutu, and satin slippers. It was also curiously shown within a glass vitrine, a means of display utilized for classical pieces or anthropological specimens. *Le tout Paris* was scandalized and critics were generous with their calumny.

Stro's "Little Dancer" was culled as much from this piece as the life of its model Marie Geneviève van Goethem, one of the three daughters of a laundress and a tailor. Since nothing more is known about Marie after being dropped from the Paris Opera Ballet corps, Stro decided to "bring her back to life" with the 'woulda, coulda, shouldas' gleaned from the sculpture's symbolic fortitude. For his part, William sketched his ballet designs reminiscent of the paintings of Degas, who was, by the way, played by Gaines in the show.

In late 2021, the world awoke from a nightmare. It had been brought to a standstill for a year and a half, in the efforts to stop, or at least slow down, the spread of covid. But even as everyone wanted to think it was all over, medical professionals knew it wasn't going to be the last epidemic. Throughout history, congested human habitations have been petri dishes for diseases of every stripe. But perhaps none stranger or more puzzling than the "dancing plague".

In 1518, the townsfolk of Strasbourg were stricken with the compulsion to shake and twist about on the streets, from one person to a few dozen to four hundred by summer's end. Exhaustion overcame many. Others, not so lucky, suffered fatal heart attacks. The only advice from flummoxed physicians was to let the malaise run its course. And it did. Sometime in September of that year, everything was back to normal. As bizarre as this all seems, accounts of the "dancing plague" are well documented. The same phenomenon, though not on the same scale, was reported in Germany, Holland, and Switzerland. There's never been a credible explanation for what happened.

———————————

Some twenty years ago, flayed cadavers posed in various acts—from kicking a ball to holding a dance pose—were on display in the controversial "Bodies: The Exhibition" at the South Street Seaport in lower Manhattan. It was one of several that was held in other cities and countries. The specimens had been treated to a process called "plastination". Developed by Gunther von Hagens, it arrests decay by removing fat and liquids from human remains, injecting polymer, and hardening them into place. Hundreds of thousands came to see the skeletons, organs, and partial or entire muscular outlines, and marvel at the internal structure and dynamism of the human body. Although exhibitors provided proper documentation, there were accusations the cadavers were illegally procured from Chinese black market sources. Much of the outrage though were based on the same hazy moral or ethical grounds that held back medical studies through the ages.

Unlikely to foment polemics are advancements in brain mapping, which shine new light on many disorders. As a species, humans are uniquely able to recognize and remember sequential data that enables the codification of dances. Physically, dance links breathing, core, spinal, homologous, homolateral and contralateral patterns that require dancers to utilize and improve more cognitive functions. But efforts at differentiating intentional from spontaneous movements complicate how dance affects the neurobehavioral sensory, motor, cognitive, social, emotional, rhythmic, and creative areas of the brain.

Some studies are showing consistently observable effects of dancing in patients suffering from Parkinson's disease, evincing improvements in their strides when they followed prescribed steady rhythmic cues. It's reckoned that symptoms like impaired balance and coordination can also be alleviated. In another study, only dancing, out of various physical activities from cycling to swimming, helped lower the risk of dementia in participants. Researchers attributed this to mental and physical exertion in combination with social interaction. After older adults went through ten weeks of ballet technique for a separate study, analysis revealed improved postural stability and balance, which may reduce risks of falls. This involves processes in the cerebellum where auditory and visual information aids the anterior vermis in synchronizing steps to music. Additionally, it's been previously discovered that the brain's plasticity seems to retard, in individuals with classical ballet training, the area in the cerebellum receiving input from the vestibular organs which triggers the sensation of dizziness.

—

The therapeutic value of dance has been reinforced in other ways. At the Imperial Ballroom Dance Studio in New York, senior citizens resumed their Sunday afternoon ballroom dance classes with renewed gusto after the lockdown. For over twenty years, this family-owned space in Chinatown has been invaluable to the neighborhood's elderly immigrants. Most of them, retired and in their seventies, come here to cope with urban isolation. And discovering a passion for dancing in their autumn years has become a way to recapture youth that's been sacrificed to work and families. Industry data discloses one thousand of these studios in New York give classes for a wide array of purposes from weddings to specific avocations such as Latin, swing, and ballroom. Other reports claim there are 10,000 in the U.S. and 55,000 worldwide.

In Damascus, Dance Nation serves a not so dissimilar kind of solace. Syrians come here to salsa away the ceaseless pressures of their war-torn country's economic and political problems. Instructors insist though that dancing shouldn't supplant reality, rather a way for locals to rekindle their sense of selves amidst the chaos. Recollections of ballroom dancing's pre-war heydays are alive and its proponents want to restore them by shoring government support for Syrian representation at major dance competitions in Arab and Asian countries.

Dance communities in those corners of the world thrive on such events. In spite of ballet's relatively late arrival there in 1911, Japan, for example, has nearly five thousand ballet companies offering classes to those who dream of competing at world class tournaments like the Prix de Lausanne in Switzerland. Several dancers like Miyako Yoshida, Morihiro Iwata, and Misa Kuranaga have joined prestigious international institutions. Japanese cultural inclinations—such as the deep respect for discipline and the 'proper' way of doing things—are also evident in how ballet is perceived. To them, a tutu is not a costume but a garment earned from years of learning and rigorous discipline.

Meanwhile, Amsterdam's fashion and dance scenes are braving new frontiers. From various elemental mediums, designer Iris Van Herpen brings forth feats of conceptual couture so experimentally alien yet clearly organic, it's as though the garments have always been there in nature. Out of glaciers or open skies, from watery depths to craggy rocks, her designs flow to the dances that often inspire her. In sustainable or upcycled materials like plastic ocean debris, exquisite dresses have been sculpted, engineered, or handcrafted in collaboration with innovative artists like James Merry or choreographer Jalet.

As for the capital of the Netherlands itself, the city has been hosting the world's biggest EDM festivals—Amsterdam Dance Event, Loveland, Dekmantel, Valhalla and others across eighty clubs—since the millennium. The importance of this $8B industry was incentive enough for the government to initiate a social experiment to gauge the safety of reopening after covid. Out of a hundred thousand people who entered a raffle, 1,300 attendees were picked and monitored on how they interacted and adhered to the mandated safety protocols. Each participant had to be tested negative and was required to test again five days after the event. Few registered positive after, but the results are unsupported by any evidence the virus was contracted at the dance.

Broadway, dark for about a year and a half, took its tentative steps toward reopening in the Fall of 2022 . In October, "New York, New York", directed and choreographed by Stro, opened at the St. James Theatre (Est. 1927 as Erlanger's Theatre). It's based on Martin Scorsese's 1977 motion picture accompanied by fresh Kander and Ebb music (additional lyrics by Lin-Manuel Miranda) with, of course, that roof shattering titular song. To the press Kander described the post WWII city "a tough, gritty, beautiful dream palace filled with youthful energy and optimism". To Stro, it is "always in motion…with its own distinct rhythm…pulling our various characters from everywhere to pursue something that can only happen (here)…because fortunes can change in a New York minute."

In May 2023, Stro received her eleventh Tony Awards nomination for choreography (she's received fifteen overall) tying her with Fosse as the most nominated choreographer in the history of the awards. Mention should be made that unlike Fosse, Stro had never been attached to an identifiable dance vocabulary. "I prefer not to impose a style and rather let it come out organically from the story," she says. If there were such a thing as a Stroman signature, it just might be the transformative power of dance. In all her shows, it is never simply a diversion nor convenient plot device. Dance is the very means by which her characters discover themselves, evolve, and waltz to their happily ever afters.

For the Chichester Festival Theatre, Stro directed and choreographed a 2022 U.K. revival of "Crazy for You", which transferred a year later for a limited engagement at the Gillian Lynne Theatre in London. The outstanding reviews were unanimous, calling it "pure music the-ater heaven" and William's costumes as "swoon-worthy".

As for "Contact", a couple of mysteries lingered on for Stro. "After the wild amount of press we got, after the billboards and posters of Deborah all over town, on Times Square, on taxis, buses, and in the subway, I thought for sure the real girl in the yellow dress who I saw that night in the club would come forward. But she never did. And, the day after the show opened, I hopped on a cab and headed down-town to find that club again. But the space had been stripped bare and was utterly unrecognizable. That one special night had disappeared like Brigadoon, only to be reborn again at Lincoln Center". And each night there closed to boisterous ovations as the company took their curtain calls to Van Morrison's "Moondance" (1970).

"One of my fondest memories is the rehearsal room of 'Contact'," confides Stro, "in that protected creative space, with dancers who inspired me to create out of the idea that dance equals the joy of life." And when joy, with all the emotional acuity of a show like "Contact" permeates throughout the theater, across the lives of so many, all that remains for anyone and everyone who's ever dedicated themselves to fashion and dance is to take a bow.

Acknowledgments

Long before now, these stories were already being written
in sweat and tears, music and memories,
But they could only have coalesced into these pages
by the kindness of these colleagues, friends, and family
With deep and unending gratitude to

Susan Stroman + William Ivey Long + Neal Boulton + Adam Garcia + Carlota Santana + Tory Dobrin + Jeff Sturdivant + Jeffrey Kazin + David Parker + Seán Martin Hingston + Talia Castro-Pozo + Larry Blum + Richard Claycomb + Keith Sherman + John Bartlett + Edward Simon + Peter Sandel + Dewey Moss + Christopher Blomquist + Patrick J. Hamilton + Jeff Peters + Liz Harler + Amy Fine Collins + Lynne Lancaster + Laura Di Orio + Sigrid Gouze + Peter Cruz + Michael Paoletta + Jono Waks + Donald Sanders + Eric Twardzik + Steve Gillon + Stefan Steil + Perri O. Blumberg + Joven Relova + Heather L. Bain + Eric Cervini + Michael Satterfield + Brian Kovener + John Sotomayor + Lauren Schuster + India Aujla + Michael Marchello + Matt Fox and Enrique Crame III + Paul Rankin + Angel Rivera + Mark Sullivan + James Scott and Phil Szuromi + Dorothy Mannfolk + Norman Villavicencio + Hilda Tiu Mauro + Marissa Mendieta Abril + Joy Buensalido + Ann and Christopher Pastrana + James Pastrana + Sigmund Tate + Susan Deiters + Matt Fust + Robin Dutt + David Black + Tracy Christensen + Jona and Mark McLenning + Sandra Nygaard + Jennifer Nuyda-Tatlonghari + Gigi Mogol + Tim Murphy and Richard Toda + Dougal Munro + Deni Robey + Dave Ryan + Terri Walsh + dancers, fashion and costume designers past, present, and future

www.ingramcontent.com/pod-product-compliance
Lightning Source LLC
Chambersburg PA
CBHW040734120726
48010CB00016B/378/J